LOCALISM
NEIGHBOURHOO

Power to the

Edited by
Sue Brownill and Quintin Bradley

P

First published in Great Britain in 2017 by

Policy Press
University of Bristol
1-9 Old Park Hill
Bristol
BS2 8BB
UK
t: +44 (0)117 954 5940
pp-info@bristol.ac.uk
www.policypress.co.uk

North America office:
Policy Press
c/o The University of Chicago Press
1427 East 60th Street
Chicago, IL 60637, USA
t: +1 773 702 7700
f: +1 773-702-9756
sales@press.uchicago.edu
www.press.uchicago.edu

British Library Cataloguing in Publication Data
A catalogue record for this book is available from the British Library

Library of Congress Cataloging-in-Publication Data
A catalog record for this book has been requested

ISBN 978-1-4473-2950-3 paperback
ISBN 978-1-4473-2949-7 hardcover
ISBN 978-1-4473-2952-7 ePub
ISBN 978-1-4473-2953-4 Mobi
ISBN 978-1-4473-2951-0 ePdf

Cover design by Hayes Design
Front cover image: Sue Brownill
Printed and bound in Great Britain by CMP, Poole
Policy Press uses environmentally responsible print partners

Contents

List of tables and figures   v
List of photographs   vi
Editors' acknowledgements   vii
Notes on contributors   ix

one   Introduction   1
            Sue Brownill and Quintin Bradley

**Part One: Understanding and characterising neighbourhood   17
            planning**
two   Neighbourhood planning and the purposes and   19
            practices of localism
            Sue Brownill
three   Neighbourhoods, communities and the local scale   39
            Quintin Bradley
four   Neighbourhood planning and the spatial practices   57
            of localism
            Quintin Bradley, Amy Burnett and William Sparling
five   The uneven geographies of neighbourhood planning   75
            in England
            Gavin Parker

Part Two: Experiences, contestations and debates   93
six   Developing a neighbourhood plan: stories from   95
            'community-led' planning pathfinders
            David McGuinness and Carol Ludwig
seven   Voices from the neighbourhood: stories from the   113
            participants in neighbourhood plans and the
            professionals working with them
            Edited by Quintin Bradley and Sue Brownill
eight   Participation and conflict in the formation of   127
            neighbourhood areas and forums in 'super-diverse' cities
            Claire Colomb
nine   Assembling neighbourhoods: topologies of power   145
            and the reshaping of planning
            Sue Brownill
ten   A passion for place: the emotional identifications   163
            and empowerment of neighbourhood planning
            Quintin Bradley

Part Three: International comparisons in community planning   **181**

eleven   Community-based planning and localism in the   183
           devolved UK
           Simon Pemberton

twelve   Citizen participation: an essential lever for urban   199
           transformation in France?
           Camille Gardesse and Jodelle Zetlaoui-Léger

thirteen   Localism and neighbourhood planning in   215
           Australian public policy and governance
           Paul Burton

fourteen   The many lives of neighbourhood planning   231
           in the US: much ado about something?
           Larry Bennett

Part Four: Reflections and conclusions   **249**

fifteen   Reflections on neighbourhood planning: 251
           towards a progressive localism
           Quintin Bradley and Sue Brownill

Index   269

List of tables and figures

List of tables

2.1   Other community rights   26
4.1   Examples of low-carbon, sustainable policies   66
      and ambitions in neighbourhood plans
5.1   Estimated and actual take-up of neighbourhood   81
      planning areas (2011–15)
5.2   Regional and qualifying body (parish/forum)   83
      distribution of neighbourhood planning (January 2016)
5.3   Index of Multiple Deprivation breakdown of   84
      neighbourhood planning qualifying bodies at the local authority
      level (January 2016)
5.4   Index of Multiple Deprivation breakdown of neighbourhood 85
      plans to referendum (by local authority) (January 2016)
11.1 Summary of community-based planning initiatives   189
      under UK devolution

List of figures

2.1   The 'hierarchy' of the English statutory planning system   26
2.2   The stages of a neighbourhood plan   27
4.1   How neighbourhood plans might speed up   58
      the delivery of new housing
5.1   Take-up of neighbourhood planning by English region   82
      (January 2016)
9.1   The Mobius strip   147
9.2   Somers Town neighbourhood development plan   153

List of photographs

1.1	Consultation begins on a draft neighbourhood plan	3
2.1	An initial open day gathers ideas about the neighbourhood	29
3.1	At the neighbourhood forum: an alternative discursive arena	43
4.1	Neighbourhood planning for sustainability	69
5.1	Wanting to shape the future	88
7.1	Doing neighbourhood planning: voices from a working group	118
8.1	Community planning workshop organised by Hackney Council for the preparation of the Stamford Hill Area Action Plan, October 2015	137
9.1	Reaching in: reshaping planning in the neighbourhood	158
10.1	A place for memory and emotion	165
15.1	Democratic planning: announcing the referendum on a neighbourhood plan	252

Editors' acknowledgements

This book emerged out of two sessions organised by the editors at the RGS-IBG (Royal Geographical Society-Institute of British Geographers) conference in August 2014. We would like to thank those who attended and presented for contributing to the emerging ideas and debates about neighbourhood planning with which this book engages. Other networks and forums have also provided an opportunity to explore the issues, including a roundtable bringing together academics and practitioners organised by the Department of Communities and Local Government and an ESRC (Economic and Social Sciences Research Council) seminar series on 'Neighbourhood Ways of Knowing and Working'. The editors would also like to acknowledge the support of the British Academy and Leeds Beckett University for funding their research into neighbourhood planning. Finally, as academics and practitioners, we, and others who have contributed to this book, have been engaged with a large number of neighbourhood planning groups through running student projects, attending meetings and research. The energy, persistence, questioning and enthusiasm of these groups remain a constant source of inspiration. While the inspiration is all theirs, the errors, of course, remain ours.

Notes on contributors

Larry Bennett earned his PhD in Urban Planning and Policy at Rutgers University and for many years has taught in the Political Science Department at DePaul University, USA. Professor Bennett's research has focused on the politics of urban redevelopment, examining this process both from the standpoint of city-scale intentions and in terms of neighbourhood impacts. His most recent books are *Neoliberal Chicago* (University of Illinois Press, 2016, co-edited with Roberta Garner and Euan Hague) and *The third city: Chicago and American urbanism* (University of Chicago Press, 2010). With Zane Miller and David Stradling, Professor Bennett edits Temple University Press' 'Urban life, landscapes, and policy' book series. He has also served on the editorial boards of *Urban Affairs Quarterly* and the *Journal of Urban Affairs*. For the last 20 years, Professor Bennett has been a member of the Board of Directors for North Branch Works, an economic development non-profit organisation serving Chicago's North River Corridor.

Quintin Bradley is a Senior Lecturer in Planning and Housing at Leeds Beckett University, UK, and leads postgraduate study in planning, housing and regeneration at the School of Built Environment & Engineering. He holds a PhD in housing studies and is active in research in the fields of community planning, housing policy and community engagement. His work has been published in peer-reviewed international journals and his monograph on the tenants' movement is published by Routledge. As a practitioner, he has extensive experience in community involvement and has worked for resident-led organisations, as well as local housing authorities and housing associations. He is active in campaigns and social movements and has a background as an investigative journalist.

Sue Brownill is a Reader in Urban Policy and Governance at the School of the Built Environment, Oxford Brookes University, UK and holds a PhD from The Centre for Urban and Regional Studies, Birmingham University. She specialises in urban planning, housing and regeneration but her particular interest is in public participation and the relationship between citizens and the state. She has experienced and written widely about this from a range of perspectives: working for a community planning organisation in London Docklands; carrying out evaluations of Planning Aid; researching neighbourhood planning;

and promoting joint work between students and community planning groups. She has worked with concepts of governmentality, modes of governance and, more recently, assemblage. Her recent work has focused on planning for affordable housing and on re-examining the hidden histories of community-led planning.

Amy Burnett is a PhD candidate in Real Estate and Planning at the Henley Business School, University of Reading, UK. Amy's research focuses on the role of civil society groups in promoting sustainable development in the context of planning and broader policy influence. Her current research explores notions of sustainability transitions and the role of networks in fostering innovation in the context of neighbourhood planning. Amy has experience in promoting sustainable communities in the UK and through her international development background in Africa and Brazil.

Paul Burton is Professor of Urban Management and Planning and Director of the Cities Research Centre at Griffith University, Australia. Paul is a founding member of Regional Development Australia, Gold Coast, and a member of the National Education Committee of the Planning Institute of Australia. Prior to joining Griffith University in 2007, he was Head of the School for Policy Studies at the University of Bristol and formerly in the School for Advanced Urban Studies.

Claire Colomb is Reader in Planning and Urban Sociology at the Bartlett School of Planning, University College London, UK, and holds a first degree in Politics and Sociology (Institut d'Etudes Politiques de Paris, France) and a PhD in Planning (University College London). Her research interests cover: urban and regional governance; planning and urban regeneration in European cities; urban social movements and public participation in planning; European spatial planning and territorial cooperation; and comparative planning systems and cultures. She is the co-author of *European spatial planning and territorial cooperation* (Routledge, 2010, with S. Dühr and V. Nadin) and the author of *Staging the new Berlin: Place marketing and the politics of urban reinvention* (Routledge, 2011).

Camille Gardesse is Associate Professor at the Urban Planning School of Paris, France, and member of the Lab'Urba research centre, in which she is co-responsible for the 'Inequalities and Discrimination' research team. She has a background in sociology and urban planning. Her PHD was on the participative process organised by the Paris municipality for the renovation project of the district of les Halles in Paris. This research analysed the possibilities for deploying participative arrangements in French urban projects. She has continued to research the relationship between urban project management and participative arrangements by participating in several collective research projects including the Concertation Décision Environnement project for the Ministry of Ecology, Environment and Sustainable Development, which focused on the interaction between citizen participation, urban planning and decision-making in the French Eco-Quatiers programme.

Carol Ludwig is a Chartered Town and Country Planning professional and scholar. Prior to academia, she was principal planner at Northumberland County Council in north-east England, where she led the Environment and Natural Resources Local Development Framework (LDF) team. Prior to this role, she was principal planner at Blyth Valley Borough Council. Both roles involved the preparation of local policy, master plans and development briefs. After almost six years working in practice, Carol moved into academia in 2010 to pursue doctoral research. In 2013, she finalised her PhD thesis, which bridges the fields of planning theory (collaborative planning and post-positivism) with critical heritage studies. Following almost two years working as a Lecturer in Planning at Northumbria University, Carol joined the University of Liverpool in October 2014 as a Lecturer in Planning (Civic Design). Her main research interests include: planning theory and practice; the theorisation of heritage, including its contestable interpretation and representation; the cultural process of identity formation; and social inclusion and community mobilisation in local planning processes.

David McGuinness is a Senior Lecturer in Planning and Urban Regeneration within the Faculty of Engineering and Environment at Northumbria University, UK. His research encompasses governance, urban regeneration, planning, sustainable development and resilience. David has been involved in major European research projects (eg FP5 STATUS and FP6 PRIMUS), resulting in the recent academic publication *Informed cities: Making research work for local sustainability* (Earthscan, 2014, with Marko Joas, Kate Theobald, Cristina Garzillo and Stefan Kuhn). He is a Fellow of the Higher Education Academy, member of the Town and Country Planning Association, and a founder member of the European Informed Cities Network.

Gavin Parker is Professor of Planning Studies at the School of Real Estate and Planning, University of Reading, UK. He is a chartered planner with research and teaching interests covering a range of topics, including community-led planning and local governance. During the period 2012–14, he was seconded as Director of Professional Standards at the Royal Town Planning Institute, where, among other responsibilities, he oversaw Planning Aid England in delivering direct support to neighbourhood planning groups across England. Gavin also chaired the Community Council for Berkshire (2006–11) and was a director of the True Food Community Cooperative (2008–15). Professor Parker has produced numerous academic and practice-oriented publications, including the books *Citizenships, contingency and the countryside* (Routledge, 2002) and *Key concepts in planning* (Sage, 2012), as well as a string of papers and reports relating to planning at the neighbourhood scale, including the October 2014 report 'User experience of neighbourhood planning' for Locality/DCLG.

Simon Pemberton, PhD, is Reader in Human Geography at Keele University, UK. During his career, Simon worked on several post-doctoral research projects before becoming Head of Regeneration for a local authority in North Wales. After four years in practice, Simon moved to become Director of the Merseyside Social Inclusion Observatory at the University of Liverpool between 2004 and 2010. Subsequently, Simon moved to the Centre for Urban and Regional Studies (CURS) at the University of Birmingham. In 2013, he moved to take up his present position at Keele. His academic work has a strong policy application and bridges the geography–planning–public policy interface. He has research interests in three main areas: (1) the rescaling of the state and implications for urban and rural regeneration; (2) super-diversity and urban planning; and (3) community-based planning. With reference to community-based planning, recent relevant papers include 'The filling in of community planning in the devolved UK' (2015; with Deborah Peel and Greg Lloyd), 'Reconciling community planning and city regionalism for efficiency gains' (2011; with Greg Lloyd) and 'Devolution, community planning and institutional decongestion?' (2008; with Greg Lloyd).

William Sparling is a PhD candidate researching the impact of Localism on the English planning system at Leeds Beckett University, UK. His research focuses on the early implications of neighbourhood planning on two urban areas of Leeds and how they attempted to fill the void left by the disappearance of spatial and regional planning. He also works in planning practice, as a senior planning policy officer, leading on neighbourhood planning for a district council in Oxfordshire and previously worked as a freelance planning consultant in Leeds.

Jodelle Zetlaoui-Léger has a PhD in Urbanism and Spatial Planning and is Professor at the École Nationale Supérieure d'Architecture Paris la Villette, France. She was previously Senior Lecturer at the Institut d'Urbanisme de Paris from 1994 to 2010. She is a member of the *Laboratoire Espaces Travail* research centre within the *Unité Mixte de Recherche CNRS LAVUE* (*Laboratoire Architecture, Ville, Urbanisme et Environnement*), and co-chairs the scientific committee for the French national EcoQuartiers programme. Her research is mainly focused on project processes, the professional practice of architecture and urban planning, and the use of evaluation approaches from both French and Anglo-Saxon perspectives. Her work considers how project organisation and the professional expertise, of both urban planners and construction professionals, have evolved in response to growing demands for sustainable development and the democratisation of urban production. Since the mid-1990s, she has undertaken ongoing collaborations with architecture and urbanism agencies aimed at integrating participative processes into urban design projects.

ONE

Introduction

Sue Brownill and Quintin Bradley

Introduction

> The coalition government will revolutionise the planning
> process by taking power away from officials and putting
> it into the hands of those who know most about their
> neighbourhood – local people themselves. (DCLG, 2010)

This statement and the legislation that followed it unleashed a new
wave of community-based planning in England. As one of a range
of rights and powers introduced by the localism agenda of 2011,
neighbourhood groups were able to draw up statutory land-use plans,
thereby creating a new tier in the planning framework. Five years later,
with close to 2,000 neighbourhoods formally engaged in the process,
it was clear that neighbourhood planning had emerged as one of the
most widespread community initiatives in recent years and one of
the most current topics within spatial planning. As such, it demands
further investigation, and the challenges it raises for new theoretical
understandings and new perspectives in planning practice need to be
explored; hence the rationale for this book.

Neighbourhood planning may well have been defined by government
as 'a *new* way for communities to decide the future of the places where
they live and work' (DCLG, 2012, p 3, emphasis added) but it builds
on a long history of community-based planning and can be seen as
the latest in a series of initiatives that have attempted to 'fix' what is
seen as the restricted and imperfect opportunities for the public to
engage in the planning system (Brownill and Parker, 2010). Neither is
localism a new concept and the tensions between attempts by citizens
to have greater control over the places in which they live and attempts
by governments to search for new forms of democratic engagement
have become a central feature of contemporary planning systems.
Within the international state rhetoric of empowerment (Painter et al,
2011), governments around the world are seeing the locality as a key

arena for restructuring the relations between the state and its citizens, promoting greater participation in planning and achieving sustainable growth. Such tendencies interact with a long-standing history of local organising that sees the locality as a site for progressive social change.

We would therefore argue that neighbourhood planning is both a particularly English phenomenon which deserves to be explored in more depth, and a microcosm of key planning issues that has resonance for wider debates on participation, localism and the purposes and practices of planning. As such, this book aims to critically explore neighbourhood planning through empirical evidence on how it is evolving and by placing these experiences in the context of existing debates on governance and planning in an international context. This is an edited volume and not a 'reader' in the strictest sense of the word; however, it addresses four central themes, which inform the structure of the book. The first is to explore whether, given the growing critique of the constrained freedoms and the uneven geographies of the 'turn to the local' (Clarke and Cochrane, 2013; Davoudi and Madanipour, 2015), initiatives such as neighbourhood planning can, indeed, represent some form of democratic renewal and 'power to the people'. Second, the book aims to extend the focus on governance and democratic engagement that has tended to characterise existing research to explore neighbourhood planning as a form of planning practice, revealing tensions between the potentially contradictory agendas for planning that inform it. Third, the book explores the rescaling of planning and participation in an international context, revealing the variety of state–citizen relationships that emerge. Finally, given the contradictory potential revealed in existing debates, we discuss whether more progressive forms of planning and localism can emerge through neighbourhood planning and similar initiatives. The book also aims to highlight these debates through privileging the experiences and voices of the situated actors within the neighbourhood planning process itself at a variety of scales and across a variety of locations. The rest of this chapter briefly introduces these four themes before outlining the structure of the book in more detail.

Localism, neighbourhood planning and empowerment

Given the prospect that neighbourhood planning can extend local control and reinvigorate democratic engagement, issues of empowerment and democracy are key to its appeal and consideration, and form the first theme that this book addresses. Neighbourhood planning also has to be seen in the context of the rise of localism,

Photo 1.1: Consultation begins on a draft neighbourhood plan

Source: Holbeck neighbourhood forum, Leeds: photograph Harvey Pritchard

characterised by the scalar and spatial dispersal of power, which has become a key feature of contemporary governance. Debates exist over the extent, nature and intent of this devolution, hence the subtitle of this book and the question mark that ends it. It is now widely rehearsed and accepted that terms like 'localism' are contested. It can be seen variously as a new form of empowerment, an example of spatial liberalism, the emergences of a co-productive planning practice, a way of resolving contradictions between economic growth and sustainability, a practice that exacerbates spatial injustice, and a site for alternative place-based politics and identities to emerge. Theoretical debates reflect this disparity characterising localism as (among other interpretations): indicative of new forms of collaborative governance and co-production (Gallant and Robinson, 2012; Healey, 2015); opening up opportunities to work the spaces of power (Newman, 2012); an example of neoliberal governmentality, engaging the public in projects that help deliver the state's objectives (Davoudi and Madanipour, 2013) and as evidence of the 'soft spaces' of spatial liberalism designed to foster economic growth (Houghton et al, 2013). Yet, while much has been written about the theoretical implications of what localism might mean (Clarke and Cochrane, 2013; Davoudi and

Madanipour, 2015), there has been less opportunity to explore how 'actually existing examples' of localism play out in practice; a gap that this exploration of neighbourhood planning seeks to fill.

Such an exploration can counter, we suggest, the tendency that arises within current debates to present neighbourhood planning and localism through dichotomies: empowerment or abandonment, central versus local, progressive or regressive. We tend to agree with Houghton et al (2013, p 219), who state that localism can be seen as inherently 'neither a good nor a bad thing ... [which] makes the key analytical challenge one of understanding how particular governance assemblages come to be formed'. This opens up the possibility for a variety of assemblages to emerge. Further, as Wills (2016, p 45) states: 'the new landscape of localism provides new political opportunities that are yet to be considered in academic debate'. We hope to contribute to this debate by delineating some of these new opportunities and the conceptual tools that can characterise and understand them. For example, is it possible to see the collective community mobilisations oriented to a 'passion for place' as a particular form of empowerment and politics beyond the expectations of state-sponsored participation exercises (Bradley, 2014)? And if so how are places remade and shaped through these practices? Other questions opened up include whether we need to move away from existing spatial metaphors of scale and networks to understand the complexities of power relations (Allen, 2016)? What forms of statecraft are emerging (Wills, 2016)? And to what purposes are the (re)constructed spaces of the neighbourhood being oriented (Clarke and Cochrane, 2013)?

This does not mean that the issues raised by existing debates should be ignored. These include the ability of neighbourhood planning to overcome previous problems of the over-representation of some sections of the public in participation in planning (the 'usual suspects') and the under-representation of others ('apathy'), and concerns over legitimacy (Davoudi and Cowie, 2013). Questions about territorial and social justice in an era of spatial liberalism (Lowndes and Pratchett, 2012) and the uneven distribution of the social and economic capital, skills and capacities needed to engage in community planning, particularly in a time of austerity, are also relevant (Holman and Rydin, 2012; Gunn et al, 2015). However, we would argue, they are evidence of the complexity of the emerging landscape of 'localisms' rather than dichotomies. We are mindful that by asking the question 'Power to the people?', we are in danger of repeating these same tendencies by judging localism against an ideal of empowerment and in opposition to centralism; however, by asking arguably the wrong question, we seek to open up new areas of debate and understanding.

Neighbourhood planning and the purposes of planning

It would be wrong to consider neighbourhood planning only within the context of governance and empowerment. The experience of neighbourhood planning strikes at the heart of debates about the purposes of planning and the differing futures that emerge through its practice. Engaging with these debates is the second theme explored in this book. Rydin (2013) draws our attention to the dominance of a 'growth-dependent paradigm' in contemporary planning systems: the restructuring of the policies, practices and governance of planning to enable economic growth, often under the ambiguous banner of 'sustainability'. Indeed, the government believed that devolving planning powers would encourage communities to say 'yes to growth'. Yet, the emerging picture of communities who are exploring the possibilities of neighbourhood planning to reassert the social, environmental and redistributive purposes of planning through, for example, promoting local policies in response to climate change, or encouraging non-speculative forms of housing delivery and community-owned land and assets, forces us to think about what other purposes of planning there are and to consider the possibilities for their implementation. The ability of neighbourhood planning to present counter-narratives to the dominant planning paradigm and localism discourse and to put forward a differing representation of the neighbourhood, not as a mere recipient of growth, but as a site of progressive alternatives, comes into play here, underlining the differing assemblages that are possible.

Similarly, neighbourhood planning speaks to debates about the practices and cultures of planning. The extent to which the prioritising of 'local' as opposed to 'expert' planning knowledge can shift planning's power dynamics towards co-production remains open to question given the skills and technicalities involved and the legal and bureaucratic nature of planning (Beebeejaun, 2015; Parker et al, 2015). Such considerations also remind us that, at the end of the day, planning is done by people – people whose experiences, conflicts, frustrations, commitment and enthusiasm are an integral part of the neighbourhood planning story. These narratives, which are given voice throughout this book wherever possible, reveal the emotions of neighbourhood working, which can themselves be part of the politics of participation (Jupp, 2008; Bradley, 2014). They illuminate how the identities of new citizen-planners are being created within the participatory spaces of neighbourhood planning and whether these conform to the normative pro-growth constructions anticipated by the state or allow for alternative identities to emerge (Inch, 2015).

Exploring planning at the neighbourhood level also reveals how planning is currently subject to contradictory forces in the UK and beyond. At the same time as initiatives such as localism claim to empower neighbourhoods, other changes to national planning frameworks and policies reinforce the opposite, centralising decision-making and reducing local autonomy (Lord and Tewdwr-Jones, 2014). Austerity governance, with its associated restrictions in funding to local authorities and public agencies, serves to further circumscribe the room for manoeuvre within the spaces of localism, and neighbourhoods are caught in the crosshairs of these paradoxical processes. While the focus of this book is on the local level, the neighbourhood experience is placed in the context of broader shifts in the spatial governance of planning and their contradictory potential.

Global perspectives on localism and planning at the local level

The largely English experience of neighbourhood planning, of course, needs to be placed in the context of how localism is evolving around the world, and this forms the third theme for the book. This enables insights into how localism can be assembled differently, take on different meanings and be shaped through different policy and political objectives in different places and at different times. As such, a variety of 'localisms' can be observed both within and between countries. Such international perspectives also speak to debates about the purposes of planning, revealing how the discourses and scope of what is seen as 'neighbourhood planning' vary, reflecting the tensions outlined earlier between the economic and social goals of planning and constructions of the role of place and publics in determining planning outcomes. Similarly, an international perspective can highlight the complexities of multi-level governance and its many configurations as the balance between tendencies towards centralisation and decentralisation change.

Possibilities for a progressive localism

It is clear, therefore, that initiatives such as neighbourhood planning can be viewed as having a contradictory potential. This leads on to the final theme addressed: whether it is possible to see alternative forms of localism emerging through the practices and experiences of neighbourhood planning. Featherstone et al (2012), Healey (2015) and others argue that a progressive localism that challenges existing power relations and the meta-narratives of growth within planning paradigms is possible. This would suggest the possibility for the neighbourhood to emerge as a space oriented to more social and grassroots planning purposes (Rydin, 2013), either on its own or in combination with other community rights such as the community ownership of land. Newman (2012) similarly argues strongly that the actors engaged in local initiatives have the opportunity for 'working the spaces of power', as opposed to being ciphers of predetermined futures. However, this optimism that neighbourhood planning can progress and prefigure alternatives within the contradictory spaces of localism is tempered by awareness of the constraints faced and is challenged by more critical analyses. Whether it is possible to balance these accounts is a key question for this book and is returned to in the conclusions.

Structure of the book

In order to address the key themes outlined earlier, the book is divided into four parts and 15 chapters. The contributory chapters speak to these themes through a variety of voices, reflecting the diversity of views on and experiences of localism and citizen-led planning in an international context. Part One introduces neighbourhood planning within the context of localism, critically exploring its theoretical and policy background and expanding on some of the key debates about empowerment, place and the nature of planning. Part Two builds on this by focusing on neighbourhood planning in practice. Drawing on a range of case studies, it investigates the issues and debates raised in Part One through the stories, experiences, emotions and contestations emerging on the ground. Part Three places the English experience in an international perspective by revealing how 'neighbourhood planning' and 'localism' are defined and understood differently in diverse contexts. The final chapter concludes the book by discussing whether neighbourhood planning contains within it the prospect of progressive forms of localism and planning.

Part One sets out the background, policies and processes of neighbourhood planning and engages with debates on the theory and practice of neighbourhood planning and localism. It discusses neighbourhood planning in the context of debates on the nature of power and how the new state spaces of localism can be characterised and understood. It identifies neighbourhood planning as a distinctive set of spatial practices and begins to explore how emerging experience relates to concerns about territorial and social inclusivity and the purposes of planning. In Chapter Two, Sue Brownill introduces the initiative of neighbourhood planning and critically examines the discourses of the localism agenda in England since 2010 within the context of global debates on the shifting spatial scales of governance. The chapter extends the arguments about the need to move beyond dichotomies, identifying a variety of propositions and purposes that inform neighbourhood planning, along with associated contradictions, tensions and counter-narratives. These propositions are: to create spaces of empowerment, and of economic growth; to remake planning's publics; and to remake planning as a collaborative activity. The chapter concludes by arguing for the need to explore how these propositions and their counter-narratives play out differently in different places, setting out the possibility of the contradictory potential of localism that is explored throughout the book.

In Chapter Three, Quintin Bradley addresses the central issue of 'power to the people' through discussing the democratic and political processes of neighbourhood planning. The chapter argues for an understanding of participation based on antagonism and conflict rather than the notions of inclusion found in policy discourses. It explores the political identities that emerge at the community level and charts the impact of direct, participatory and representative democracy on new and existing relations of power.

Two chapters follow that examine the theme of neighbourhood planning as a form of planning practice, exploring processes, outcomes and implications. In Chapter Four, Quintin Bradley, Amy Burnett and William Sparling explore the implementation of neighbourhood planning as a specific set of spatial practices. Through examining examples of published plans, the chapter explores how key planning issues, such as the provision of sites for housing and achieving low carbon futures and social sustainability, are being dealt with in neighbourhood planning in the light of government expectations. The authors argue that neighbourhood planning has been able to develop distinctive and locally identified spatial practices that potentially enable neighbourhoods to balance social, economic and environmental sustainability while also challenging the strategies of the growth-dependent planning paradigm.

Gavin Parker's chapter (Chapter Five) draws primarily on recent research that surveyed 120 groups involved at different stages of the neighbourhood planning process in England. Focusing on both the experiences of those involved in urban and rural areas, it provides a source from which to draw out some wider observations about the overall neighbourhood planning experience. In particular, it gives insights into the evolution of neighbourhood planning groups in terms of their motivations and capacities to engage, their location and socio-economic background, the issues that they are focusing on, and the barriers that they have been facing. In the light of debates on localism, it discusses the extent to which neighbourhood planning is producing an uneven and unequal geography and adds new dimensions to debates on capacity building and the over- and under-representation of certain interests in neighbourhood planning.

In Part Two, the focus shifts to neighbourhood planning in practice. This section explores how the spaces of engagement created by neighbourhood planning are experienced by those involved and what the emerging histories of neighbourhood planning reveal about how localism moves from a set of propositions to a series of practices on the ground. The chapters shed further light on the key themes that the book is addressing, raising questions about whether the rhetoric of power to the people contained in policy is an emerging reality and the extent to which a variety of purposes of planning are evident. The chapters reveal the motivations, frustrations, achievements and conflicts involved and, in turn, use this empirical experience to raise further theoretical questions about the ability of neighbourhood planning to present alternative representations of the neighbourhood, political activity and localism.

In Chapter Six, David McGuinness and Carol Ludwig tell the story of two neighbourhood plan 'front-runners' – Upper Eden in rural Cumbria and North Shields on the Tyneside coast – drawing on extensive interviews with key stakeholders. The chapter reveals the different local contexts and trajectories in the two neighbourhoods and also the challenges, compromises and frustrations faced by those involved, particularly in relation to the skills and social capital required. It also critically explores the wider lessons that can be drawn from these two advanced case studies about the reality of localism at the neighbourhood level, questioning whether areas can *really* influence their future via neighbourhood plans.

The following chapter (Chapter Seven) continues the emphasis on the lived realities of neighbourhood planning by bringing together a range of participants to talk about their experiences in their own words. Presented as a series of verbatim narratives, the accounts from neighbourhood planners, local authority officers, developers and consultants reveal a vivid picture of the energy, passion and frustrations in navigating the spaces of neighbourhood planning. They also lay bare some of the conflicting rationales of localism and divergent views on how the role of these different actors can and should be constituted. While intending these narratives to stand on their own, the editors encourage readers to consider how some of the book's broader themes of power relations, democratic renewal and the remaking of planning and places are made real through these stories of the everyday practices of planning at the neighbourhood level and the lives of those engaged in them.

In Chapter Eight, Claire Colomb asks whether neighbourhood planning has the potential to bring about more progressive, socially equitable forms of decision-making or, on the contrary, whether it promotes inter-group conflict and exclusionary forms of planning. It analyses cases of neighbourhood planning and community mobilisation in the London Borough of Hackney, an area of ethnic and socio-economic super-diversity. The chapter argues that in the context of a highly unequal city like London, the concept of a homogeneous or potentially articulate and cohesive community that often underpins policy assumptions about neighbourhood planning rarely makes sense. Contrasting case studies indicate how, in this context, neighbourhood planning has the potential to both divide and unite 'communities'.

By examining examples of completed neighbourhood plans as they enter the planning system, Sue Brownill, in Chapter Nine, revisits one of the central themes of the book: the extent to which neighbourhoods are empowered within the constrained freedoms of localism. Given the complex dynamics revealed, the chapter argues for a topological view of power, focusing not on the scalar relations between different *levels* of state and other power, but on how these reach into and interact in the same space. The chapter goes on to explore how the shifting power relations around neighbourhood planning are creating spaces with the potential to either reinforce the expected outcomes of growth-dependent planning or to reshape and even replace them.

Chapter Ten engages with the emotional attachments of place that often form the basis of the motivations to engage in neighbourhood planning but which can be excluded from accounts of its practice. In it, Quintin Bradley explores how place identity and place attachment are mobilised in neighbourhood plans and how they can form the basis of collective neighbourhood action. The chapter considers neighbourhood working as a form of political activity in itself, over and above the intent of writing land-use policies, and argues that 'emplacement' and how place is experienced can be a route to empowerment.

Part Three places the English experience of neighbourhood planning into an international context, drawing on experience from a range of countries engaged (or not) in promoting planning at the local level. It reveals further the different meanings and interpretations of the scope of neighbourhood planning and localism that can emerge, with neighbourhood planning seen variously as land-use planning, the interface between communities and authorities in the improved delivery of services (including social projects, community development and health), and citizen engagement. Such contrasts put the confines of official English localism and attempts by communities to embrace wider rationalities than the economic into context. The section also shows that while multi-level governance may well be an international phenomenon, the political and rhetorical significance given to the neighbourhood level within this can vary significantly. It reveals how different state structures, ideologies and priorities influence neighbourhood planning and how attempts to remodel state–citizen relationships evolve. This underlines the need to understand how neighbourhood planning can be assembled differently in different places. Similarly, the chapters come to some differing conclusions on the possibilities for the emergence of a more progressive localism.

In Chapter Eleven, Simon Pemberton begins this section by exploring localism and what is termed here 'community-based planning' in the context of the devolved nations of the UK. It does this, first, through considering some broader debates about the rescaling of governance, arguing that a 'strategic-relational approach' can help understand the disparate processes of the 'hollowing out' and 'filling in' of the state that characterise devolution. The chapter highlights how policy ideas and knowledge are socially constructed and spatially constituted, meaning that a variety of 'localisms' have emerged in the UK. While English community-based planning can be seen as focusing on economic growth and lacking strategic coordination, in Wales and Northern Ireland, the concern has been more with modernising and democratising service delivery. Meanwhile, the chapter suggests that the Scottish emphasis on securing equality through locally flexible yet vertically linked community-based planning arrangements may provide evidence of a more progressive localism.

In Chapter Twelve, Camille Gardesse and Jodelle Zetlaoui-Léger reflect on the evolution of participation in planning and the prospects for localism in the French context of a centralised and republican state. They show how a hierarchical governance structure, a conception of the public official as the custodian of the 'general interest' and the exclusion of the idea of community from the construction of republican citizenship severely limited participation until the 2000s, creating a 'French exception' to the increasingly participatory norm in other Western democracies. Although not immune to a more recent turn to the neighbourhood, including the policy transfer of 'English' participatory techniques and a rediscovery of the neighbourhood in urban policy linked to the social crisis of the *banlieues*, the authors conclude that the pervasiveness and inertia of previous eras, as well as the increasing role of the private sector in managing large-scale urban projects, mean that these are unlikely to fulfil their potential. However, they also point to more positive examples where local authorities more committed to participation can use their powers to open up the 'common territorial good', raising the question of whether a strong state is needed to ensure that the freedoms of localism can develop.

This is followed by two chapters that discuss localism and community-based planning under federal systems. In Chapter Thirteen, using Evans et al's threefold classification of representative, managerial and community localism, Paul Burton contrasts the devolved managerial responsibilities to local authorities of Australian localism with the promotion of citizen and neighbourhood rights in the community localism in England. Focusing on examples of localism in practice, the chapter outlines how, while many state and territory governments extol the virtues of refocusing attention on local levels of government, the ways in which apparently devolutionary programmes are constructed in practice suggests that more complex processes of multi-level governance are at work. In addition, concerted attempts to devolve power to the neighbourhood level are conspicuous by their absence. As Burton concludes, localism in Australia is 'a principle yet to be applied with any degree of enthusiasm' (this volume, p 228).

In Chapter Fourteen, Larry Bennett similarly shows how the federal nature of government in the US has contributed to the emergence of a diverse neighbourhood planning landscape. Defining neighbourhood planning in the US context as being centred on the bringing together of professionals and residents to produce locally responsive plans or services rather than the devolution of power, the chapter traces its 'many lives' from its origins in the settlement movement in disadvantaged Chicago neighbourhoods (another policy transfer from England), through responses to the protest movements of the 1960s, to a much broader current agenda encompassing such diverse activities as schooling, community policing, participatory budgeting and neighbourhood coalitions. Within these, the recurring concerns of domination by more affluent residents, the uneven nature of the capacity of communities to engage and the ability of higher levels of governance to override local decisions are apparent. Given these limitations, the chapter cautions that what is in effect a limited restructuring of local governance is unlikely to deliver significant social change.

The final chapter (Chapter Fifteen) reflects on the themes addressed throughout the book. In doing so, Quintin Bradley and Sue Brownill return to the key question of whether or not it is possible to see a more progressive form of localism emerging through the practices of neighbourhood planning – one that addresses social justice, is open and democratic, and reasserts the social and redistributive purposes of planning. Drawing on the debates and evidence presented in the preceding chapters, they discuss the possibilities for progress evident through new forms of democratic engagement and place identity, the emerging counter-narratives to the purposes of localism being pursued by government, and the potential realisation of these purposes through the tools of land-use policies and development. However, they also question the extent to which this potential can be realised within the current constraints of localism apparent in England and elsewhere. Nevertheless, while neighbourhood planning may or may not represent 'power to the people', it is obvious that it has changed the landscape and the dynamics of planning, and will do so in ways that will continue to ripple through planning thought and practice for years to come.

References

Allan, J. (2016) *Topologies of power*, Abingdon: Routledge.

Beebeejaun, Y. (2015) 'Co-production and neighbourhood planning', presentation to the ESRC Seminar on 'Neighbourhood Ways of Knowing and Working', London, 24 June.

Bradley, Q. (2014) 'Bringing democracy back home: community localism and the domestication of political space', *Environment & Planning D: Society & Space*, vol 32, no 4, pp 642–57.

Brownill, S. and Parker, G. (2010) 'Why bother with good works? The relevance of public participation(s) in planning in a post-collaborative era', *Planning Practice and Research*, vol 25, no 3, pp 275–82.

Clarke, N. and Cochrane, A. (2013) 'Geographies and politics of localism: the localism of the United Kingdom's Coalition government', *Political Geography*, vol 34, pp 10–23.

Davoudi, S. and Cowie, P. (2013) 'Are English neighbourhood forums democratically legitimate?', *Planning Theory and Practice*, vol 14, no 4, pp 562–6.

Davoudi, S. and Madanipour, A. (2013) 'Localism and neo-liberal governmentality', *Town Planning Review*, vol 84, no 5, pp 551–61.

Davoudi, S. and Madanipour, A. (2015) *Reconsidering Localism*, Abingdon: Routledge.

DCLG (Department for Communities and Local Government) (2010) 'Planning power from town halls and Whitehall to local people', press release, 6 December. Available at: https://www.gov.uk/government/news/planning-power-from-town-halls-and-whitehall-to-local-people

DCLG (2012) 'Neighbourhood planning'. Available at: https://www.gov.uk/government/uploads/system/uploads/attachment_data/file/229749/Neighbourhood_planning.pdf

Featherstone, D., Ince, A., Mackinnon, D., Strauss, K. and Cumbers, A. (2012) 'Progressive localism and the construction of political alternatives', *Transactions of the Institute of British Geographers*, vol 37, pp 177–82.

Gallant, N. and Robinson, J. (2012) *Neighbourhood planning*, Bristol: The Policy Press.

Gunn, S., Brookes, E. and Vigar, J. (2015) 'The community's capacity to plan: the disproportionate requirements of the English neighbourhood plan initiative', in S. Davoudi and A. Madanipour (eds) *Reconsidering localism*, Abingdon: Routledge, pp 147–67.

Healey, P. (2015) 'Civic capacity, place governance and progressive localism', in S. Davoudi and A. Madanipour (eds) *Reconsidering localism*, Abingdon: Routledge, pp 105–25.

Holman, N. and Rydin, Y. (2012) 'What can social capital tells us about planning under localism?', *Local Government Studies*, vol 39, no 1, pp 71–88.

Houghton, G., Allmendinger, P. and Oosterlynck, S. (2013) 'Spaces of neoliberal experimentation: soft spaces, postpolitics and neoliberal governmentality', *Environment and Planning A*, vol 45, no 1, pp 217–34.

Inch, A. (2015) 'Ordinary citizens and the political cultures of planning: in search of the subject of a new democratic ethos', *Planning Theory*, vol 14, no 4, pp 404–24.

Jupp, E. (2008) 'The feeling of participation: everyday spaces and social change', *Geoforum*, vol 39, pp 331–43.

Lord, A. and Tewdwr-Jones, M. (2014) 'Is planning under attack? Chronicling the deregulation of urban and environmental planning in England', *European Planning Studies*, vol 22, no 2, pp 345–61.

Lowndes, V. and Pratchett, L. (2012) 'Local government under the Coalition government: austerity, localism and the "Big Society"', *Local Government Studies*, vol 38, no 1, pp 21–40.

Newman, J. (2012) *Working the spaces of power: Activism, neo-liberalism and gendered labour*, London: Bloomsbury.

Painter, J., Orton, A., Macleod, G., Dominelli, L. and Pande, R. (2011) 'Connecting localism & community empowerment: research review and critical synthesis for the ARHC Connected Community Programme', project report, Department of Geography & School of Applied Social Sciences, Durham University, Durham.

Parker, G., Lynn, T. and Wargent, M. (2015) 'Sticking to the script? The co-production of neighbourhood planning in England', *Town Planning Review*, vol 86, no 5, pp 519–37.

Rydin, Y. (2013) *The Future of Planning*, Bristol: The Policy Press.

Wills, J. (2016) 'Emerging geographies of English localism; the case of neighbourhood planning', *Political Geography*, vol 53, pp 43–53.

Part One:
Understanding and characterising
neighbourhood planning

This section introduces neighbourhood planning and localism in policy and practice and begins to outline the significance of the initiative and what it reveals about the key themes that we are addressing in relation to democracy, participation and the purposes of planning. Four chapters bring together theoretical analysis and field research to lay out these key themes, test them in practice and flag up the continuing lines of inquiry. In Chapter Two, Sue Brownill provides a comprehensive introduction to neighbourhood planning and situates it within an international context of community-led planning, citizen engagement and shifting scales of governance. She explores the social, spatial and political assemblages of localism, and highlights the counter-narratives and challenges revealed through neighbourhood planning, discussed further throughout the book. In Chapter Three, Quintin Bradley articulates the democratic practices of neighbourhood planning, as well as its themes of autonomy, self-management and insurgent citizenship. He charts a tradition of collective direct action in the planning system, exploring the political identities of the locality and the impact of neighbourhood planning on the regulation of participation and the inequalities of political space.

From this engagement with the possibilities, tensions and contradictions of neighbourhood planning, Chapters Four and Five examine planning practice and begin to clarify the operation of these themes at the neighbourhood level. In Chapter Four, Quintin Bradley, Amy Burnett and William Sparling highlight the distinctive spatial practices of neighbourhood planning that aim to balance social, economic and environmental sustainability in housing, regeneration and low carbon futures. In Chapter Five, Gavin Parker provides a vivid depiction of the geographical spread of neighbourhood planning and the motivations and abilities of the community groups engaging in it. He explores the tensions between local and technical knowledge, participative democracy, and the socio-spatial inequalities of localism as they are experienced in neighbourhoods, and provides an evidence base from which to draw out the book's wider observations about the dynamics of neighbourhood planning.

TWO

Neighbourhood planning and the purposes and practices of localism

Sue Brownill

Introduction

This chapter situates neighbourhood planning within the context of the evolution of community-led planning, citizen engagement and the shifting scales of spatial planning at the national and international levels. It critically examines neighbourhood planning as a key element of the localism that has evolved in England since 2010, outlining the contradictory propositions and powers at its heart. The chapter is in three parts. The first explores international trends in planning policy and governance and ways of characterising and understanding these, arguing that we have to move away from dichotomies to look at the complexities of the social, spatial and political relations involved. The second section critically examines the localism and the neighbourhood planning initiatives of recent UK governments in the context of these debates, while the third section highlights the counter-narratives, tensions and challenges that are revealed and which are examined in later chapters in the book.

The turn to the local

Neighbourhood planning may appear to be a particularly English initiative but it can only be fully understood within the context of international trends in planning and governance. Ideals of decentralising power and changing the boundaries between the state and its citizens have increasingly found expression in a range of countries and initiatives. Indeed, as Yetano et al (2010, p 784) state: 'nowadays it is difficult to find a government that is not claiming to be pursuing opportunities for citizen engagement'. Rose (1996, p 332) refers to this as the rise of 'government through community': a shift in the discourses, territory and practices of governing that appear to signal a move to a more participatory approach to decision-making and the devolution of power from central governments to what is variously termed the 'community', 'locality' or 'neighbourhood'. As we shall see throughout this book, the reality is more complex.

This turn to the local is not confined to particular times or places, taking on different forms and labels in particular social and political contexts. In the UK, it can be traced to the Community Development Projects of the late 1960s (Loney, 1983; Gallent and Robinson, 2012) and through the communitarianism of New Labour (Imrie and Raco, 2003; Wallace, 2010). It is evident, inter alia, in rural community councils in India, participatory budgeting in Brazil and the participatory rural appraisal carried out by aid agencies. Within this shifting landscape, the term 'localism' has come to encapsulate the most recent attempts to govern through community, particularly in England.

The rise of localism has been linked paradoxically to increasing globalisation, which is rendering national governments less relevant in what Rhodes (1994) terms the 'hollowing out of the state'. As power flows upwards and outwards to complex networks of quasi-state agencies, this scalar shift from government to governance can create a 'democratic deficit' and a disengagement of the public with politics, intensified by the increasing cultural and political fragmentation of contemporary society. In this context, the local becomes the space where publics can be re-engaged, and experiments in 'better government' carried out.

This spatiality is entwined with a strong rhetoric of empowerment: a commitment to 'meaningful consultation' and to handing power over to 'where it belongs' (DCLG, 2011, p 1). General arguments about the decentralisation of power can be made real and manifest at the local level, accompanied by attempts to develop new forms of deliberative and participatory democracy. However, Rose's term 'government *through* community' (emphasis added) suggests another intent: not to empower, but to use the local to frame political problems and solutions in particular ways. However, it would be wrong to see local action as just another tool of contemporary governance. There is a long history of activism in resisting development and more radical attempts to develop alternative visions and secure greater local control through, for example, the common ownership of land and other assets. The local therefore holds out possibilities for alternative forms of governance and the use of space. Its contradictory potential is one of the central themes of this book.

Understanding localism: beyond dichotomies

Given that localism presents diverse and apparently conflicting possibilities, there are inevitably difficulties and debates when it comes to understanding and defining it. Despite, or perhaps because of, its prevalence, 'the use of the term is often couched in political rhetoric and conceptual uncertainty' (Gallant and Robinson, 2012, p 23). This suggests that it is more useful to identify the many meanings and purposes associated with localism than to define it. Clarke and Cochrane (2013), for example, identify four such main (political) meanings. First, it can be seen as 'a positive disposition to localism as the necessary challenge to centralism' (Clarke and Cochrane, 2013, p 10). This encapsulates the stress on better government, on the belief that devolving control to local areas is preferable to 'big government' and on people actively engaging in improving service delivery and decision-making. Second, localism can refer to those 'actual instances' of the variety of government and other initiatives that have been termed 'localism', such as neighbourhood planning. Third, there is the sense that some interests will seek to mobilise locally. Finally, they talk about the uses and construction of locality as 'spaces of engagement oriented to a variety of ends' (Clarke and Cochrane, 2013, p 11). These could include a myriad of contradictory purposes within one construction of localism, such as promoting growth or developing prefigurative alternatives to capitalism.

Such an approach is important in avoiding the tendency to turn this contradictory potential of localism into dichotomies. Davies and Pill (2012), for example, present a choice between 'empowerment or abandonment', and Lowndes and Pratchett (2012) refer to areas 'sinking or swimming' in the tides of localism. While useful in cutting through the political rhetoric surrounding localism, such understandings are unlikely to capture the complex and fluid relations revealed throughout this book. Dichotomous thinking can be linked to 'epochal, mono-causal and uni-directional accounts of change' (Newman and Clarke, 2009, p 17). So, for some (Innes and Booher, 2004; Gallent and Robinson, 2012), localism can be seen as providing new spaces of empowerment through the rise of deliberative democracy, networked localised governance and the new forms of public ownership associated with it (Healey, 1997). Other accounts see localism not as empowerment, but as a manifestation of neoliberal governmentality (Davoudi and Madanipour, 2013; Houghton et al, 2013). Government *through* as opposed to *by* community devolves constrained responsibilities to localities within the context of creating the conditions for the marketisation of social and political relations (Brenner and Theodore, 2002; Harvey, 2005). While such an approach may bring localities into focus, these are seen as limited concessions aimed at legitimising broader political and economic shifts and reducing public dissent (Peck and Tickell, 2002), while power is, in reality, displaced from the central state to the market and those with economic power (Flyvbjerg, 1998). Related to this are accounts that see the growth of multi-scalar and networked forms of governance as signalling a shift to a post-political world, with the displacement of debate and the turning of political decisions into managerial processes undertaken by non-elected and unaccountable agencies (Swyngedouw, 2009).

In contrast, Allen and Cochrane (2010) argue that there is a need to move beyond dichotomies, such as seeing the power relations of localism as a simple movement up or down between the centre and the local (empowerment/abandonment). They reveal the more complex topologies of the web of relations, whereby, for example, central actors can exist within the local, leading to particular relations, tensions and outcomes. What constitutes the local is therefore not necessarily just 'local'; rather, it is an assemblage of ideas, actors, policies and visions held together in an uneasy and constantly changing tension. Madanipour and Davoudi (2015, p 27) likewise suggest that we see localism as an 'institutional–representational–territorial nexus with multiple and contested meanings'. This nexus is formed by the institutions and agencies that engage in a locality (again, that are not always local), the different ways in which the local is imagined and projected, and the territorial arrangements that shape it. Both accounts stress a relational view of space rather than seeing the local as bounded and static.

Newman (2012) further highlights that moving away from dichotomous thinking affords the possibility for diverse and alternative forms of localism to be identified within the focus on contradictory processes and spaces. In particular, by focusing on the changing roles of the situated actors – the officers, politicians, members of the public and others – the potential for 'working the spaces of power' is highlighted and explored rather than celebrated as empowerment or dismissed as incorporation.

In this way, localism can be seen as 'neither a good nor a bad thing' (Houghton et al, 2013, p 219). This makes it important to explore the meanings associated with it, the purposes to which it is put, the propositions of what is expected from it and the alternative forms that it could take. The rest of this chapter does this by, first, outlining localism and neighbourhood planning as it has emerged in the UK and, second, exploring the purposes of localism and the mechanisms and technologies of governance that have been put in place to achieve them.

Localism and neighbourhood planning in England: a 'new era of people power'?

> The coalition government will revolutionise the planning process by taking power away from officials and putting it into the hands of those who know most about their neighbourhood – local people themselves. (DCLG, 2010a)

It can be argued that localism has become the defining motif of UK governments since 2010. Initiatives such as the Big Society, the Localism Act and neighbourhood planning have come to constitute one of the 'actual instances' of localism outlined by Clarke and Cochrane. This remodelling of the relationship between the state and society was initially evident in the idea of the 'Big Society', with its three key principles of community empowerment, opening up public services and social action (Cabinet Office, 2010), representing to David Cameron, the then Prime Minister, 'the biggest, most dramatic redistribution of power from elites in Whitehall to the man and woman on the street' (Cameron, 2010).

Introduced at the same time as the largest public sector cuts in a generation, the Big Society struggled to be seen as anything but a way of encouraging participation to compensate for austerity, and it slipped down the political agenda. Nevertheless, the ideology behind it was embedded in different initiatives, including the 2010 Localism Bill. The government press release on the Bill's launch heralded it as starting a 'new era of people power' (DCLG, 2010b), and Erick Pickles, Secretary of State for the Environment from 2010 to 2015, famously repeated the mantra by saying:

> I have three very clear priorities: localism, and we'll weave that into everything we do from parks to finance to policy. My second priority is localism, and my third is … localism. If you want people to feel connected to their communities. Proud of their communities. Then you give people a real say over what happens in their communities. And the power to make a difference. (Pickles, 2010)

Contained within the Localism Act passed in 2011 were a wide range of initiatives for a 'fairer, more democratic and more effective' planning system (DCLG, 2011, p 11). Central to these was the devolution of planning powers, including powers for neighbourhoods to draw up their own statutory neighbourhood plans (HM Government, 2011, s116 and schedules 9, 10 and 11) (see Box 2.1). This had been prefaced through a pre-election policy paper, *Open source planning* (Conservative Party, 2010), written by John Howell, MP for Henley, in whose constituency one of the first neighbourhood plans (Thame) was situated. He said: 'Communities should be given the greatest possible opportunity to have their say and the greatest possible degree of local control. If we get this right, the planning system can play a major role in decentralising power and strengthening society' (Conservative Party, 2010).

Other changes included the abolition of the regional tier of planning outside London, which had previously directed strategic policy and set housing targets, giving local planning authorities (LPAs) more powers and flexibility in relation to their local plans. Following the Act, a National Planning Policy Framework (NPPF) was introduced in 2012, which simplified planning guidance and practice, introduced a presumption in favour of sustainable development, and enshrined planning devolution (DCLG, 2012). The Localism Act also introduced a range of 'community rights' alongside neighbourhood plans (see Table 2.1). Before going on to discuss the particular meanings associated with English localism, this 'neighbourhood planning regime' (House of Commons, 2015, p 3) is set out in more detail.

The neighbourhood planning regime

According to the Localism Act, a Neighbourhood *Development* Plan (NDP), to use the full title (a point that will be returned to), 'is a plan which sets out policies (however expressed) in relation to the development and use of land in the whole or any part of a particular neighbourhood area specified in the plan' (HM Government, 2011, schedule 9). They are statutory plans drawn up by local groups setting out the land-use policies that 'can guide and shape development in a particular area' (House of Commons Library, 2015). This means that unlike previous advisory participatory initiatives, such as Parish Plans or Planning for Real, NDPs carry legal weight. However, they have to fit within, and conform to, the existing planning hierarchy (see Figure 2.1). In order to be approved, NDPs have to go through various stages (see Figure 2.2 and Table 2.1).

Box 2.1: Neighbourhood plans in summary

What is a neighbourhood plan?

A neighbourhood development plan 'will set out a vision, policies and proposals for the future development of an area. If adopted it would become the statutory plan for that area' (Localism Act).

How is the neighbourhood area defined?

This is the area covered by a town or parish where one exists. If not, a neighbourhood area is defined by residents. All areas have to be approved by a LPA following an application by a town or parish council or a neighbourhood forum.

How are they regulated?

Through national planning policy (the NPPF) and neighbourhood plan regulations, which set out procedures and so on.

Who can draw one up?

Either a parish or town council (these are the lowest tier of the English local government hierarchy) or, where there is none, a neighbourhood forum. A neighbourhood forum has to be approved by the LPA and should consist of at least 21 people and be representative of the local area. In addition, a business forum can be established for a business-led plan consisting of local employers and businesses, as well as residents.

How are they funded?

All groups can apply to Locality (a non-governmental organisation funded by government) for funding for technical support. This is limited (eg in 2015, to £9,000) but subsequent applications are allowed. Town and parish councils can use income from their precepts or rates (local taxes) and general reserves.

How are they approved?

Following consultation with residents and stakeholders, a draft plan is put forward for a 'light-touch' inspection. This involves a planning inspector but is less onerous than an examination of a local plan and does not involve legal representation. If the plan is approved, it goes to a referendum and has to be approved by over half of those voting. Those eligible to vote are people registered on the electoral roll. In the case of a business-led plan, each business has one vote. Once the referendum has been passed, the local authority adopts or 'makes' the plan and it is then taken into consideration when decisions are made on planning applications.

Table 2.1: Other community rights

Neighbourhood Development Orders	Grants planning permission for specified developments in a neighbourhood area. Once established, there would be no need for anyone to apply to the council for planning permission if it is for the type of development covered by the order	The same regulations relating to NDPs apply
Community Right to Build Orders	Allows local communities to undertake small-scale, site-specific, community-led developments without going through the normal planning application process	Have to be drawn up by a recognised body, be approved by more than 50% in a vote and comply with local and national planning policy
Community Right to Bid	Allows communities to have important buildings, such as shops, pubs and so on, listed by the local authority as assets of community value. If the owner wants to sell, the community has six months in which to put in a bid	
Community Right to Challenge	Allows groups to bid to run a local public service if they think they can do it better	
Community Right to Reclaim Land	The Community Right to Reclaim Land helps communities to improve their local area by giving them the right to ask that underused or unused land owned by local councils and other public bodies is sold so that it can brought back into use	Applications sent to the secretary of state for approval

Figure 2.1: The 'hierarchy' of the English statutory planning system

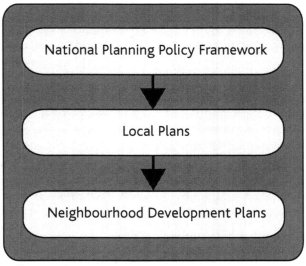

Source: S. Brownill.

Figure 2.2: The stages of a neighbourhood plan

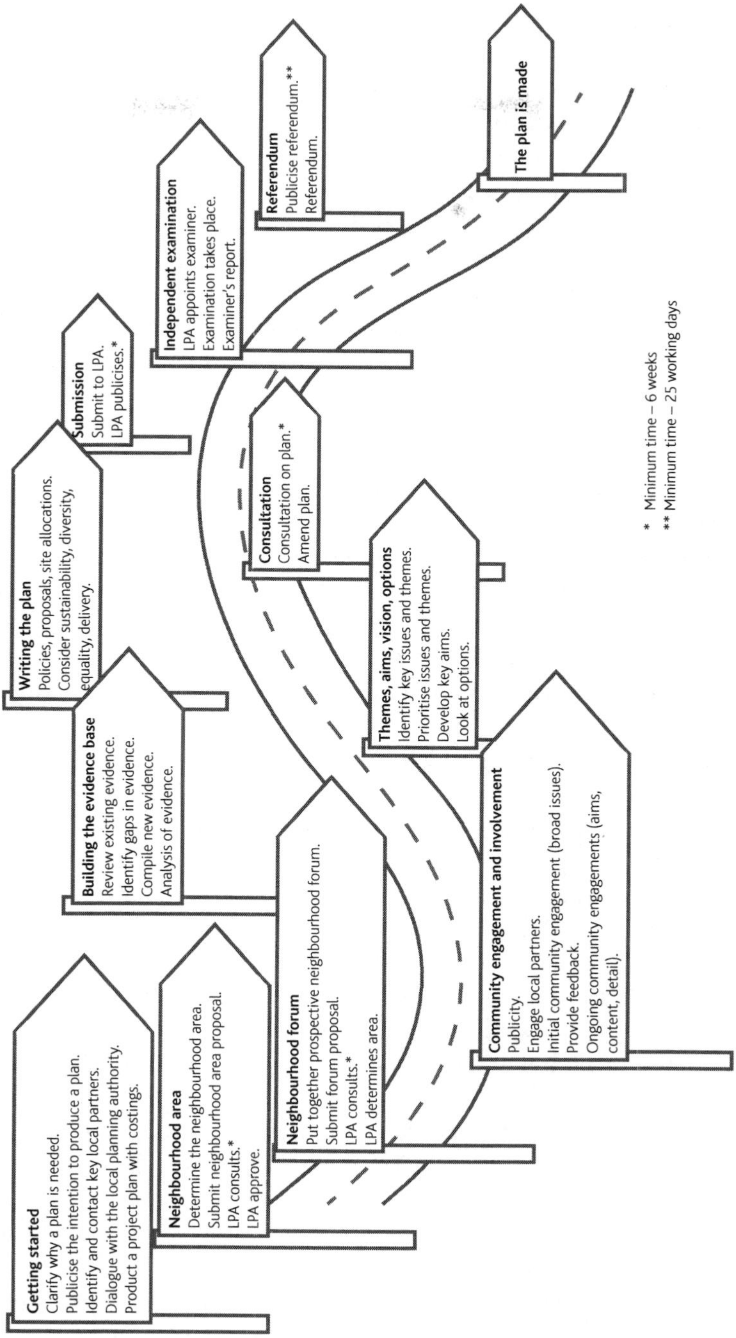

Getting started
Clarify why a plan is needed.
Publicise the intention to produce a plan.
Identify and contact key local partners.
Dialogue with the local planning authority.
Produce a project plan with costings.

Neighbourhood area
Determine the neighbourhood area.
Submit neighbourhood area proposal.
LPA consults.*
LPA approve.

Neighbourhood forum
Put together prospective neighbourhood forum.
Submit forum proposal.
LPA consults.*
LPA determines area.

Community engagement and involvement
Publicity.
Engage local partners.
Initial community engagement (broad issues).
Provide feedback.
Ongoing community engagements (aims, content, detail).

Building the evidence base
Review existing evidence.
Identify gaps in evidence.
Compile new evidence.
Analysis of evidence.

Themes, aims, vision, options
Identify key issues and themes.
Prioritise issues and themes.
Develop key aims.
Look at options.

Writing the plan
Policies, proposals, site allocations.
Consider sustainability, diversity, equality, delivery.

Consultation
Consultation on plan.*
Amend plan.

Submission
Submit to LPA.
LPA publicises.*

Independent examination
LPA appoints examiner.
Examination takes place.
Examiner's report.

Referendum
Publicise referendum.**
Referendum.

The plan is made

* Minimum time – 6 weeks
** Minimum time – 25 working days

Source: Adapted from Locality (http://locality.org.uk).

These include the approval of a responsible group to lead the process, either a town or parish council or, where none exists (largely in urban areas), a newly formed neighbourhood forum consisting of 21 individuals can be approved by the local authority. In addition, business-led forums have the right to draw up plans, as in Milton Keynes. Other stages follow: designating an area, establishing an evidence base and consulting with the community. In addition a 'light-touch' inspection is required to ensure that the plan meets the 'basic conditions' of: being in line with national planning policy; being in 'general conformity' with the local plan for the area; and meeting European Union (EU) and human rights obligations. Finally, the plan has to receive over half the votes cast in a local referendum before it is adopted by the LPA. These stages are covered by regulations that sit alongside the Localism Act and that set out guidelines and procedures covering the NDP process (HM Government, 2012), shaping, in effect, the associated technologies and practices of governance. Under the Act, LPAs are required to provide support for neighbourhood planning groups, organise the inspection and referendum, and adopt a plan that has passed a referendum. They are given limited financial support from central government to carry out this role. In addition, neighbourhood groups can access financial support (up to £9,000 per year) from a scheme set up by government and run by the non-governmental organisation (NGO) Locality and technical aid through a host of other websites, organisations and consultants.

Other neighbourhood planning initiatives (see Table 2.1) include Neighbourhood Development Orders (NDOs), which permit development proposals such as for shops and housing without the need for a planning application. For example, in Cockermouth, Cumbria, an NDO set out approved shop frontages and elevations for the local high street. Like NDPs, they need to go through an independent inspection and referendum. Community Right to Build Orders (CRBOs) are a special kind of NDO that gives permission for small-scale site-specific developments, for example, for affordable housing. As well as following the same procedures and referendum, they have to be put forward by a fully constituted not-for profit community group.

There is also a suite of other community rights included in the Localism Act: to bid, to challenge and to reclaim land that is not covered by the same regulations. The community right to bid allows communities to list 'assets of community value' in the form of open space, shops, pubs and buildings. Should these come up for sale, there is a six-month moratorium during which time the community can attempt to buy the building (which raises obvious questions about resources and financing). The community right to challenge enables communities to take over the running of local services if they think they are not being adequately done by a local authority or other provider, and the right to reclaim land enables communities to force the sale of underutilised public sector land. Under previous New Labour legislation, groups also have the right to set up community land trusts, which can own and develop land and buildings. Together, these rights form 'an infrastructure of localism' (Brownill and Downing, 2013), which has the *potential* to enable neighbourhoods to both influence and deliver local development.

Neighbourhood planning and propositions of localism

If localism is about using these tools to create spaces oriented to a variety of aims, what *are* the aims of English localism? It is possible to identify four propositions of the localism of neighbourhood planning: to create spaces of empowerment; to create spaces that will accept economic growth and new development; to remake planning's publics as 'citizen-planners'; and to remake planning as a collaborative and non-professional activity. Each of these is based on a particular view of the neighbourhood as consensual and biddable. All of these can be contested and contain their own contradictions, as the following discussions reveal.

Photo 2.1: An initial open day gathers ideas about the neighbourhood

Source: Clifford Neighbourhood Planning Group, Leeds

Creating spaces of empowerment

A clear disposition towards empowerment is evident in neighbourhood planning. The extent to which this is realised forms a major theme throughout later chapters in this book but here it is important to note that, as Brownill and Carpenter (2009) state, localism only ever exists 'in the shadow of centralism', and a variety of constraints were placed on the flexibility and freedoms promised by the Localism Act. First, NDPs have to be 'in conformity' with local, national and European policy (see Figure 2.1). While representing a retreat from the almost total local freedom outlined in *Open source planning* (Conservative Party, 2010), this is, nevertheless, a more complex relationship than the simple hierarchy implied in Figure 2.1 (as will be shown in later chapters in this book). Second, the UK planning system is, at heart, discretionary. NDPs work through the LPA, taking neighbourhood plan policies into consideration when making decisions on planning applications, hence the wording from government that they 'can' rather than 'will' guide development and must be 'considered' rather than 'followed'. Even the suggested referendum question asks whether the LPA should use the NDP 'to *help* it decide planning applications in the neighbourhood area'. Third, despite the Localism Act, the government has continued to make changes to the planning regime that, in effect, recentralise power or hand it to other interests, particularly landowners and developers. For example, permitted development rights, such as the change of use from commercial to residential, enable schemes to go ahead in NDP areas without the need for planning permission and therefore without the need to conform to the plan. Coalition localism can therefore be seen as a form of spatial liberalism. However, as Clarke and Cochrane (2013) remind us, these freedoms are allowed only in so far as they are oriented towards particular objectives.

Spaces oriented to growth

In line with this, a key objective of neighbourhood planning for government is about creating spaces that will accept growth, particularly in the south-east of England, where planning is perceived as blocking housing development and thereby contributing to shortages and high house prices. John Howell made this clear in an interview when he stated that neighbourhood planning is about 'overcoming opposition to growth and getting housing numbers delivered', although this is placed in more nuanced language in the document itself: 'Our conception of local planning is rooted in civic engagement and collaborative democracy as the means of reconciling economic development with quality of life' (Conservative Party, 2010, p 1). The locality becomes the place where these apparently contradictory aims can be mediated. Neighbourhood plans are seen as providing an alternative governance mechanism to the top-down targets of the previous regional planning regime to deliver this growth, creating a 'virtuous circle' where communities 'consent to development because they feel ownership and can integrate it into a vision' (DCLG, 2013a; see also Figure 4.1 in Chapter Four).

Incentives were introduced in line with the 'nudge' thinking of the Conservatives, which aimed to enable and encourage rather than enforce such a predisposition to growth. In particular, 25% of the Community Infrastructure Levy, a flat-rate charge to developers on the square metreage of new developments, could be assigned to constituted bodies who have prepared an NDP, while areas with no NDP get 15%: 'Instead of hectoring people and forcing development on people the government believes that we need to persuade communities that development is in everyone's interest' (DCLG, 2013b). However, at the end of the day, as the government briefing paper states, 'policies produced in a NDP cannot block development that is already part of a local plan. NDPs can, however, shape and influence where that development will go and what it will look like' (House of Commons Library, 2015, p 4), hence the fact that these are called neighbourhood *development* plans.

For Davoudi and Madanipour (2013), this is an example of how localism should be seen in Foucauldian terms as a form of neoliberal governmentality, whereby governance through community leads to the outcomes determined by government. However, counter-narratives to this proposition exist, setting out alternative rationales for neighbourhood planning and alternative forms of growth. Somers Town NDP in inner London, for example, sees neighbourhood planning as a way of preserving a working-class neighbourhood in the face of growth and addressing issues of social exclusion (STNF, 2016). West Ferring in Sussex includes proposals for a CRBO for affordable homes and a community centre delivered through a community land trust, putting the community in control of new development, and others such as Woodcote are seeking to intervene in the delivery model of the volume house-builders. These examples underline the contested meanings of localism and the possible spaces opened up for alternatives.

Remaking planning's publics

The rhetoric of neighbourhood planning is about shifting power from officials and higher levels of government to 'the folks'. As Erick Pickles went on to say in his localism speech: 'because we like the folks. We don't think we know better than they do. And we trust them to know what's best for them' (Pickles, 2010). However, under localism, they are encouraged to participate in the spaces of neighbourhood planning in a particular way. In effect, it is about turning 'the folks' into local citizen-planners who accept the need for development and who willingly engage to deliver this. Inch (2015) raises a key set of questions in relation to who is invited to participate and, more to the point, what is the model of the local citizen-planner that they are expected to adopt.

If localism is about promoting growth, it therefore goes without question that these citizens should not be opposed to development, but should embrace it. Original characterisations of NDPs as 'Nimby Charters' following the *Open source planning* document were headed off by the requirement that they be in conformity with other plans. This quote from one of the chairs of a resident association in Thame would give some support to this: "we *are* all nimbies but we can't be so we will have to compromise". It is easy to see how this is meant to depoliticise planning and achieve consensus; the fact of new development is non-negotiable but the community can influence where it goes and how it looks. Yet, despite these constraints, neighbourhood planning has been taken up by a large number of areas. By September 2016, almost 2,000 areas had started the process (DCLG, 2016), though this is short of the 8,000 that the government hoped for when they were introduced (Young, 2015).

In terms of who is invited to participate, by being carried out closer to the ground through a parish or town council or a recognised neighbourhood forum, the assumption is that neighbourhood planning will involve more citizens in planning. This is hoped to resolve the apparent unrepresentativeness of past participation regimes, which were criticised for engaging only certain (largely educated and middle-class) sections of the population and being geographically patchy (Brownill and Parker, 2010). However, the extent to which this is possible is questionable given the availability of time and skills, as is revealed in later chapters of this book. Neighbourhood planning is an 'invited' participatory space, as opposed to previous forms of localism under New Labour that prioritised areas of greatest need. This has led to concerns that it will be those areas with the desire and/or capacity to engage that will take up the invitation, hence Lowndes and Pratchett's (2012) focus on 'sinking or swimming'. Partly to offset this, a range of support was made available for groups of residents; initially set at £7,000, this was increased to £9,000, with an additional £6,000 for groups in 'deprived' areas. Chapter Five provides evidence that these have not overcome the barriers to involvement. Similarly, Davoudi and Cowie (2013) question the representativeness of neighbourhood planning bodies such as neighbourhood forums, as well as their democratic legitimacy.

Remaking planning

Another proposition of localism is the desire to change the nature of planning itself. Instead of it being a distant and technical exercise carried out by 'experts', as the title of the initial *Open source planning* document suggests, it is an activity that can be democratised and thereby made more effective. Implicitly, this not only requires the devolution of planning powers, but also a change in the way planning is carried out. This extends previous attempts at 'culture change' in planning under New Labour and calls for the co-production of plans between communities and planners (Parker et al, 2015). Neighbourhood planning aims to include local knowledge in planning and to break down the notion of planning expertise. The local citizen–planner is therefore seen as capable of undertaking a range of activities: surveys, consultation, needs assessments and building an evidence base. A battery of web sites, tool kits, planning camps, road maps and newsletters exist to support them in this process, as well as the limited funding mentioned. Inch (2015) refers to these as the 'technologies of citizenship', and Davoudi and Madanipour (2015) also refer to the governmental 'technologies of agency', as opposed to control, that characterise English localism. Does this remaking of planning therefore enable the democratisation of planning and the ideal of the co-production of policy between citizens and the state, or is it about steering agency towards the hoped-for outcomes? In practice, many NDPs 'buy in' expertise, and large numbers of NDPs have planning and other professionals on their steering groups. Again, this raises questions about which neighbourhoods can engage and what type of citizen can enter the arena. Furthermore, this practice of governance is not without its risks as local groups may well not want to adopt the role that is set out for them. They may have other motives and rationales; they may also use the infrastructures provided to develop a different conception of localism – to work the spaces of power.

This remodelling of planning also puts the focus on LPAs, who are a crucial but often neglected actor in neighbourhood planning. They are put under contradictory pressures by the government to ensure speedy development and to support neighbourhood planning. Despite the resources available,[1] LPAs have no flexibility in whether they want to support NDPs or not and are facing severe budget restrictions. LPA responses to neighbourhood planning are as variable as the occurrence of NDPs themselves, with some actively supporting them and others less enthusiastic and even obstructive.

This agenda is also about opening up planning not just to local people, but to a range of other interests, such as employers, landowners and developers, who may or may not have local concerns at their hearts. The fact that NDPs can be business-led and that neighbourhood forums should contain a range of interests is significant here and is used to underscore critiques that localism is continuing the neoliberalisation of planning policy and practice.

Spatial imaginaries

The government's perception of neighbourhood planning is based on a spatial imaginary that sees the neighbourhood as homogeneous, persuadable and consensual, containing groups and interests that are locally dependent, meaning that neighbourhoods can be assembled to achieve certain ends. It does not see as problematic the fact that some neighbourhoods will be able to engage more than others, and this conception of space is also based on an assumption that the local is truly local.

This spatial imaginary can be challenged in a number of ways. Later chapters in the book reveal that, in practice, there have been conflicts within neighbourhoods around setting boundaries, between rival proposals for neighbourhood forums for the same area and within NDP groups over priorities and policies. Neighbourhoods are revealed as not being wholly biddable and of resisting the purposes of localism, in particular, by challenging the growth assumptions in local and national planning policy, as well as by creating their own counter-narratives and alternative purposes of localism. Spatial liberalism therefore presents particular difficulties for governments in achieving their objectives.

The idea that the local is 'local' can also be challenged by replacing the Euclidian static and bounded view of space on which official versions of neighbourhoods are based with a relational one. By way of illustration, we can re-look at Figure 2.1 not as a hierarchy of discrete and cascading spatial scales, but as a more complex picture where the local is a field in which different scalar processes and interests operate in the same space.

Conclusions: localism and its discontents

This chapter has argued that while the rise of localism has to be seen in the context of global trends in spatial planning and governance, how localism evolves in particular places will vary. Further, to fully understand and characterise this complexity means moving away from dichotomous and unidirectional thinking to explore the meanings, uses and practices of localism as it emerges over time and space. Using this lens to explore the neighbourhood planning initiative of recent UK governments as an example of one of these 'actually existing' forms of localism, the chapter has revealed a narrative based on the purposes of devolving power, remaking the neighbourhood as the location of growth and recasting planning's publics as citizen-planners.

In doing this, the chapter has revealed how this narrative contains major contradictions and questions. Key among these is how the constrained freedoms of spatial liberalism mediate the devolution of power but there are also issues about the unequal geographies of engagement, the extent to which neighbourhood planning can overcome barriers to involvement in planning and the dynamics of the relations between the different actors involved. Another set of questions revolve around whether counter-narratives can emerge that seek to develop a different kind of localism – one that addresses social inequalities, challenges the type of economic growth being put forward and reasserts the social purposes of planning.

All these and other questions are explored throughout this book and particularly in Chapter Four, which explores the movement from a set of meanings and purposes to the practices of neighbourhood planning.

Note
[1] In 2015, these were: £5,000 for each area designated, up to 20 per year; a further £5,000 for each forum designated; another £5,000 when a plan is submitted; and a final £20,000 for each successful examination.

References

Allen, J. and Cochrane, A. (2010) 'Assemblages of state power: topological shifts in the organization of government and politics', *Antipode*, vol 42, no 5, pp 1071–89.

Brownill, S. and Carpenter, J. (2009) 'Fit for purpose? Governance and integrated planning in the Thames Gateway, England', *Urban Studies*, vol 46, no 2, pp 251–74.

Brownill, S. and Downing, L. (2013) 'Neighbourhood planning: is an infrastructure of localism developing?', *Town and Country Planning*, vol 82, pp 9–12.

Brownill, S. and Parker, G. (2010) 'Same as it ever was: introduction to special edition on rethinking participation', *Planning Practice & Research*, vol 25, no 3, pp 409–15.

Brenner, N. and Theodore, N. (2002) *Spaces of neoliberalism: Urban restructuring in North America and Western Europe*, Oxford: Blackwell.

Cabinet Office (2010) 'Big Society – Overview'. Available at: http://www.cabinetoffice.gov.uk/content/big-society-overview (accessed 12 June 2011).

Cameron, D. (2010) 'The Big Society speech', 19 July. Available at: http://www.number10.gov.uk/news/big-society-speech/

Clarke, N. and Cochrane, A. (2013) 'Geographies and politics of localism: the localism of the United Kingdom's Coalition government', *Political Geography*, vol 34, pp 10–23.

Conservative Party (2010) *Open source planning*, London: Conservative Party.

Davies, J.S. and Pill, M. (2012) 'Empowerment or abandonment? Prospects for neighbourhood revitalisation under the Big Society', *Public Money and Management*, vol 32, no 3, pp 193–200.

Davoudi, S. and Cowie, P. (2013) 'Are English neighbourhood forums democratically legitimate?', *Planning Theory & Practice*, vol 14 no 4, pp 562–6.

Davoudi, S. and Madanipour, A. (2013) 'Localism and Neo-liberal governmentality', *Town Planning Review*, vol 84, no 5, pp 551–60.

Davoudi, S. and Madanipour, A. (2015) *Reconsidering localism*, London: Routledge.

DCLG (2010a) 'Planning power from town halls and Whitehall to local people', press release, 6 December. Available at: https://www.gov.uk/government/news/planning-power-from-town-halls-and-whitehall-to-local-people

DCLG (2010b) 'Localism Bill starts a new era of people power', press release, 10 December. Available at: https://www.gov.uk/government/news/localism-bill-starts-a-new-era-of-people-power

DCLG (2011) *A plain English guide to the Localism Act*, London: The Stationary Office.

DCLG (2012) *The national planning policy framework*, London: DCLG.

DCLG (2013a) 'Neighbourhood planning versus planning with the local plan', presentation to Neighbourhood Planning Roundtable, 4 October.

DCLG (2013b) 'Communities to receive cash boost for choosing development', press release, 10 January. Available at: https://www.gov.uk/government/news/communities-to-receive-cash-boost-for-choosing-development

DCLG (2016) 'New landmark with 200 communities now approving neighbourhood plans'. Available at: https://www.gov.uk/government/news/new-landmark-with-200-communities-now-approving-neighbourhood-plans (accessed 22 July 2016).

Flyvbjerg, B. (1998) *Rationality and power: Democracy in practice*, Chicago, IL: University of Chicago Press.

Gallant, N. and Robinson, J. (2012) *Neighbourhood planning*, Bristol: The Policy Press.

Harvey, D. (2005) *A brief history of neoliberalism*, Oxford: Oxford University Press.

Healey, P. (1997) *Collaborative planning: Shaping places in fragmented societies*, London: Macmillan.

HM Government (2011) *The Localism Act*, London: The Stationary Office.

HM Government (2012) *Neighbourhood planning (general) regulations*, SI 2012/637.

Houghton, G., Allmendinger, P. and Oosterlynck, S. (2013) 'Spaces of neoliberal experimentation: soft spaces, postpolitics and neoliberal governmentality', *Environment and Planning A*, vol 45, no 1, pp 217–34.

House of Commons Library (2015) 'Briefing paper 05838, neighbourhood planning'.

Imrie, R. and Raco, M. (2003) *Urban renaissance?*, Bristol: The Policy Press.

Inch, A. (2015) 'Ordinary citizens and the political cultures of planning: in search of the subject of a new democratic ethos', *Planning Theory*, vol 14, no 4, pp 404–42.

Innes, J. and Booher, D. (2004) 'Reframing public participation: strategies for the 21st century', *Planning Theory and Practice*, vol 5, no 4, pp 419–36.

Loney, M. (1983) *Community against government*, London: Heineman.

Lowndes, V. and Pratchett, L. (2012) 'Local government under the Coalition government: austerity, localism and the "Big Society"', *Local Government Studies*, vol 38, no 1, pp 21–40.

Madanipour, A. and Davoudi, S. (2015) 'Localism: institutions, territories, representations', in S. Davoudi and A. Madanipour (eds) *Reconsidering localism*, London: Routledge, pp 11–29.

Newman, J. (2012) *Working the spaces of power: Activism, neo-liberalism and gendered labour*, London: Bloomsbury.

Newman, J. and Clarke, J. (2009) *Publics, politics and power: Remaking the public in public services*, London: Sage.

Parker, K., Lynn, T. and Wargent, M. (2015) 'Sticking to the script? The co-production of neighbourhood planning in England', *Town Planning Review*, vol 86, no 5, 587–609.

Peck, J. and Tickell, A. (2002) 'Neoliberalising space', *Antipode*, vol 34, no 3, pp 380–404.

Pickles, E. (2010) Speech given at Queen's Speech Forum, 11 June. Available at: https://www.gov.uk/government/speeches/queens-speech-forum

Rhodes, R. (1994) 'The hollowing out of the state: the changing nature of the public service in Britain', *The Political Quarterly*, vol 65, no 2, pp 138–51.

Rose, N. (1996) 'The death of the social? Refiguring the territory of government', *Economy and Society*, vol 25, no 3, pp 327–56.

STNF (Somers Town Neighbourhood Forum) (2016) 'Somers Town neighbourhood plan'. Available at: http://somerstownplan.info/plan/

Swyngedouw, E. (2009) 'The antinomies of the postpolitical city: in search of a democratic politics of environmental production', *Urban Studies*, vol 33, no 3, pp 601–20.

Wallace, A. (2010) *Remaking community? New Labour and the governance of poor neighbourhoods*, Aldershot: Ashgate.

Yetano, A., Royo, S. and Acerete, B. (2010) 'What is driving the increasing presence of citizen participation initiatives?', *Environment and Planning C: Government and Policy*, vol 28, pp 783–802.

Young, C. (2015) 'Emerging neighbourhood plan refusals hit barriers', *Planning Resource*, 15 May. Available at: http://www.planningresource.co.uk/article/1347047/legal-viewpoint-emerging-neighbourhood-plan-refusals-hit-barriers

THREE

Neighbourhoods, communities and the local scale

Quintin Bradley

Introduction

This chapter situates international debates on participation and the widening of democratic engagement in the context of initiatives in the English planning system. It discusses the devolution of neighbourhood planning powers to local communities from 2011 and draws parallels with traditions of citizens' control and direct action in land-use planning. It asks whether neighbourhood planning can be said to devolve some kind of 'power to the people'. In doing so, the chapter argues for an understanding of participation not as a process of inclusion, but as a political practice founded on the inevitability of antagonism and conflict. It begins by exploring the theory and practice of participation in planning and its relation to community action. It then introduces neighbourhood planning within the context of community opposition to development and considers the emergence at the local scale of new collective identities structured around participation as a democratic political practice.

Participation, citizens and communities

The spectre of hierarchical power continues to haunt all attempts to deepen democratic participation in land-use planning. In the community engagement practices of Australasian, European and US states, and in the development programmes of the global South, participation still eludes its anticipated empowerment. Debates over the theory and practice of participation have centred on tensions between representative and participatory democracy and the conflicting rationales of consumer voice and citizenship in the context of liberalised development markets (Brownill and Carpenter, 2007; Brownill, 2009; Bailey, 2010). The stubborn knot at the heart of these debates has been the extent to which participation recognises and challenges the inequalities embedded in market societies and hierarchical structures of government (Flyvbjerg, 2002). The theoretical distinctions between consumerist and citizenship models of participation were first advanced four decades ago to distinguish a collective approach to democratic engagement from the individualised consultation of market research (Croft and Beresford, 1996; Cairncross et al, 1997). These distinctions are now difficult to discern in practices of public participation, where the consumerist model has long since acquired ubiquitous orthodoxy. In the rise of the global liberal project, political engagement is equated with the acquisition of capital while citizenship has been distilled down to the civil rights of ownership and exchange (Barron and Scott, 1992). Participation appears to serve an international political programme in which the market is taken as the organisational principle for society. Empowerment is conceptualised in this programme as a non-zero-sum transaction that has no effect on the established social order and instead serves to incorporate citizens more actively in their own governance. The noticeable failure of participation programmes to bring about fundamental change has sharpened the scepticism of those commentators who regard it as a mechanism for legitimising existing power relations (Marinetto, 2003; Newman et al, 2004; Taylor, 2007). The continuing contradiction between participation as process and empowerment as outcome has directed attention to more radical notions of collective action. A dichotomy is asserted between the top-down desire of service providers to enlist users in business improvement and the bottom-up challenge to state and market hegemony posed by grassroots movements for self-determination and empowerment (Mohan and Stokke, 2000; Somerville, 2004; Parker and Murray, 2012).

One strand in the development of participation practice originates in protests against bureaucratic and paternalist state services, as typified by neighbourhood campaigns against the demolition and dispersal schemes associated with land-use planning in the 1960s and 1970s. The participation championed by these community protests was a political process of disruptive and oppositional civic engagement to 'achieve change in a society whose problems are endemic in its very structures' (Hague, 1990, p 244; Della-Porta and Diani, 2006). As a transformation of power relations, this model of participation was associated with citizens' control (Arnstein, 1969), with 'counter-publics' or locally organised groups of residents and service users who challenged professional definitions of needs and services and articulated 'oppositional interpretations of their identities, interests and needs' (Fraser, 1997, p 81). The desire for autonomy and self-organisation has been a persistent thread in the history of community action in

England, as it has been in social movements across the world (Böhm et al, 2010). The foundation of self-governing communities by religious and political dissenters in the 16th and 17th centuries was reflected in the cooperatives, communes and mutual aid societies that signalled the making of a working-class movement, and a tradition of informal settlements and community self-build continues into the present day (Ward, 1974). This trajectory of dissident autonomy has been consistently captured and incorporated into the institutional processes and structures of the state and capital. Its enduring legacy has been the mobilisation of themes of self-management and the privileging of local knowledge and local residence in state strategies of localism, manifested as active citizenship and enlisted in the outsourcing of public services, the fragmentation of organised labour and the policing of behaviour (Gaventa and Valderrama, 1999; Mosse, 2001). Promises of territorial autonomy made to community organisations provide the populist accompaniment to the commodification of the local as the base unit of a reordered society: a self-governing entity liberated by the dismantling of welfare systems and the deregulation of markets. The autonomous neighbourhood is a potent symbol for the cause of liberalism and for its dissenters. As a simultaneity of complicity and subversion, it remains a site of potential conflict over definitions of freedom and empowerment (Roy, 2006).

A localising rhetoric in planning policy increasingly situates the neighbourhood or community as the agent of governance and makes commonplace the assertion that local residents know best about their area. The community in these visions of liberalism is imagined as something other than the grassroots citizens' groups and community-based social movements that continue to challenge professional assessments of need (Wainwright, 2003). Governments construct for themselves a public that can contribute responsibly to planning decisions while seeking to deny community engagement in the more contentious elements of planning, such as major infrastructure projects (Cowell and Owens, 2006). Questions of outcome, or the democratisation of development decisions, appear to have been sidestepped in favour of innovations in process that promote inclusion as an ethics of professional conduct (Fainstein, 2000; Allmendinger and Tewdwr-Jones, 2002). A definition of participation as the pursuit of deliberative consensus characterises community engagement in land-use decisions and privileges the range and quality of interactions between planners and the public. The power of the sponsoring agency in convening the deliberation, selecting the participants and orchestrating the outcome goes largely unchallenged, while market-research notions of essentialist identity are used to construct a public whose views can be deemed legitimate (Barnes et al, 2003; Beebeejaun, 2012). The denial of the conflict and antagonism intrinsic to planning as an intervention in land and property markets suggests that political questions of environmental quality are amenable to 'common sense' and can be determined by a simple aggregation of individual choices, sampled through surveys, exhibitions and forums (Allmendinger and Haughton, 2012). The arena of participation has been re-imagined as a marketplace where information is exchanged between equals and a mutually beneficial definition of the common good is agreed (Newman, 2001; Campbell and Marshall, 2002; Bradley, 2012). Local communities are deprived of the ability to advocate their own interests and are induced into conformity with social norms that are heavily weighted in favour of established power relations and structural inequalities. A more equitable planning process might be one that consciously encourages the articulation of alternative and conflicting visions of the common good. In an unequal society 'shot through with antagonistic fractures', conflict and opposition are fundamental to the democratic process (Purcell, 2009, p 151). Participation takes place in a contested political field, across boundaries that define conflicting collective interests. In this argument, participation is a political practice rather than an inclusive process of consensus-building and it is ignited by the partisan challenge of collective identities (Mouffe, 1993, 2005; Hillier, 2010).

Communities, protest and planning

The collective action of community groups and social movements is still an internationally familiar feature of participation in land-use planning. Regeneration and urban development schemes have been conceived and initiated by community groups, while local campaigns have lobbied against, obstructed and delayed road-building programmes, airport runway extensions, energy and waste plants, and mineral extraction plans. What is significant about collective participation in planning, however, is the way in which community organisations and campaign groups are routinely dismissed as illegitimate and irrational. The acronym 'NIMBY' ('not in my back yard') originated in the US and became widely used as a derogatory term to condemn the planning objections of citizen groups as either ill-informed and ignorant, or selfish and materialistic, with the term typically expressing the absurdity of protestors who admit the social need for development but object to it taking place in their vicinity (Dear and Taylor, 1982; Dear, 1992).

Photo 3.1: At the neighbourhood forum: an alternative discursive arena

Source: Hyde Park neighbourhood forum, Leeds: photograph Magdalena Szymanska

Community organisations are summarily dismissed as privileged groups exerting protectionist property claims and exercising unfair influence at the expense of civic interests (DeVerteuil, 2013). The empirical and conceptual rationale for the use of the term 'NIMBY', and its assertion that place-based protestors suffer from an irrational syndrome, has been effectively contested (Burningham, 2000; Wolsink, 2006). In another light, community campaign groups opposing development in their locality can be described as environmental movements concerned with the just distribution of costs and benefits (McClymont and O'Hare, 2008). Their collective action, whether arguing for just or seemingly unjust outcomes, points to the exclusions and inequalities concealed by the formal participatory process (Hillier, 2002; Devine-Wright, 2012). The binary dichotomy between civic interest and narrow self-interest breaks down even in studies of affluent place-based groups opposing services such as homelessness shelters or drug treatment centres (Gibson, 2005). A more complex struggle between alternative visions of the common good emerges once the pejorative language is discarded. The participation of citizens' groups in land-use planning reveals a scalar clash of political and economic interests. The depiction of one set of those interests as illegitimate and selfish indicates the success of the more powerful in universalising their particular perspective (Burningham and O'Brien, 1994; Irwin et al, 1994).

Collective protests against development plans have enlarged the definition of participation to include acts of civil disobedience and non-violent direct action, and the occasional coercive use of illegal occupations and sabotage. As one veteran of the anti-roads protests of the 1970s explained, they resolved not to play 'the game according to the rules which (in so far as they are revealed) are devised by their opponents, but by working out a new game altogether, with rules devised by themselves' (Tyme, 1978, p x). Neighbourhood-based objectors were often aided by national and international environmental campaigns, and began to identify themselves with global struggles (Wall, 1999; Dury et al, 2003). The rise of an environmental justice movement committed to direct action at a grassroots level posited a global failure of trust in the democratic legitimacy of formal planning processes (Mihaylov and Perkins, 2015). As environmental movements became institutionalised at national and global scales, a wave of grassroots protests continued to challenge conventional political processes. The compelling nature of these local movements suggested the likelihood that increasingly effective institutionalised means of managing and domesticating them would be developed (Rootes, 1999).

A surge in rural protests from the late 1990s, with countryside and agrarian movements organising in US, Britain and France, caused a further blurring of boundaries between protests inspired by material interest and those motivated by environmental protection (Woods, 2003). These new campaigns were opposed to development and dedicated to the safeguarding of heritage and rural tradition and they brought direct action and the politics of protest further into the mainstream democratic process. Rural protesters were networked within a paternalist institutional structure associated with established property rights and a tradition of conservative political allegiances. This did not inhibit them from employing the tactics of disruptive and obstructive protest and spectacular mass action, alongside more mainstream political practices of lobbying and argumentation (Woods et al, 2012). The characterisation of these, sometimes affluent, rural protests as new social movements serves as a reminder that 'insurgent citizenship' is not confined to marginalised and oppressed communities (Holston, 2009), but describes a tactical connection to a tradition of empowerment through direct action (Doherty et al, 2003). The broadening of the repertoire of practices associated with public participation in land-use planning has been described as 'insurgent planning', a term that recognises 'the oppositional practices of the grassroots as they innovate their own terms of engagement' (Miraftab, 2009, p 41). Rural protests, and the collective action of relatively affluent local communities, indicate the limits of inclusion when environmental and cultural concerns are threatened by land and property market decisions. In the place of a sanctioned engagement, whose purpose is to implicate citizens in governance, insurgent collective planning asserts the irreconcilability of difference. It institutes antagonism and conflict in the place of dominance through consensus (Roy, 2006). The potency of collective action in planning is a challenge to state processes of participation. It can be managed through public order strategies but can it be effectively incorporated into the plan-making consensus (Brenner and Theodore, 2002)? Such a process of institutionalisation might offer communities a contained and bounded empowerment in the sphere of local plan-making. It is as such a displacement strategy that neighbourhood planning in England may be understood. The next section situates the political framework of neighbourhood planning in the context of conflict and the domestication of collection action in the planning system.

The political identities of neighbourhood planning

The Localism Act 2011 in England marked a radical transformation in state spatial strategies. Its response to grassroots planning protest was to grant statutory planning powers to neighbourhoods within a bounded system of exclusions aimed to domesticate their contentions and negate their impact on economic development. This gave legal definition to the territorial claims of community organisations in urban neighbourhoods and recognised the aspirations of rural areas. It legitimised insurgent planning and constructed the autonomous neighbourhood not as liberal inclusion, but as self-managed containment. It effectively corralled a territorial reservation for the practices of collective participation in planning and enclosed it within the supposedly benevolent state systems of rationalism and representation (Brownill and Downing, 2013; Farnsworth, 2013).

Boundary conditions were laid down to define the parameters of what could be conceived and delivered under these neighbourhood plans. Municipal planning authorities were empowered to rule on the boundaries of the neighbourhood and adjudicate on boundary conditions, and in urban areas, they were granted the power to designate, or legally recognise, the right of community organisations to claim representation as a neighbourhood forum. Neighbourhood plans that conformed to these boundary conditions and were approved by popular referendum became statutory instruments as part of the local development framework. Within these boundaries, collective participation in planning acquired a narrow political domain where the decisions of professionals and the edicts of hierarchical power could be challenged legitimately and distinct collective identities might emerge (Bradley, 2015).

The bounded neighbourhood-as-planning-polity resembled more the protected spaces championed in the social movement literature than the state-sanctioned invited spaces of planning participation (Miraftab, 2009). As a territory granted its own collective representation, the neighbourhood could appear as a haven or shelter from the direct gaze of the state and the modulation of public officials (Fantasia and Hirsch, 1995). It formed an 'alternative discursive arena' where local knowledge was valued and needs could be identified and debated at some distance from the rationalities and imperatives of planning policy (Fraser, 1997, p 81). The boundary conditions of neighbourhood planning placed a limit on the outcome of these debates, and acted to filter the more contentious resolutions. Predetermined by law to support development, neighbourhoods were forced into compliance with a pro-growth agenda. This explicit exclusion, however, implicitly recognised the intelligibility of neighbourhood opposition to unwanted development. Neighbourhood planning greeted opponents of development not as irrational NIMBYs, but as rational collective actors responsible for their own planning policy. It brought planning protestors from an 'outer region of indifferent, questionable, or impossible being' to an accepted identification as statutory agents of plan-making (Butler, 1993, p 21). It was an official recognition and, at the same time, a reprimand – a call to order by the law (Althusser, 2001 [1971]).

Participation in planning operates an invisible 'horizon of intelligibility' behind the illusionary search for consensus (Norval, 1996, p 4). There are limits to what is open to discussion, but they are unacknowledged; there are unwritten ground rules that govern the conduct of debate and establish the extent of legitimacy (Barnes et al, 2003). Neighbourhood planning made those boundaries visible. It established formal restrictions on what could be planned, and only by accepting those constraints could neighbourhood groups acquire their right to citizenship. Neighbourhood planning made power visible and cemented it as a formal 'frontier of exclusion' (Laclau, 2007, p 38). The power relations of the planning system and its democratic engagement became transparently 'a force that says no' (Foucault, 1980, p 119). The boundaries of neighbourhood planning organised political space. They became political lines of demarcation between different democratic practices, between different expressions of identity and between unequal mobilisations of political power (Laclau, 1990).

Boundaries are symbolic but not imaginary, and neighbourhood planning in England has etched them into geography and people's lives.

The boundaries established for neighbourhoods delineated territory to define the local and mark out a fixed place in the flow of networks and connections (Amin, 2004). They provided the lines of inclusion and similarity that made it possible to mobilise a shared experience of place and plan for collective goals (Defilippis et al, 2006). The significance of spatial boundaries is in the demarcation of equivalence and difference: they symbolically define belonging and exclusion. Boundaries create an 'inside' that has the semblance of homogeneity and belonging. They transform the reality of difference into the appearance of similarity through the act of exclusion: 'the boundary encapsulates the identity of the community' (Cohen, 1985, p 12). The boundary effect is to establish a 'we–they' distinction between collective identities. For the political philosopher Chantal Mouffe, this constitution of collectives is the foundation of political practice. The establishment of boundaries signals the explicit demarcation of the political community into a confrontation between 'clearly differentiated positions' (Mouffe, 1993, p 4). A tangible division is forged that opposes one force against another, more powerful one, and constitutes a line of antagonism that suggests the ever-present potential for conflict.

The boundaries of neighbourhood planning returned control over the processes, quality and outcomes of community engagement to the community. They marked out the permissions and restrictions of collective participation as a political process that cited the right of autonomous citizen groups to speak for themselves. This regulatory framework established the legitimacy of the neighbourhood, instituted its subordination and specified the political practices of adversarial opposition that it could engage in. All the antagonism inherent in the unequal system of land, property and planning decisions became concentrated in a set of regulations or boundary conditions. At the boundaries of neighbourhood planning, the conditions for an agonistic politics of planning became possible (Mouffe, 2005).

The democratic politics of neighbourhood planning

Agonistic planning has been discussed principally as a critique of the deliberative model of participation and its pursuit of consensus (Purcell, 2009; Hillier, 2010). More broadly, the politics of agonism have provided an ideal model of democratic practice with which to oppose the exclusion of radical alternatives in the liberal spatial imaginary (Swyngedouw, 2010; Allmendinger and Haughton, 2012; Clarke and Cochrane, 2013; Metzger et al, 2015). Mouffe's concept of agonistic politics describes an adversarial relationship where irreconcilable collectives, 'although acknowledging that there is no rational solution to their conflict, nevertheless recognise the legitimacy of their opponents. They are adversaries not enemies' (Mouffe, 2005, p 20). Different political projects confront each other, advocating clearly distinct alternative pathways, and instead of attempting to overcome their adversaries, they channel their conflict into political practices and institutions that ensure coexistence and order 'in the context of conflictuality' (Mouffe, 2005, p 8). Agonistic politics can never escape a constituent antagonism, but it manages these passions and directs them into pluralist democratic practice.

The argument advanced here is that neighbourhood planning has given licence to a politics of collective participation that involves a range of agonistic democratic practices. Neighbourhood planning was designed to domesticate the antagonism between neighbourhoods and the planning system. It offered place-based groups the opportunity to influence development planning in the expectation that this would reduce their opposition to market growth (DCLG, 2011). However, neighbourhood planning did not dispel the antagonism inherent to planning; instead, it established boundaries that channelled it into an uneven relationship of agonism. The neighbourhood emerges as a collective identity characterised by the practice of participatory democracy, subordinated to the local planning authority, yet enabled to initiate policy – a new planning polity in the political arbitration of land use.

The antagonism that is channelled into this agonistic relationship emerges clearly in the discourse of neighbourhood planning groups. Many of those establishing a neighbourhood planning forum were driven by anger at the opaque rationality of the planning system and the hierarchical decision-making of the local state. They were motivated by the desire for a more empowered engagement in decision-making (Parker et al, 2014; Bradley, 2015). Planning was not always the main concern of these neighbourhood groups; instead, it served as a proxy for all government systems from which local people felt excluded. Their frustration was given collective voice and provided with a ration of statutory power through which they could begin to assert a neighbourhood identity against the hierarchies of institutional power. The articulation of a grievance, the attribution of blame on an external agent and the belief that change is possible are all necessary conditions for the 'we–them' distinction that generates the development of collective identity (Benford and Snow, 2000).

Defining the boundaries of neighbourhood planning areas involved making territorial claims, negotiation with other collectives and outright conflict between rival groups seeking to stamp their particular cultural identity on the neighbourhood. The boundary determination could intensify the divisions within neighbourhoods and sharpen the conflict between communities. Conversely, the assertion of belonging and inclusion implicit in boundary marking, coupled with the community engagement encouraged by neighbourhood planning, has been cited as leading to a renaissance of democratic participation in plan-making parish and town councils. The turnout in neighbourhood plan referenda in some rural areas compared favourably with voting in general elections, and average turnout overall demonstrated an enthusiasm for place greater than that aroused in local authority elections. The requirement for a referendum ensured that the plan was sensitive to the radical plurality of neighbourhood interests and was produced through a political process of negotiation and compromise. The urban neighbourhood forum gave institutional shape to the claims of community organisations to represent a constituency and designation by the local authority provided additional legitimacy. The expectation of enacting a statutory vision for an area generated a wave of organisation-building as residents' associations merged and new ones formed to explore their planning rights. Many neighbourhood forums expanded their interests from planning to wider governance roles, and continued to exercise a representative role once their plan was made, with some formally establishing as parish councils (Bradley, 2015; Wills, 2016).

The designation of a boundary has both practical and symbolic importance in not only constituting the identity of the neighbourhood, but also drawing a line between the neighbourhood and the planning authority – a political divide that channels conflict. Local authorities commonly used their boundary designation powers as an exercise in subordination and the lines of antagonism implicit in the process were made evident in the judicial review brought in 2013 by Daws Hill Neighbourhood Forum after Wycombe District Council redrew its planning boundary. Confrontation over boundary designation could expand beyond the initial point of antagonism to generate 'frontier effects' that impact on power relations between the authority and the neighbourhood more generally and are likely to spill over into further episodes of conflict (Laclau and Mouffe, 1985, p 134). The impact of neighbourhood planning in forging new boundaries of antagonism between citizens and local authorities was recognised and welcomed by central government. The Housing and Planning Act 2016 limited the discretion of local authorities in boundary designation and granted neighbourhoods a new right of appeal to government. It signalled the neighbourhood's potential enlistment as a political ally or foil in the fractious relationships between nation-state and its networks of local governance. The emergence of new collective identities at the neighbourhood level was recognised by the judiciary, and, belatedly, by the development industry, and a string of planning appeals and judicial reviews evidenced the antagonism caused by the advent of the neighbourhood as a new planning polity. There were indications that a distinctive planning practice might be initiated by neighbourhoods concerned to enhance place identity and environmental quality within the context of liberalised development. As an emerging political identity, the neighbourhood has erupted into an agonistic field of power relationships, intruding into institutions of government, networks of governance and hegemonies of capital. Participation in planning has become a political practice where differentiated interests with conflicting visions now confront each other. The illusive pursuit of manufactured consensus has been replaced by adversarial antagonism, negotiation and compromise.

Conclusion

The subtitle of this book asks whether neighbourhood planning should be interpreted as representing some form of 'power to the people'. This chapter has tried to answer that question by situating neighbourhood planning within a tradition of community self-management and direct action in development decisions. It has contrasted the collective action of neighbourhood groups with the sanctioned inclusion of community engagement in planning and its pursuit of illusory consensus, and it has argued for an understanding of participation as political practice founded on the inevitability of conflict. Neighbourhood planning returned the principle of collective mobilisation to public participation and created authentic sources of community power in the planning system. Its response to grassroots planning protest was to legitimise the claims for self-governance advanced by community organisations. It demarcated a territorial reserve for collective participation and constructed an autonomous public licensed to determine policy within regulatory boundaries. These boundaries presented an attempt to domesticate insurgent planning while acknowledging the antagonism inherent to property markets. As an institutional recognition of conflict, they established the lines of inclusion and exclusion from which collective identities could develop. They inaugurated the neighbourhood as an autonomous planning polity, subordinate but enabled to devise policy and to author distinctive spatial practices. The political space of participation was reoriented towards antagonism not inclusion. Neighbourhood planning signals the potential for a widening of democratic engagement in planning, with the neighbourhood as the upstart voice of participative democracy. A partisan political practice may now emerge in the heart of the liberal consensus.

References

Allmendinger, P. and Haughton, G. (2012) 'Post-political spatial planning in England: a crisis of consensus?', *Transactions of the Institute of British Geographers*, vol 37, pp 89–103.

Allmendinger, P. and Tewdwr-Jones, M. (2002), The communicative turn in urban planning: unravelling paradigmatic, imperialistic and moralistic dimensions', *Space and Polity*, vol 6, no 1, pp 5–24.

Althusser, L. (2001 [1971]) *Lenin and philosophy and other essays*, New York, NY: Monthly Review.

Amin, A. (2004) 'Regions unbound: towards a new politics of place', *Geografiska Annaler*, vol 86, B 1, pp 33–44.

Arnstein, S. (1969) 'A ladder of citizen participation', *American Institute of Planners Journal*, vol 35, no 4, pp 216–24.

Bailey, N. (2010) 'Understanding community empowerment in urban regeneration and planning in England: putting policy and practice in context', *Planning Practice & Research*, vol 25, no 3, pp 317–32.

Barnes, M., Newman, J., Knops, A. and Sullivan, H. (2003) 'Constituting "the public" in public participation', *Public Administration*, vol 81, no 2, pp 379–99.

Barron, A. and Scott, C. (1992) 'The Citizens' Charter programme', *Modern Law Review*, vol 55, pp 526–46.

Beebeejaun, Y. (2012) 'Including the excluded? Changing the understandings of ethnicity in contemporary English planning', *Planning Theory & Practice*, vol 33, no 4, pp 529–48.

Benford, R. and Snow, D. (2000) 'Framing processes and social movements: an overview and assessment', *Annual Review of Sociology*, vol 26, pp 611–39.

Böhm, S., Dinerstein, A.C. and Spicer, A. (2010) '(Im)possibilities of autonomy: social movements in and beyond capital, the state and development', *Social Movement Studies*, vol 9, no 1, pp 17–32.

Bradley, Q. (2012) 'A "performative" social movement: the emergence of collective contentions within collaborative governance', *Space and Polity*, vol 16, no 2, pp 215–32.

Bradley, Q. (2015) 'The political identities of neighbourhood planning', *Space and Polity*, vol 19, no 2, pp 97–109.

Brenner, N. and Theodore, N. (2002) 'Cities and geographies of "actually existing neoliberalism"', *Antipode*, vol 34, no 3, pp 349–79.

Brownill, S. (2009) 'The dynamics of participation: modes of governance and increasing participation in planning', *Urban Policy and Research*, vol 27, no 4, pp 357–75.

Brownill, S. and Carpenter, J. (2007) 'Increasing participation in planning: emergent experiences of the reformed planning system in England', *Planning Practice and Research*, vol 22, no 4, pp 619–34.

Brownill, S. and Downing, L. (2013) 'Neighbourhood plans – is an infrastructure of localism emerging', *Town & Country Planning*, vol 82, no 9, pp 372–6.

Burningham, K. (2000) 'Using the language of NIMBY: a topic of research not an activity for researchers', *Local Environment*, vol 5, no 1, pp 55–67.

Burningham, K. and O'Brien, M. (1994) 'Global environmental values and local contexts of action', *Sociology*, vol 28, no 4, pp 913–32.

Butler, J. (1993) *Bodies that matter: On the discursive limits of sex*, London: Routledge.

Cairncross, L., Clapham, D. and Goodlad, R. (1997) *Housing management, consumers and citizens*, London: Routledge.

Campbell, H. and Marshall, R. (2002) 'Utilitarianism's bad breath? A re-examination of the public interest justification for planning', *Planning Theory*, vol 1, no 2, pp 163–87.

Clarke, N and Cochrane, A. (2013) 'Geographies and politics of localism: the localism of the UK's Coalition government', *Political Geography*, vol 34, pp 10–23.

Cohen, A. (1985) *The symbolic construction of community*, London: Tavistock Publications.

Cowell, R. and Owens, S. (2006) 'Governing space: planning reform and the politics of sustainability', *Environment & Planning C: Government and Policy*, vol 24, pp 403–21.

Croft, S. and Beresford, P. (1996) 'The politics of participation', in D. Taylor (ed) *Critical social policy: A reader*, London: Sage Publications.

DCLG (Department for Communities and Local Government) (2011) *Localism Bill: neighbourhood plans and community right to build impact assessment*, London: Department for Communities and Local Government.

Dear, M. (1992) 'Understanding and overcoming the NIMBY syndrome', *Journal of the American Planning Association*, vol 58, no 3, pp 288–300.

Dear, M. and Taylor, S. (1982) *Not on our street. Community attitudes to mental health care*, London: Pion.

Defilippis, J., Fisher, R. and Shragge, E. (2006) 'Neither romance nor regulation: re-evaluating community', *International Journal of Urban and Regional Research*, vol 30, no 3, pp 673–89.

Della-Porta, D. and Diani, M. (2006) *Social movements: An introduction*, Oxford: Blackwell.

DeVerteuil, G. (2013) 'Where has NIMBY gone in urban social geography?', *Social and Cultural Geography*, vol 14, no 6, pp 599–603.

Devine-Wright, P. (2012) 'Rethinking NIMBYism: the role of place attachment and place identity in explaining place-protective action', *Journal of Community and Applied Social Psychology*, vol 19, pp 426–41.

Doherty, B., Plows, A. and Wall, D. (2003) 'The preferred way of doing things: the British direct action movement', *Parliamentary Affairs*, vol 56, pp 669–83.

Dury, J., Reicher, S. and Stott, C. (2003) 'Transforming the boundaries of collective identity: from the "local" anti-road campaign to "global" resistance?', *Social Movement Studies*, vol 2, no 2, pp 191–221.

Fainstein, S. (2000) 'New directions in planning theory', *Urban Affairs Review*, vol 35, no 4, pp 451–78.

Fantasia, R. and Hirsch, E. (1995) 'Culture in rebellion: the appropriation and transformation of the veil in the Algerian revolution', in H. Johnston and B. Klandermans (eds) *Social movements and culture*, London: UCL Press.

Farnsworth, D. (2013) 'Informed choice – the future for town planning?', *Town and Country Planning*, vol 82, no 2, pp 85–7.

Flyvbjerg, B. (2002) 'Bringing power to planning research: one researcher's praxis story', *Journal of Planning Education and Research*, vol 21, pp 353–66.

Foucault, M. (1980) *Power/knowledge: Selected interviews and other writings 1972–1977*, London: Harvester Wheatsheaf.

Fraser, N. (1997) *Justice interruptus: Critical reflections on the 'post socialist' condition*, London: Routledge.

Gaventa, J. and Valderrama, C. (1999) 'Participation, citizenship & local governance', background note prepared for workshop on 'Strengthening participation in local governance', Institute of Development Studies, 21–24 June.

Gibson, T. (2005) 'NIMBY and the civic good', *City and Community*, vol 4, no 4, pp 381–401.

Hague, C. (1990) 'The development and politics of tenant participation in British council housing', *Housing Studies*, vol 5, no 4, pp 242–56.

Hillier, J. (2002) 'Direct action and agonism in democratic planning practice', in P. Allmendinger and M. Tewdwr-Jones (eds) *Planning futures: New directions for planning theory*, London: Routledge, pp 110–35.

Hillier, J. (2010) 'Agonising over consensus: why Habermasian ideals cannot be real', *Planning Theory*, vol 2, no 1, pp 37–59.

Holston, J. (2009) 'Insurgent citizenship in an era of global uncertainties', *City & Society*, vol 21, no 2, pp 245–67.

Irwin, A., Georg, S. and Vergragt, P. (1994) 'The social management of environmental change', *Futures*, vol 26, no 3, pp 323–34.

Laclau, E. (1990) *New reflections on the revolution of our time*, London: Verso.

Laclau, E. (2007) *Emancipation(s)*, London: Verso.

Laclau, E. and Mouffe, C. (1985) *Hegemony and socialist strategy*, London: Verso.

Marinetto, M. (2003) 'Who wants to be an active citizen? The politics and practice of community involvement', *Sociology*, vol 37, pp 103–20.

McClymont, K. and O'Hare, P. (2008) '"We're not NIMBYs": contrasting local protest groups with idealised conceptions of sustainable communities', *Local Environment*, vol 13, no 4, pp 321–35.

Metzger, J., Allmendinger, P. and Oosterlynck, S. (2015) *Planning against the political: Democratic deficits in European territorial governance*, London: Routledge.

Mihaylov, N. and Perkins, D. (2015) 'Local grassroots environmental activism', *Behavioural Sciences*, vol 5, pp 121–53.

Miraftab, F. (2009) 'Insurgent planning: situating radical planning in the global South', *Planning Theory*, vol 8, no 1, pp 32–50.

Mohan, G. and Stokke, K. (2000) 'Participatory development and empowerment: the dangers of localism', *Third World Quarterly*, vol 21, no 2, pp 247–68.

Mosse, D. (2001) '"People's knowledge", participation and patronage: operations and representations in rural development', in B. Cooke and U. Kothari (eds) *Participation: The new tyranny*, London: Zed Books.

Mouffe, C. (1993) *The return of the political*, London: Verso.

Mouffe, C. (2005) *On the political*, London: Verso.

Newman, J. (2001) *Modernising governance: New Labour, policy and society*, London: Sage Publications.

Newman, J., Barnes, M., Sullivan, H. and Knops, A. (2004) 'Public participation and collaborative governance', *Journal of Social Policy*, vol 33, no 2, pp 203–23.

Norval, A. (1996) *Deconstructing apartheid discourse*, London: Verso.

Parker, G. and Murray, C. (2012) 'Beyond tokenism? Community-led planning and rational choices: findings from participants in local agenda-setting at the neighbourhood scale in England', *Town Planning Review*, vol 83, no 1, pp 1–28.

Parker, G., Lynne, T., Wargent, M. and Locality (2014) *User experience of neighbourhood planning in England research*, Reading: University of Reading.

Purcell, M. (2009) 'Resisting neoliberalisation: communicative planning or counter-hegemonic movements?', *Planning Theory*, vol 8, no 2, pp 140–65.

Rootes, C. (1999) *Environmental movements: Local national and global*, London: Frank Cass Publishers.

Roy, A. (2006) 'Praxis in the time of empire', *Planning Theory*, vol 5, no 1, pp 7–29.

Somerville, P. (2004) 'State rescaling and democratic transformation', *Space and Polity*, vol 8, no 2, pp 137–56.

Swyngedouw, E. (2010) 'Apocalypse forever? Post-political populism and the spectre of climate change', *Theory, Culture & Society*, vol 27, pp 213–32.

Taylor, M. (2007) 'Community participation in the real world: opportunities and pitfalls in new governance spaces', *Urban Studies*, vol 44, no 2, pp 297–17.

Tyme, J. (1978) *Motorways versus democracy: public inquiries into road proposals and their political significance*, Basingstoke: Macmillan.

Wainwright, H. (2003) *Reclaim the state: Experiments in popular democracy*, London: Verso.

Wall, D. (1999) 'Mobilising Earth First in Britain', in C. Rootes (ed) *Environmental movements: Local, national and global*, London: Frank Cass Publishers, pp 81–100.

Ward, C. (1974) *Tenants take over*, London: Architectural Press.

Wills, J. (2016) 'Emerging geographies of English localism: the case of neighbourhood planning', *Political Geography*, vol 53, pp 43–53.

Wolsink, M. (2006) 'Invalid theory impedes our understanding: a critique on the persistence of the language of NIMBY', *Transactions of the Institute of British Geographers*, vol 31, pp 85–91.

Woods, M. (2003) 'Deconstructing rural protest: the emergence of a new social movements', *Journal of Rural Studies*, vol 19, pp 309–25.

Woods, M., Anderson, J., Guilbert, S. and Watkin, S. (2012) 'The countryside is angry: emotion and explanation in protest mobilization', *Social & Cultural Geography*, vol 13, no 6, pp 567–85.

FOUR

Neighbourhood planning and the spatial practices of localism

Quintin Bradley, Amy Burnett and William Sparling

Introduction

Whether the state strategy of localism delivers on its promise of empowerment depends on the extent to which it devolves effective instruments of policy to citizens and communities. The devolution of localism is commonly conveyed by invitation to citizens to join local governance structures or be included in neighbourhood management projects (Lowndes and Sullivan, 2008). Citizens seldom acquire the right to make decisions as a collective, and it is rare for statutory power to be designed to be wielded by public participants rather than public officials (Bradley, 2015). This chapter examines the use of statutory planning powers to effect spatial change by neighbourhoods in England. Neighbourhood planning is unusual in that a tailor-made set of statutory powers was devised and offered to communities to give them distinct rights within the development planning framework. Where much research on neighbourhood planning, including in this book, has focused on its impact on community governance and the management of place, this chapter is concerned with the implementation of a set of spatial practices, and the use by neighbourhoods of a specific, and quite limited, framework of land-use planning to achieve their goals.

Neighbourhood planning emerged as the new and most local scale of the planning system in England in a series of reforms intended to overhaul the process of land-use allocation in order to liberalise the regulation of development markets. The concern of the planning system to adjudicate on questions of the public good in land use was rhetorically redirected towards a presumption in favour of sustainable development. Neighbourhood planning was presented to communities as the power to align the imperatives of economic growth with the requirements of social and environmental sustainability (DCLG, 2011a). This chapter reviews the spatial practices that have emerged as a result and discusses the extent to which communities have been able to use neighbourhood plans to achieve their aims in balancing economic, social and environmental sustainability. It begins by addressing the approach taken by neighbourhoods to the key challenge of housing supply; then, it reviews the use of planning policy to highlight the goals of social sustainability in regeneration and public infrastructure, and considers the environmental measures and low-carbon alternatives promoted in neighbourhood plans. The chapter concludes with an assessment of what is distinctive about the spatial practices of neighbourhood planning and their impact on land and property markets.

Housing and neighbourhood planning

A policy intention behind the launch of neighbourhood planning in England was to overcome community opposition to new housing development, blamed as one of the key reasons why building had failed to keep pace with household growth (Archer and Cole, 2014). It was anticipated that giving communities 'real power in respect of the design and precise location' of development would secure their compliance with a pro-growth agenda and increase the number of land sites allocated for housing (DCLG, 2011b, p 10). Neighbourhood plans were seen as a way to provide more certainty for developers (see Figure 4.1), and one of the key indicators of the success of the policy was to be a reduction in the number of planning appeals and legal challenges.

Figure 4.1: How neighbourhood plans might speed up the delivery of new housing

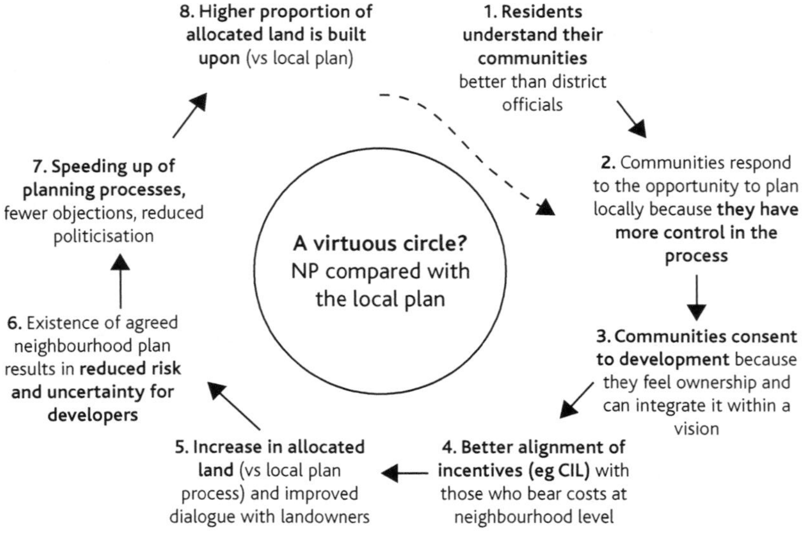

Note: CIL – Community Infrastructure Levy; Neighbourhood Plan.
Source: Stanier (2014).

In November 2015, the housing and planning minister announced the success of this policy. Neighbourhood planning had increased house-building by more than 10%. Selective analysis of neighbourhood plans showed that they had allocated more sites for housing than required in strategic local plans (Mountain, 2015). Far from ending a system that pitted communities against house-builders, however, the policy of neighbourhood planning had, if anything, exasperated this antagonism (Bradley and Sparling, 2016). The house-building industry in England is dominated by a small number of volume builders who produce 44% of all new homes. These developers regarded neighbourhood plans as an obstruction to speculative house-building (Peters, 2014). Neighbourhood planning powers were set out in a new *National Planning Policy Framework* that required local authorities to provide more than five years' worth of specific, developable housing land sites and identify broad locations for new housing up to nine years ahead (DCLG, 2012). If the local plan did not provide the requisite land, it would be found 'out of date', enabling speculative building that did not reflect assessments of housing need (Burroughs, 2015). This liberal planning regime had dramatically boosted planning approvals for house-building in England and resulted in a string of appeal victories for developers, who succeeded in winning access to greenfield sites. While neighbourhood plans had to be in 'general conformity' with the local plan, in non-strategic matters, they could circumvent the local planning authority. They could be developed in the absence of a local plan and were subject to a much-reduced form of examination. Where neighbourhood planning posed an obstacle to the volume builders was when a local plan was found to be 'out of date' but the neighbourhood plan passed examination and subsequently took precedence over local housing policies.

The first legal challenge from house-builders came when the neighbourhood plan for the parish of Tattenhall in rural Cheshire set a ceiling of no more than 30 homes per site in the built-up part of the village. The Tattenhall neighbourhood plan was produced in the absence of strategic policies since the local planning authority, Cheshire West and Chester Council, was still preparing its own local plan and could not evidence a five-year housing land supply. The Tattenhall neighbourhood plan was approved at examination and it was successful at referendum in September 2013 on a convincing 52% turnout. House-builders Barratt Homes and Wainhomes sought a judicial review of Cheshire West's decision to go to referendum, arguing, among other things, that the neighbourhood plan sought to restrict the delivery of housing and therefore did not comply with pro-growth national planning policy. Mr Justice Supperstone dismissed the house-builders' case, ruling that the neighbourhood plan did not seek to limit the overall number of homes and had established its case for housing development at a scale that reflected the existing character of the area.[1]

The right of neighbourhood plans to identify their own sites for house-building was also challenged by the volume house-builders in legal action. Larkfleet Homes sought a judicial review of the Uppingham neighbourhood plan in Rutland on the grounds that housing site allocation was a strategic matter and the responsibility of the planning authority. Uppingham had allocated three sites for at least 170 homes but Larkfleet had a commercial interest in land not included in the plan and demanded that the referendum result be quashed. Mr Justice Carter dismissed the claim since neighbourhood planning regulations expressly allowed neighbourhoods to allocate sites for development.[2] Larkfleet appealed to the High Court and the Court of Appeal and when defeated tried to take their challenge to the Supreme Court only to be refused again.

The neighbourhood plan for Broughton Astley, a large village near Leicester, was agreed in January 2014 after a referendum on a turnout of 38%, with an 89% vote in favour. Prior to the referendum, an application by a developer to build 111 homes on a site not included in the neighbourhood plan was rejected by Harborough District Council, a decision overturned on appeal, but then reinstated by the secretary of state and endorsed by the High Court.[3] The developer's central challenge was that the Broughton Astley neighbourhood plan was based on a local plan that was 'out of date' and could not demonstrate a five-year supply of housing. The sites allocated for housing in the neighbourhood plan, while meeting some of the local housing need, might not meet all needs therefore. The secretary of state's judgement cuts to the heart of the dichotomy between devolution and liberal market growth, and it is worth quoting:

> In this appeal case he considers that the key issue in applying the presumption is whether any adverse impacts of the proposal would significantly and demonstrably outweigh the benefits, when assessed against the policies in the Framework taken as a whole including its policies on neighbourhood planning as well as policy on housing supply.
>
> Paragraph 185 of the Framework states that, outside the strategic elements of the Local Plan, neighbourhood plans

will be able to shape and direct sustainable development. The Secretary of State regards this purpose as more than a statement of aspiration. He considers that neighbourhood plans, once made part of the development plan, should be upheld as an effective means to shape and direct development in the neighbourhood planning area in question. (DCLG, 2014, p 4)

The secretary of state found that the neighbourhood's right to determine the location of development outweighed the need to ensure housing growth. The intervention of the secretary of state in this and other house-builder disputes over neighbourhood plans evidenced a political will to defend the right of neighbourhoods to exercise a level of autonomy over housing development. A complex framework of case law was established in which: draft neighbourhood plans might be given the same substantial weight as those that had been approved at referendum; plans based on out-of-date housing numbers could be upheld; and plans that did not demonstrate site viability or conform to European directives might still be allowed. The spatial practices of neighbourhood plans with regard to house-building were shaped by such judgements and appeared, as a result, to offer considerable latitude for communities to direct and contain housing development within an overall vision of place. Although, in early 2016, the remit of neighbourhood plans was severely constrained where no five-year supply of land could be evidenced in the local plan, the intention to devolve power to neighbourhoods initially appeared to be as important to national planning policy as the imperative to maximise growth, meaning that, in some cases, the will of the neighbourhood overruled policies on housing supply.

Over half the neighbourhood plans successful at referendum allocated sites for housing, and most had policies on housing, and specifically on affordable housing (DCLG, 2015). Where neighbourhood plans aimed to boost housing, they prioritised small, previously developed or 'brownfield' sites, where development would cause minimum disruption to environmental quality and local character. They were especially concerned to meet local housing need and favoured resident-led approaches like custom-build or community land trusts that might 'lock in' affordability for the future, and they aimed to restrict the growth of housing not used for primary residence. Many neighbourhood plans made explicit their opposition to the dominant housing market model and the speculative approach of the volume house-builders. Neighbourhood planning policies for housing can be understood as a set of spatial practices that seek to encourage a new model of house-building. With their advocacy of small brownfield sites, small to medium builders, and the priority they placed on affordability and local need, neighbourhood planning groups appeared as the proponents of sustainability and social purpose in the English housing market, in conflict with the corporate interests of liberalised housing development. The aim of neighbourhood planning was to redirect the behaviour of citizens to support house-building but it directed citizens to an awareness of community housing needs not the market needs of the volume house-builders. Opposition from developers to these spatial practices might suggest that the problems of housing supply lie not with the refusal of communities to support growth, but with the dominant model of house-building and its dysfunctional market.

Contentions around house-building were inextricably connected in neighbourhood planning to a desire to maintain the character and quality of a local community and its social solidarity. In the next section, we review the approach taken by neighbourhood plans to social sustainability through regeneration and renewal of the built environment.

The social goals of neighbourhood plans

The spatial planning powers of neighbourhood plans were oriented towards private development not public infrastructure. Neighbourhood plans could not bring about investment; they could only regulate development decisions. They were restricted to shaping the criteria against which planning applications might be judged. This was a severe limitation on the ability of neighbourhoods to deliver social sustainability. Urban neighbourhoods, in particular, demonstrated a greater zeal for economic growth than rural plans, but the fulfilment of their vision depended on land availability and a market with appetite for development (Peters, 2014).

In the deprived east end of Preston, the neighbourhood forum of Fishwick and St. Matthews wanted to improve the quality of their inner-city environment. The main problems they sought to tackle were traffic pollution and the lack of green space (FOFS, 2014). The opportunities for changing Inner East Preston were, however, very limited without public investment. Development sites were few, there was little market interest and the changes that the community wanted to see required the creation of new parks and road improvements, which required significant public finance. The Preston Council planning officer working with Fishwick and St. Matthews explained her concerns over the limits of what the plan could achieve:

> "I have this worry that it's one thing to write a plan but how do you actually put it into action? It is the delivery which is the difficult part. I mean there's no harm in having a few aspirations, but the area won't be completely transformed. It will still be the same area." (Interview, 2013)

The limits of neighbourhood planning were very apparent in urban areas of deprivation. Out of the 1,700 neighbourhoods drawing up plans at the time of writing, one third were urban areas, many of them disadvantaged inner-city neighbourhoods that had benefited from previous publicly funded regeneration programmes. The interest in neighbourhood plans in these deprived areas was often evidence of the proactive involvement of local authorities, who saw a potential resource in the wake of the withdrawal of regeneration funding and in the face of budget cuts that had reduced services to the statutory minimum (Lowndes and McCaughie, 2013). Neighbourhood planning became almost the only available framework through which the politics of urban renewal could be pursued.

However, planning policy could prove to be a blunt tool when applied to the post-industrial urban landscape of inner cities, especially in the context of the liberalisation of development. Neighbourhoods seeking to preserve the character of a high street or regulate residential design were hampered by government edicts that exempted certain changes in use and extensions to property from the requirement to seek planning permission (HMG, 2015). It was difficult for neighbourhood forums to address community concerns over traffic and parking issues, or crime and nuisance, through planning policy. Some of the problems facing urban areas were illustrated by the Heathfield Park neighbourhood plan in Wolverhampton, which was made in September 2014 after a referendum that engaged only 8% of the electorate. Heathfield Park was ranked among the most deprived areas in the country and the plan aimed to address a regeneration agenda concerned with identity and image, employment, transport, traffic, and health. In translating these issues into planning policy, the Heathfield Park neighbourhood plan expressed its support for planning applications that conformed to its goals, and provided guidance to developers on neighbourhood priorities. It identified particular sites where the development of employment and training opportunities would be supported, and where infrastructure changes could benefit the community. The neighbourhood plan became a manifesto for the improvement of the area written in the language of land-use regulation; however, it could not make these changes happen, and it could not ensure that developers would act upon its policies. It might advocate the use value of specific investments but its policies would be implemented only to realise the exchange value of development sites (Heathfield Park Local Neighbourhood Partnership, 2014).

Where planning policies were limited in their outcomes, neighbourhood plans could at least identify community projects that might benefit from developers' contributions through the Community Infrastructure Levy (CIL) or other sources of capital funding. Such community projects are seen as a way to amplify the planning policies and to encourage people to get involved in plan-making. The Fortune Green & West Hampstead Neighbourhood Development Forum included recommendations for complementary action in support of its planning policies, intended to 'reflect the will of the community'. Many of them were addressed to the local authority and other public agencies, and they advocated specific actions on the basis of consultation with residents (Fortune Green & West Hampstead NDF, 2014). A distinction between planning policies and projects was established by Exeter St James, the first urban neighbourhood plan to go to referendum in 2012. The inclusion of projects in the plan enabled the neighbourhood forum to identify the public investment that was required in the area and remind public agencies of the improvements needed. It also provided a means to address some of the concerns raised by residents, so that the neighbourhood plan became more than a package of spatial policies and evolved into a plan for the development and regeneration of the community as a whole. The first community project put into action by the Exeter St. James Forum was the renovation of a neglected urban green space, known as Queen's Crescent Gardens. This project involved the setting up of a community benefit society to take ownership of the public open space and lead on other neighbourhood projects (Exeter St James Forum, 2015). In seeking to expand the spatial practices available to them, neighbourhood forums, like Exeter St. James, had little choice but to embrace the rhetoric of self-management and enterprise that accompanied the localisation of planning policy. These spatial practices were resourced by volunteer labour, depended on limited supplies of social capital and underscored the impact on disadvantaged areas of the retreat of the public sector and the shrinkage of the space of public responsibility. They emphasised in stark terms the failure of planning to articulate an inclusive strategy of social sustainability.

The opportunities for neighbourhood plans to advance sustainable environmental strategies are considered in the next section.

Neighbourhood planning and low-carbon policies

A role of planning in England is to 'support the transition to a low carbon future in a changing climate' (DCLG, 2012, para 17), and neighbourhood planning has opened up space for grassroots actors to influence the scope of local low-carbon policies. This section draws on interviews with neighbourhood planning groups and a thematic review of policies in selected plans to assess opportunities for grassroots contributions to low-carbon planning.

The Climate Change Act 2008 commits the UK government to cutting greenhouse gas emissions (GHG) by 80% from 1990 levels by 2050 (HMG, 2008). More recently, in June 2016, the government passed the 5th Carbon Budget, committing to a 57% reduction from 1990 levels between 2028 and 2032. Under European Union (EU) legislation, the UK is also committed to generating 15% of the country's energy from renewables by 2020; leaked government estimates suggest that only 11.5% will be achieved (EC, 2009; The Ecologist, 2015). Change to 'Emissions from buildings account for 17% of the UK's direct GHG emissions (Committee on Climate Change, CCC, 2016).[4]

Recent policy changes have curtailed localised policy responses to low-carbon neighbourhood plans. Until recently, local planning authorities and some early neighbourhood plans had sought to introduce additional measures for sustainable housing. In March 2015, the government's 'Housing Standards Review' withdrew the Code for Sustainable Homes (CSH) as the framework for sustainable house-building. Its implementation through the Deregulation Act 2015 prevented local plans and neighbourhood plans from setting 'additional local technical standards or requirements relating to the construction, internal layout or performance of new dwellings' (Pickles, 2015). This meant that any policy in a neighbourhood plan or local plan that included an ambition to achieve CSH 5 or 6 was redundant. Supportive policies that looked favourably on high levels of performance were still possible, but these could not mandate increased performance over and above building regulations.

From 2016, building regulations will be the equivalent of (almost) CSH level 4 – an increase of 20% in energy efficiency compared to the 2010 standards (DCLG, 2015). However, the government ended much-touted pledges for domestic dwellings to be zero-carbon by 2016. The mechanism of 'allowable solutions' for offsetting energy savings above building regulations will no longer be required. This would have bolstered additional low-carbon measures, such as district heating schemes or investing in energy-efficiency measures in existing housing stock. These changes led to concern that the UK government was promoting a pro-growth agenda influenced by house-builders in efforts to prioritise economic development over wider issues of environmental sustainability. Despite these changes, there is still a degree of policy uncertainty, particularly for EU directives, such as the target of achieving 'nearly carbon-zero' for new buildings by 2021 (EC, 2010; see also RICS, 2016), due to the UK's decision to leave the EU. Moreover, emerging guidance suggests that where neighbourhood plans set *additional* housing allocations, there may be scope to demand more stringent energy-related measures (CSE, 2016).

Neighbourhood plans can apply both planning and non-plan-making mechanisms to achieve low-carbon outcomes (CSE, 2016). While neighbourhoods cannot set technical standards, they can indicate a preference for how local funding from new developments may be spent through the CIL. These ambitions could reflect wider community priorities; however, to date, there are limited examples of neighbourhood plans identifying CIL for low-carbon measures. Table 4.1 sets out a sample of the range of low-carbon and sustainability ambitions in existing neighbourhood plans (draft and made).

Table 4.1: Examples of low-carbon, sustainable policies and ambitions in neighbourhood plans

Area	Non-plan-making mechanisms	Examples
Low-carbon ambitions (general)	Aspiration to be carbon-neutral Adhere to 'One Planet Living' principles	*Draft* – Bradford on Avon, Ashton on Hayes, Frome
Area	**Plan-making mechanism**	**Examples**
Energy (renewables)	Supporting community energy schemes	*Draft* – Boston Spa *Made* – Coniston, Hough on the Hill
	Establishing a community energy enterprise	*Draft* – Frome, Wye
	Specific types of renewable energy	*Draft* – Haberton *Made* – Anslow, Much Wenlock
	Targets for onsite renewables generation in new development	*Made* – Tickhill
	District heating	*Made* – Wolverton

Area	Non-plan-making mechanisms	Examples
Energy efficiency	BREEAM (for commercial properties only)	*Draft* – Frome
		Made – Wirksworth
	Upgrading existing dwellings	
Sustainable transport	Criteria for new-builds to be walking distance from the town centre	*Made* – Wye, Chapel-en-le-Frith
	Encouraging cycle pathways	*Draft* – Frome, Buckfastleigh
		Made – Arundel, Barnham and Eastergate, Thame
	Reorder priorities between cars and pedestrians	*Draft* – Frome, Old Market
Biodiversity	Protection of ecosystems through wildlife corridors	*Made* – Ascot, Sunninghill and Sunningdale, Yapton, Anslow
	New development should integrate with existing green infrastructure	*Made* – Barnham and Eastergate
	Habitat creation, woodlands and wetlands	*Made* – Wye
	Local green space designation	*Made* – Hough on the Hill
Water	Encourage the use of sustainable urban drainage	*Draft* – Frome, Bloxham *Made* – Tattenhall, Bersted, East Preston, Yapton, Buckingam
CIL spending	Bus interchange, cycle routes	*Draft* – Laurence Weston *Made* – Barnham and Eastergate

Note: For further examples, see Centre for Sustainable Energy (CSE) (2016). BREEAM (Building Research Establishment Environmental Assessment Method).

Representatives from environmental organisations, such as Transition Towns and Friends of the Earth (FoE), have begun to engage in neighbourhood plans as a means to advance alternatives to growth-dominated discourses. In particular, transition initiatives (TIs) encourage localised economies centred upon the use of local materials and resources. This research uncovered a number of strategies used by such groups to advance an environmental, low-carbon agenda. For instance, where these groups had produced plans in the past, such as an energy descent plan or a sustainable transport strategy, this could then feed into the evidence base of low-carbon policies in the neighbourhood plan (eg Frome). Where Green Party councillors are involved at a town, district or county level, some have been able to leverage the presence of environmental groups within the neighbourhood planning process. The chair of one neighbourhood plan suggested making sure that the TI was included initially has enabled it to drive its own agenda forward through the neighbourhood planning process. In this case, the sustainability working group of the neighbourhood plan was co-opted into the TI itself. In Wivenhoe, a member of a TI suggested that they were accepted into the neighbourhood planning group because the former was seen as 'not too threatening' or likely to disrupt the status quo; there were synergies in using the neighbourhood plan to build a stronger community and promote well-being: "a sort of carbon reduction through increased liveability" (interview).

While there is clearly a significant level of ambition to include low-carbon policies by environmental groups and other actors, many of the neighbourhood representatives spoken to as part of this research took an incremental approach, rather than a radical one. A key challenge for such actors was developing a neighbourhood plan that was ambitious and, at the same time, implementable. As part of the formal governance of the neighbourhood planning groups, environmentalists have taken care to avoid radical sustainability discourse. A member of FoE Alnwick suggested that they did not believe more radical policies would be accepted by more conservative members of the steering committee, and they were therefore left off the agenda. Another TI member said that they faced a lack of support at the local level and had to engage other sympathetic groups in consultations to make it appear as if the environmental voice was louder than it actually was on the ground. Other groups had proactively sought to enrol national-level supporters of a low-carbon agenda, such as CSE or planning consultants with a reputation for low-carbon policymaking (eg Welton and Lawrence Weston, Bristol).

The reformed English planning system still significantly hampers the extent to which some of the more radical ideas of grassroots sustainability can gain traction to challenge existing regimes, and the room for neighbourhood planning groups to develop novel policies has been squeezed. While there are opportunities for neighbourhoods to state their preferences for allocations of CIL, which could promote alternative low-carbon action, the dampened ambition of many groups – whether through political, practical or economic constraints – may be adversely affecting the number of neighbourhood groups who will seize these financial mechanisms to innovate.

Energy is an example of how recent policy reforms have weakened low-carbon ambitions. Solar Photovoltaics (PV), wind and hydro are

Photo 4.1: Neighbourhood planning for sustainability

Source: Hyde Park neighbourhood forum, Leeds: photograph Magdalena Szymanska

covered by the Feed-in-Tariff (FiT), which groups may have considered for community energy schemes. Members of the neighbourhood planning group in Boston Spa, Leeds, identified a weir as a site for hydro-electric power generation. The group actively encouraged the parish council to part-fund a feasibility study and to promote community generation of energy in the neighbourhood plan (Boston Spa NP Steering Group, 2015, p 10). However, significant cuts to the FiT – up to 66% for domestic Solar PV – undermine the viability of future community schemes. Options for renewable heat, such as district heating schemes, are facing similar cuts in subsidies (currently under consultation).

Hargreaves et al (2013) suggest that niche innovations gain traction when different groups become federated. Neighbourhood planning forums can be 'like a tree trunk, helping networks to grow', in the words of Angela Eoch, of Imagine Places (Eoch, 2014). However, experiences in the development of low-carbon neighbourhood plans echo Hodson and Marvin's (2013) notion of disconnected grassroots alternatives. Many of the groups who were interviewed as part of this research did not consider themselves as engaged in networking opportunities among planning groups, either on a regional or a thematic basis.

Efforts to broker between neighbourhood groups with similar low-carbon ambitions are under way, however. For instance, CSE's (2016) 'Guidebook for low-carbon neighbourhood planning' has been downloaded over 2,500 times, indicating the appetite for neighbourhood planning groups to respond to climate change. The scope of ambition reflected in some neighbourhood plans has already helped to attract a constellation of new actor networks, particularly in the south-west, where strong regional networks for low-carbon localism have developed.

Neighbourhood plans are only one response to the wider challenge of promoting a low-carbon society. While challenges remain in terms of securing and implementing low-carbon policies, neighbourhood planning has enabled some grassroots actors to make links into mainstream processes of government. Dan Stone from CSE, who supports such groups to develop low-carbon policies, suggested that while neighbourhood plans cannot insist on high environmental standards, they have helped to normalise discussions about climate change at a local level.

More needs to be done to capitalise on this greater level of engagement once a neighbourhood plan has been made. Mapping of existing communication channels between neighbourhood plan groups, planning practitioners and business and community actors could strengthen an awareness of key areas to achieve synergies for low-carbon development (Doak and Parker, 2002). Whether these new relationships can counteract recent government policy changes, support the role of planning in the transition to a low-carbon economy and meet the historic commitment in Paris to set global climate change targets remains to be seen; particularly in light of the UK's decision to leave the EU and to dissolve the Department for Energy and Climate Change (DECC), causing environmentalists to fear that climate change may fall down the UK political agenda.

Conclusion

This chapter has reviewed the lexicon of spatial practices devised by neighbourhood planning to guide development towards social, environmental and economic sustainability. We have highlighted these spatial practices in three specific ways in this chapter, discussing the impact of neighbourhood planning on house-building, social renewal and low-carbon initiatives, in order to review the extent to which communities are able to balance the demands of economic development against their social and environmental concerns. Neighbourhood plans have enabled communities to adapt the strategic development plans of local planning authorities to reflect local priorities, and can be understood in the context of the deregulation of planning policy.

In establishing a new statutory planning polity at the neighbourhood level, this deregulation demonstrated that local support for growth was not always compatible with the spatial ambitions of the development market and underlined the structural weakness of a housing industry dominated by volume builders. The liberalising rhetoric of localisation, coupled with government concern to provide tangible benefits to neighbourhoods, enabled some communities to prioritise local needs over strategic planning priorities. In devolving land-use and site allocation powers together with significant influence over non-strategic development to neighbourhoods, this new scale of plan-making has underlined the disparity between the exchange values that motivate private development markets and the use values that guide communities. A new set of imperatives must now be considered in the mix of policy, legislation and case law that surrounds neighbourhood development plans.

Neighbourhood planning has proved a blunt tool to define the social needs of sustainable development, though there have been some resourceful and imaginative attempts to map out public investment programmes in the restricted language of land-use regulation. The gap in social provision left by the forced contraction of the public sphere has been partially filled by the rhetoric of community self-management that accompanies the government strategy of localism. While small-scale community projects may be achievable through voluntary endeavour, any major regeneration is beyond the capacity of neighbourhood planning, which can only reinforce the spatial inequalities of uneven capitalist development. In the absence of any clear government direction for environmental policies, and with restrictions on what can be achieved through planning policy, neighbourhood plans have still demonstrated a grassroots commitment to low-carbon development. The majority of neighbourhood plans have sought to protect and promote green space and green infrastructure, and to shape the spatial practices of the development industry to plan for cycle and walking routes and wildlife corridors, with new house-building contained in small sites and settlement boundaries kept distinct. There have been few radical propositions but neighbourhood planning groups have forged some connections to environmental causes and created an infrastructure that might enable the networking and ideas generation needed to support grassroots environmental innovation.

If it can be said that a distinctive spatial practice is emerging from neighbourhood planning, it is characterised by a more intimate knowledge of space and spatial relations, and it is distinguished by a paramount desire to promote environmental quality, place identity and social well-being. The localisation of plan-making at the neighbourhood scale has deepened the political complexity of land-use and property market regulation and challenged the strategies of developers. The neighbourhood has emerged as a precocious new actor in the contested production of space.

Acknowledgement

The authors would like to thank Dan Stone from CSE for his invaluable comments to the low-carbon section of this chapter.

Notes

[1] Barratt Homes & Wainhomes Developments v Cheshire West & Chester Borough Council, Stephen Robinson & Tattenhall & District Parish Council [2014] EWHC 1470 Q.B.

[2] Larkleet Homes v Rutland County Council & Uppingham Town Council [2014] EWHC 4095 Q.B.

[3] Crane v SSCLG [2015] EWHC 425 (Admin).

[4] See: https://www.theccc.org.uk/charts-data/ukemissions-by-sector/buildings/

References

Archer, T. and Cole, I. (2014) 'Still not plannable? Housing supply and the changing structure of the housebuilding industry in the UK in "austere" times', *People, Place and Policy*, vol 8, no 2, pp 97–112.

Boston Spa NP Steering Group (2015) 'Boston Spa neighbourhood plan', draft for informal consultation, 3 September.

Bradley, Q. (2015) 'The political identities of neighbourhood planning in England', *Space and Polity*, DOI: 10.1080/13562576.2015.1046279.

Bradley, Q. and Sparling, W. (2016) 'The impact of neighbourhood planning and localism on house-building in England', *Housing Theory and Society*, DOI: 10.1080/14036096.2016.1197852.

Burroughs, L. (2015) *Getting homes built*, Housing Foresight Paper No 4, London: Campaign for the Protection of Rural England.

Committee on Climate Change (2016) 'UK emissions by sector: buildings'. Available at: www.theccc.org.uk/charts-data/ukemissions-by-sector/buildings/ (accessed 19 October 2016).

CSE (Centre for Sustainable Energy) (2016) 'A guidebook for low carbon neighbourhood planning', Bristol.

DCLG (Department of Communities and Local Government) (2011a) *Localism Bill: Neighbourhood plans equalities impact assessment*, London: Department of Communities and Local Government.

DCLG (2011b) *Impact assessment to the Localism Bill: Localism Bill: neighbourhood plans and community right to build*, London: DCLG.

DCLG (2012) *National Planning Policy Framework*, London: HMG.

DCLG (2014) 'Town and Country Planning Act 1990 – section 78 appeal by Mr. I. P. Crane – site at land south of Hallbrook Primary School, Crowfoot Way, Broughton Astley, Leicestershire'. Available at: www.gov.uk/government/uploads/system/uploads/attachment_data/file/305142/14-04-17_3-in-1_Crowfoot_Way_Harborough_2183563.pdf (accessed 10 August 2015).

DCLG (2015) *Notes on Neighbourhood Planning 16*, London: DCLG.

Doak, J. and Parker, G. (2002) '"Pre-plan mapping", networks, capital resources and community strategies in England', Working Papers in Land Management and Development 11/02.

EC (European Community) (2009) 'Renewable Energy Directive', 2009/28/EC.

EC (2010) 'Energy Performance of Buildings Directive (EPBD)', Directive 2010/31/EU.

Eoch, A. (2014) 'Neighbourhood planning in London 2014', Conference in Ealing, London, 28 May.

Exeter St James Forum (2015) 'ESJ Community Trust'. Available at: http://www.exeterstjamesforum.org (accessed 12 August 2015).

FOFS (Friends of Fishwick & St Matthews) (2014) *Inner East Preston neighbourhood development plan 2014–2029*, Submission Version, Preston: Friends of Fishwick & St Matthews.

Fortune Green & West Hampstead NDF (Neighbourhood Development Forum) (2014) 'Fortune Green & West Hampstead neighbourhood plan'. Available at: http://www.camden.gov.uk (accessed 12 August 2015).

Hargreaves, T., Longhurst, N. and Seyfang, G. (2013) 'Up, down, round and round: connecting regimes and practices in innovations for sustainability', *Environment and Planning*, vol 45(A), pp 202–420.

Heathfield Park Local Neighbourhood Partnership (2014) *Heath Town, Springfield, New Park Village Neighbourhood Plan: Your Plan Your Future 2014–2026*. Wolverhampton: Heathfield Park Local Neighbourhood Partnership.

HMG (Her Majesty's Government) (2008) *The Climate Change Act*, London: The Stationery Office Limited.

HMG (2015) *Town and country planning, England, the Town and Country Planning (General Permitted Development) (England) Order 2015*, London: The Stationery Office Limited.

Hodson, M. and Marvin, S. (2013) *Low carbon nation?*, Oxford: Routledge.

Lowndes, V. and McCaughie, K. (2013) 'Weathering the perfect storm? Austerity and institutional resilience in local government', *Policy & Politics*, vol 41, no 4, pp 533–49.

Lowndes, V. and Sullivan, H. (2008) 'How low can you go? Rationales and challenges for neighbourhood governance', *Public Administration*, vol 86, no 1, pp 53–74.

Mountain, C. (2015) *Neighbourhood planning: Progress on housing delivery*, London: DCLG Neighbourhood Planning Team.

Peters, R. (2014) *Neighbourhood plans: Plan and deliver?*, London: Turley.

Pickles, E. (2015) *Written statement to Parliament: Planning update March 2015*, London: HMG.

RICS (Royal Institution of Chartered Surveyors) (2016) 'The future of policy and standards for low and zero carbon homes', London.

Stanier, R. (2014) 'Local heroes: neighbourhood planning in practice', *Journal of Planning and Environment Law*, issue 13, pp 105–16.

The Ecologist (2015) 'Leaked letter: Rudd admits 25% green energy undershoot, misled Parliament'. Available at: www.theecologist. org/News/news_analysis/2986190/leaked_letter_rudd_admits_25_ green_energy_undershoot_misled_parliament.html (last accessed 19 October 2016).

FIVE

The uneven geographies of neighbourhood planning in England

Gavin Parker

Introduction

While neighbourhood planning is still emerging as an active component of planning practice and as part of the wider project of planning reform taken up by the UK government since 2010, it is revealing to narrate how it has been designed and responded to. The political and theoretical implications of neighbourhood planning are clearly important to understand and reflect upon (see Bradley, 2015; Davoudi and Madanipour, 2015; Parker et al, 2015; see also Chapters Two and Nine), but this chapter focuses on how, where and on what basis this non-mandatory, voluntary approach to statutory planning has been taken up by communities over the first four years or so of its operation.

Alongside the take-up (and non-take-up) of neighbourhood planning, the basis for engagement with planning issues offered by neighbourhood planning and the conditions and capacities existing across the thousands of very different 'neighbourhoods' in England provide just some of the cleavages likely to affect engagement with this set of planning tools. This is true not only of communities, but also of the different attitudes and responses from local authorities that have been produced given their statutory role as partners in neighbourhood planning (Smith, 2014). Moreover, the resource and control implications felt by at least some local authorities appear to be affecting the progress of neighbourhood planning. Thus, there have been issues identified in terms of the unevenness of take-up and equity concerns, the terms of engagement offered (which act to shape the 'possibilities' of neighbourhood planning), and the level of burdens shouldered by participants (see Gunn et al, 2015; Parker et al, 2015).

An overview of the evolution of the neighbourhood planning initiative in England, including the location and types of active areas, is outlined here to provide some empirical perspective on the first period of neighbourhood planning on the ground. The 'user experience' of neighbourhood planning research (see Parker et al, 2014) and subsequent consideration of how communities have operated (Parker et al, 2015) are drawn upon in the narrative, along with some contemporary critique and additional material relating to the socio-economic status of active neighbourhood planning areas. A brief contextual precis is set out before detailing the profile of neighbourhood planning activity in England during 2011–15. The chapter concludes with a short critical assessment.

Neighbourhood planning and neoliberal localism

Neighbourhood planning is framed and orchestrated to help deliver centrally determined priorities (notably, growth) with limited scope for diversion and embellishment (Parker et al, 2015). The neighbourhood planning arrangements also rely on the motivation and organising capacities found within a neighbourhood in order to effectively respond to this 'invitation'. Such conditions of operation do raise questions of practical accessibility and the likely benefits of participation in neighbourhood planning across a wide range of socio-economic circumstances.

Overall, neighbourhood planning is underpinned by a belief held by government that local people have sufficient interest in planning to invest time and energy – and, moreover, to do so over a sustained period – in order to unlock the potential of individuals at the neighbourhood scale. Ultimately, undertaking neighbourhood planning is a significant investment and could involve a (possibly continuous) cycle of preparation, adoption, implementation and review. At the time of the launch of neighbourhood planning, the governmental rhetoric surrounding the Localism Bill appeared to downplay asymmetries of knowledge and capacity, or other differences existing between one neighbourhood and another. Instead, an unproblematic or uniform view of neighbourhood propensities was apparent. Governmental assumptions about (inclusive) voluntary take-up have been questioned, based partly on the experience of past participatory opportunities and given known variation in capacity and prevalent issues across localities. Furthermore, the most organised and articulate, that is, those able to mobilise and draw on networks of social capital, were likely to be most able to manipulate the new environment to serve their own ends and possibly leave others 'adrift' (Lowndes and Pratchett, 2012). This doubt is recognisable in concerns expressed in past research involving parish plans and community-led plans operated in England (eg Parker, 2008; Parker and Murray, 2012).

It was envisaged that the unevenness of take-up and possible inequitable outcomes could well be exacerbated by the design of the tools and the approach to support for neighbourhood planning offered by central government. It was feared that some areas would use the approach to protect themselves from development in a form of 'defensive localism' (Weir, 1994; Fung, 2009), while others could be left to take poor-quality or higher levels of unwanted development and miss out on opportunities to facilitate needed development in their own area, or otherwise to shape their environment through their own deliberations. Indeed, the anticipation was that some would not be able to draw on resources and possibilities that enable process benefits derived from participation, including the establishment or refiguring of links within the community, with their local authority (as local planning authority) and with others.

This raises questions about the experiences of neighbourhood planning so far and how neighbourhood planning has been emerging in terms of neighbourhood planning support, the spatial distribution of neighbourhood planning take-up, the diversity of areas who are participating, the capacities required and the navigability of neighbourhood planning, as discussed in the following.

The take-up of neighbourhood planning

There was concern about the accessibility of neighbourhood planning and it has clearly been difficult for some communities to grapple with it, as Gunn et al (2015) highlight and as discussed in Parker et al (2015). These queries and their dynamics are considered in reference to the actual take-up of neighbourhood planning, after considering how support for neighbourhood planning/planners has been organised.

Support for neighbourhood planning

A total of 278 neighbourhood planning 'Frontrunners' were launched in five waves from April 2011 (labelled at the time as 'vanguard' communities) and in advance of the Localism Bill being enacted. The Frontrunners were selected from across England after applying to participate, along with their local authority, and indicating that they were committed to the neighbourhood planning initiative. At this stage, four external agency groupings were engaged through a central government support contract to provide advice and to assist those neighbourhoods involved (Parker, 2012). The resources provided were mainly for training, advice and direct support to the

Frontrunner communities. The multi-agency approach was found to be somewhat problematic in that four different approaches and forms of advice and guidance were being shaped and made available. Some neighbourhood planning groups were listening and responding to more than one of these sources and this ultimately acted as much to confound as to supplement knowledge or effect practical progress. In 2012, neighbourhood planning was mainstreamed beyond the Frontrunner areas, although no formal evaluation of the early experience was conducted. This widening of availability also signalled a change in the support arrangements in 2013 and an increase in the numbers becoming involved in neighbourhood planning.

The next support tranche (2013–15) saw one consortium led by Locality with Planning Aid England/RTPI (Royal Town Planning Institute) and a grants plus 'direct support' offer that was made available to groups that applied. The resources offered after 2013 were on a 'first come, first served' basis, with no selection criteria applied, but it is notable that from April 2015 (the third tranche of support), the Department of Communities and Local Government (DCLG) did adjust their approach and adopted the idea that some areas needed to be prioritised. They have subsequently sought to address this by directing some funding support towards 'priority areas', that is, 'typically those with neighbourhood forums, in deprived locations, high growth areas, or areas with populations over 25,000' (Moore, 2015), and offered technical support to eligible areas. This was prompted by the emerging and uneven geographies discussed in the following, notably, the skew towards rural (parished areas) (see Table 5.1) and other issues identified in Parker et al (2014). Overall, central government had committed around £40 million for neighbourhood planning during the period 2011–18 (in three tranches), as well as establishing a team of DCLG civil servants to support neighbourhood planning.

The DCLG had estimated in 2012 that neighbourhood development plans (NDPs) would cost £20,000 to £86,000 per plan (DCLG, 2012), and each plan was to attract a 'burdens' payments to the relevant local authority of up to £30,000 per plan (payable on completion). Ostensibly, this approach was designed to offset local authority costs, including the administration of the neighbourhood referendum. Despite such arrangements, it is likely that neighbourhood planning costs have been underestimated given that the full costs are quite difficult to disentangle. A number of elements would need to be considered, including: engagement costs; volunteer time; consultant time; local authority officer time; referendum costs; plan production costs; and other incidental costs (eg room hire, materials). Some of these cannot be accurately discerned or priced and there is a suspicion that the estimated average costs, while attempting to account for the elastic nature of NDPs (ie they may be more or less ambitious in terms of policy breadth and may cover a larger or smaller population), do not give a clear picture of actual costs. Feedback from respondents in the Parker et al (2014) study indicated that a large amount of volunteer time had invariably been expended but was not recorded or costed. Clearly, cost obstacles could practically exclude some communities or groups within neighbourhoods or impair the quality of the process.

Neighbourhood planning partners

It is notable that little comment was passed on how local authorities as partners in neighbourhood planning were likely to respond to the national government agenda – largely because assumptions about their role were wrapped up in a rather vague 'duty to support' that the Localism Act imposed on local authorities. In essence, neighbourhood planning was imposed on local authorities at a time when other reforms to planning were occupying their resources – which were also under pressure as part of austerity cuts. This has made for a rather uneven welcome, and, notably, more than a quarter of local authorities in England had no neighbourhood plans in progress by the winter of 2015. The interactive map of the distribution of neighbourhood plans and the stage reached (see: http://www.neighbourhoodplanner. co.uk/map) highlights areas where fewer neighbourhood plans are in production and indicates the stage reached. The 2014 research indicated that the qualifying bodies' experience of local authority involvement in neighbourhood planning was variable.

In terms of the private sector, there was also little overt recognition that so many communities would turn to planning consultants to help prepare their plan, although the rounds of neighbourhood planning programme support offered by government actively invited private consultants to support neighbourhood planning groups. Parker et al (2014) found that around 70% of active neighbourhood planning areas had drawn on private consultants in various ways. Critically, this was to assist in (re)writing policy in many cases given that many areas had found the guidance difficult to interpret and apply and the overall process to be burdensome.

Consideration of how national government, local authorities, private consultants and other support or intermediary organisations have acted to shape the implementation and form of neighbourhood planning is recognised as a research topic that needs further attention. Further work specifically exploring how local authorities have responded to neighbourhood planning and why would be useful given that their role was also seen to be very influential on the success, or at least the experience, of the neighbourhood planning effort led by the qualifying bodies (Parker et al, 2014).

Speed and timing of neighbourhood planning take-up

The recent research with neighbourhood planning participants highlighted a stronger take-up in the parishes of southern England, with many early adopters enjoying a history of active community planning in the past (Parker et al, 2014). Given that many parished (very often rural) areas are unlikely to be able to accommodate large numbers of housing or other new significant development, a view has been expressed that more attention might usefully be paid to neighbourhood types that are more likely to accommodate development sustainably. In short, neighbourhood plans may be less needed in many rural areas (if the enterprise is to be judged against the government's growth agenda), as well as given the recognised housing crisis, which requires many thousands more houses to be built year on year than has actually been achieved since 1980. As such, a more targeted approach may be beneficial, as well as one that is more integrated with strategic planning, if neighbourhood planning is to play a role in shaping larger agendas as part of a responsibility to address wider societal needs.

Equally, in such areas where large-scale development *is* feasible, NDPs may not necessarily be the appropriate tool and qualifying bodies may not be able to 'keep up' with the speed of change (including the number of planning applications and decisions) generated in such areas. Indeed, there has been frustration at ongoing change, which sometimes jeopardises the progress and integrity of NDPs. Moreover, larger urban extension-type schemes are traditionally conceived and implemented by higher-level authorities – with scope instead for local detailing and refinement, with or without community engagement. This reflects the perceived difficulties of reaching consensus or managing land and property markets prior to neighbourhood plan publication and dealing with large-scale long-term projects – which quite possibly cross administrative boundaries. The backdrop to the first years of neighbourhood planning has featured such tensions and has added a degree of confusion about the primacy or status of emerging neighbourhood plans and their relationship with local plans or emerging local plans (PAS, 2015).

The DCLG Select Committee report of December 2014 on the effectiveness of the 2012 National Planning Policy Framework (NPPF) raised a number of points about neighbourhood planning. In the report, neighbourhood plans were strongly supported in principle but it was recognised that they should not become the preserve of the middle classes or of the rural middle class – given that the early wave of neighbourhood planning activity had been dominated by rural (parished) areas (Defra, 2013; Parker et al, 2014; Turley, 2014). Particularly, there should be interest in those plans that are formulated (and abandoned) in urban neighbourhoods and how they are negotiated.

A commentary on how others have facilitated neighbourhood planning activity thus far is provided to agitate this wider agenda. The actual and estimated take-up of neighbourhood planning is shown in Table 5.1 from spring 2013 (ie after neighbourhood planning had been open to all communities in England). This shows take-up to be largely as the DCLG estimated in broad terms.

Table 5.1: Estimated and actual take-up of neighbourhood planning areas (2011–15)

Neighbourhood planning designated areas	DCLG forecast take-up	Actual NP take-up[a]	Number of NPs to referendum (actual)[a]
Spring 2013	762	500	1
Spring 2014	1143	1000	8
Spring 2015	1524	1400	60
Summer 2015	n/a	1500	80
Winter 2015	n/a	1600	100

Note: [a] Indicative numbers given the rolling nature of neighbourhood plan figures. NP – neighbourhood plan.
Source: Based on DCLG (2012) and successive 'Neighbourhood planning notes' produced by the DCLG.

The take-up year on year shows that while many have initiated the neighbourhood planning process, few have progressed to the final stages (ie referendum). Only 92 neighbourhoods had successfully progressed to the referendum stage by December 2015, with this rising to 130 by the end of January 2016. Overall, the progress to referendum has been much slower than anticipated, with the time taken to complete (ie to reach referendum stage) in many cases going well beyond two years and the average time taken being 27 months. This highlights that NDPs have taken longer than parish plans/community-led plans, which averaged less than two years to complete – largely due to fewer regulatory steps involved in the latter and set consultation periods required in the former (see Parker, 2008).

Take-up of neighbourhood planning geographically

There was a slow adoption of neighbourhood planning despite the neighbourhood planning option being open to all in 2012. By spring 2013, only around 500 groups had been designated as neighbourhood planning areas – a net increase of only 270 groups. In terms of the regional breakdown, Figure 5.1 shows the take-up of neighbourhood planning by region by January 2016. This indicates a larger number of areas active in the south of England, with the South East and South West regions accounting for 42% of neighbourhood planning take-up overall.

Figure 5.1: Take-up of neighbourhood planning by English region (January 2016)

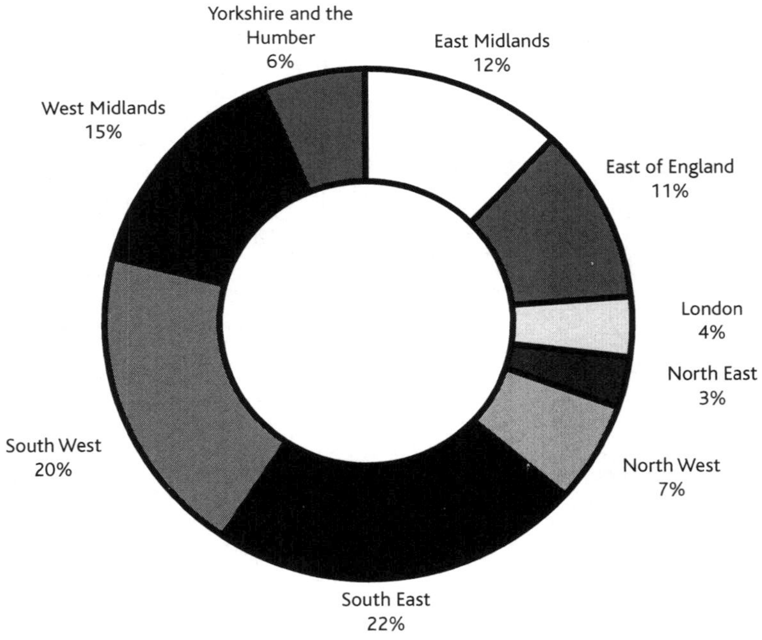

Source: G. Parker.

Table 5.2 sets out the overall take-up since 2011/12, which shows that 1,625 neighbourhood areas had been formally designated by January 2016. The overall cohort shows that the great majority were in parished areas, with only 150 (9%) in forum areas. The wider cohort is, however, spread more evenly across England, with more than 850 groups embarking on neighbourhood planning outside of the South East, South West and London. The latter three regions had 749 neighbourhood areas designated between them.

In terms of regional take-up and progress, we can see that almost half of those passing a referendum were located in the south of England. Table 5.2 also shows that of the 130 plans that had passed a referendum by the end of January 2016, most were in parished (rural) areas, with only 12 in forum areas.

Table 5.2: Regional and qualifying body (parish/forum) distribution of neighbourhood planning (January 2016)

Region (England)	NP to referendum: parish/forum (total)	NP qualifying bodies: parish/forum (total)
London	0/3 = (3)	1/63 = (64)
South East	50/2 = (52)	340/20 = (360)
South West	15/1 = (16)	312/13 = (325)
West Midlands	12/4 = (16)	231/6 = (237)
East Midlands	21/0 = (21)	189/8 = (197)
East of England	10/0 = (10)	181/1 = (182)
Yorks & Humber	2/0 = (2)	86/16 = (102)
North West	7/2 = (9)	90/18 = (108)
North East	1/0 = (1)	44/5 = (49)
England (total)	118/12 = (130)	1475/150 = (1625)

Note: NP – neighbourhood plan.

In terms of urban/rural classification, around one third were in urban areas: of the 92 that had passed the referendum by autumn 2015, based on the Lower Super Output Area (RUC11) classification, 24 were in E1/E2 settings (rural village), 14 were in E1/D1 or E2/D2 settings (rural village/rural town), 22 were in D1/D2 (rural town), and 32 were in A1, B1 and C1 categories (urban). These statistics tend to correspond with concerns that many urban areas have faced extra hurdles in establishing forums and in agreeing the neighbourhood area, and that progress has been slower as a result. However, in some urban areas, there are signs of greater uptake and support, for example, Leeds had 23 active neighbourhood planning areas by summer 2015 and London as a whole had 64 qualifying bodies designated (as shown in Table 5.2). Further work is needed to understand how some local authorities are enabling and shaping neighbourhood planning in different ways and how some others appear to be downplaying neighbourhood planning and the possible effect on neighbourhood enthusiasm or use of alternative planning tools.

Diversity of neighbourhood planning take-up

As indicated earlier, there have been concerns raised about how more deprived communities may respond to neighbourhood planning. In terms of the socio-economic profile of those participating in neighbourhood planning, the distribution of the larger group of qualifying bodies ($n = 1625$) shows that 23% were ranked in the lower two Index of Multiple Deprivation (IMD) quintiles– 255 were in the fourth and only 122 were in the fifth quintile (7.5%) – leaving 77% in the top three quintiles at the local authority level (see Table 5.3). This indicates that initial concerns about weaker uptake from disadvantaged areas also appear to be somewhat justified.

Table 5.3: Index of Multiple Deprivation breakdown of neighbourhood planning qualifying bodies at the local authority level (January 2016)

Region (Population)	IMD Q1	IMD Q2	IMD Q3	IMD Q4	IMD Q5	Totals
London (8.174 million)	1	1	2	19	40	64
South East (8.635 million)	214	61	57	23	5	360
South West (5.289 million)	46	122	73	76	8	325
West Midlands (5.602 million)	41	25	149	16	6	237
East Midlands (4.533 million)	48	82	38	20	9	197
East of England (5.847 million)	58	61	39	17	7	182
Yorks & Humber (5.284 million)	3	19	8	46	26	102
North West (7.052 million)	3	52	27	13	14	109
North East (2.597 million)	0	0	17	25	7	49
All (53.865 million)	414 (25.4%)	424 (26.1%)	410 (25.2%)	255 (15.7%)	122 (7.5%)	1625 (100%)

Note: Based on 2015 IMD classifications and 2013 Office for National Statistics population projections. Q1 = least deprived to Q5 = most deprived.

Take-up across all regions shows a reasonable spread, but the take-up in the South East is markedly skewed towards less-deprived areas (see Tables 5.3 and 5.4). However, a more fine-grained examination is needed as more or less affluent neighbourhoods will be scattered across local authority areas (see also Parker and Salter, 2016).

As to the relative affluence of those that had reached referendum by January 2016 ($n = 130$) according to their IMD quintile group ranking at the local authority level, around 18% were from the lower two quintile (more deprived) groups, while 42 were in the first quintile. We should be aware of the danger of drawing conclusions too early given that the sample size is small (see also Parker and Salter, 2016), but this indicates that less deprived communities were dominating in the early years. However, the types of communities that are subsequently taking up neighbourhood planning still requires further investigation in detail.

Table 5.4: Index of Multiple Deprivation breakdown of neighbourhood plans to referendum (by local authority) (January 2016)

Region	IMD Q1	IMD Q2	IMD Q3	IMD Q4	IMD Q5	Totals
East Midlands	7	6	5	3	0	21
East of England	5	3	0	2	0	10
London	0	0	0	3	0	3
North East	0	0	1	0	0	1
North West	0	3	4	0	2	9
South East	26	6	17	3	0	52
South West	3	5	5	3	0	16
West Midlands	1	2	8	2	3	16
Yorks & Humber	0	0	0	0	2	2
Total	**42**	**25**	**40**	**16**	**7**	**130**

Note: Based on 2015 IMD rankings. Q1 = least deprived to Q5 = most deprived.

The work reported in the study by Parker et al (2014) did not extend to a full socio-economic profiling of participating areas; indeed, it was a little too early in terms of take-up and cohort progress to reach firm conclusions in any case. How to ensure that areas in need of support and development can be activated either in neighbourhood planning or similar participatory/co-creative activity still remains to be deliberated upon, and any impact of DCLG targeting towards priority areas since 2015 is something to be observed.

Neighbourhood plan policy content

The government was clear that NDPs could contain fewer or a greater number of policies according to the wishes of the neighbourhood, and this was intended to offer flexibility in scope and associated preparation burdens. As a result, the number of policies contained in emerging neighbourhood plans varies (Turley, 2014; DCLG, 2015; PAS, 2015) and some have argued that the policy orientation of those NDPs coming forward have appeared quite balanced, with both 'protectionist' and pro-development policy. Most plans considered in the *User experience* research (Parker et al, 2014, 2015) had policies on housing, and over half had allocated sites for housing. When the DCLG took a snapshot in December 2015, they calculated that the average number of policies in NDPs stood at 19 (DCLG, 2015) and confirmed that while just over half of the NDPs had *allocated sites* for housing, most (89%) had policies that addressed local housing. What remains unclear and somewhat hypothetical is what housing numbers would have been facilitated in any case and therefore whether neighbourhood plans are actually increasing net housing numbers. A small number of NDPs have sought to allocate more housing units in their areas than the relevant local plan. Examples include Broughton Astley in Leicestershire, Thame in Oxfordshire and Tattenhall in Cheshire, but where a local plan is not in place, the allocations in neighbourhood plans cannot necessarily be said to represent net increases in development. There is a picture also emerging of other components of plans relating to landscape protection and heritage protection, and this may be seen as part of a subtle squeeze being put on development by some neighbourhoods. However, there are also a number of cases where proposed content is being ruled out by local authorities, consultants and or examiners if it is deemed not to be 'land-use planning' or, indeed, if it fails to meet the 'basic conditions', which has caused some frustration (Parker et al, 2015).

Clearly, more study on the process by which content has been shaped is required and this could usefully include a reflection on how a 'land-use' versus 'spatial' planning scope and focus could be usefully reconceptualised at this scale. This is relevant as many other 'place-shaping' issues are identified as important by neighbourhoods, which may also speak loudly about the diverse needs and geographies across neighbourhoods, and such matters have been accommodated in community-led planning in the past (Parker, 2014).

Motives and aims of participants

Given the effort and frustrations that many participants have reported with neighbourhood planning, the goal of creating a statutory plan clearly holds some motivating power as many neighbourhoods have opted to undertake this work. The Parker et al (2014) study reported that the majority of those embarking on NDPs expressed their main motivation as a desire to take control of decisions over their own area, with many voicing dissatisfaction with their local authorities in the past. They wanted to shape the future and provide a vision for the neighbourhood. Many highlighted that this included retaining or enhancing the desirable characteristics of their locality. In terms of their attitudes towards new development, the respondents understood that neighbourhood plans were tools to enable development. In that position, and also due to pressure for housing in particular, they wanted to be able to shape the design, timing, location and scale of development in their own area – and in a way that their local planning authority had not in the past. In terms of the latter point, the study did reveal a gap in trust and understanding between the local authority and many of the neighbourhoods.

Discussion and conclusion: navigating neighbourhood planning

The assumption that the government has carried forward into policy is that communities are willing and able not only to engage with planning, but also to *lead* planning activity for their own area. This doctrinal approach prefigures a significant culture change in planning. This wider project aims to reallocate roles and responsibilities for planning across the sectors. The experience of neighbourhood planning so far has seen significant controversy surrounding the internal capacities and distribution of social and economic capital, and the time and skills needed to draw upon neighbourhood planning tools effectively. Such disparities appear to have been underestimated by the government. Many of those involved in the Parker et al (2014) *User experience* study signalled how burdensome and challenging it had been to navigate their way through the NDP requirements, and most of these had (of necessity) received some form of support from third parties, that is, consultants. This has led many to comment that they would not wish

Photo 5.1: Wanting to shape the future

Source: Holbeck neighbourhood forum, Leeds: photograph Harvey Pritchard

to undertake such a process again. It is possible, given this situation, that urban and more deprived communities have been deterred by the likely burdens involved (see also Gunn et al, 2015) or have been slower to take up or progress NDPs.

Thus, despite a significant level of take-up overall, a slower rate of progress to completion has been achieved than the government had hoped for. This has prompted central government to seek ways of 'speeding up' neighbourhood planning, highlighted in the adjustments to the neighbourhood planning process in the 2015 Housing and Planning Bill (Prime Minister's Office, 2015; Wilson and Smith, 2015). Ironically, the 'light-touch' approach that had been advocated by the government for neighbourhood planning has apparently acted to create a degree of confusion rather than to enable or expedite progress, and had left neighbourhood groups calling for more support and guidance.

In terms of what is needed, the respondents in the 2014 study clearly felt that face-to-face support was most important and that they had had variable experiences with local authorities. The support contracts for neighbourhood planning from 2012 to 2015 featured direct support from agencies such as Planning Aid England, and this enabled independent advisors to give guidance and advice in a bespoke fashion. Experiences thus far demonstrate that intermediary input from local authorities and consultants has been critical for 'successful' neighbourhood planning activity, and if such support is not available and targeted where most needed, then neighbourhood planning does run the risk of succeeding only in pockets across England and possibly burning itself out after the first cycle of NDPs.

The quality of neighbourhood planning processes and the transaction costs issues (ie time, value-adding, costs) are also important. Consideration of how the neighbourhood planning process creates wider process benefits– around awareness raising and understanding of the need for good planning, as well as enabling needed development – is of value. Further navigation issues have arisen with neighbourhood planning working groups who need the completed document to speak to their own community, as well as to meet governmental needs (see Brand and Gaffikin, 2007; Parker et al, 2015). It seems that at least some local authorities and consultants are largely concerned that the plans conform to the requisite 'basic conditions' and will be implementable rather than actually reflect community views.

The chapter has highlighted the uneven take-up and the difficulties experienced with neighbourhood planning. While the support and use of neighbourhood planning will be of more benefit where it can have most impact, many other planning and development tools are equally also available already (see RTPI, 2011; Parker, 2012), and finding a creative way of including and enabling the use of these as part of a broader localist planning array is also a useful task in itself. What is certain is that neighbourhood planning alone cannot form the basis for planning policy in England. In finding a stable role in statutory planning in the future, the integration of policy and interaction vertically and horizontally with other plans is necessary and the maintenance of quality in NDP production will be needed – as will a much greater take-up.

References

Bradley, Q. (2015) 'The political identities of neighbourhood planning in England', *Space and Polity*, vol 19, no 2, pp 97–109.

Brand, R. and Gaffikin, F. (2007) 'Collaborative planning in an uncollaborative world', *Planning Theory*, vol 6, no 3, pp 282–313.

Davoudi, S. and Madanipour, A. (eds) (2015) *Reconsidering localism*, London: Routledge.

DCLG (Department of Communities and Local Government) (2012) *Neighbourhood planning impact assessment*, London: TSO.

DCLG (2015) *Notes on neighbourhood planning No. 17*, December, London: DCLG.

Defra (Department for Environment, Food and Rural Affairs) (2013) *Neighbourhood planning. The rural frontrunners: Research and case studies*, London: Defra.

Fung, A. (2009) *Empowered participation: Reinventing urban democracy*, Oxford: Princeton University Press.

Gunn, S., Brooks, E. and Vigar, G. (2015) 'The community's capacity to plan: the disproportionate requirements of the new English neighbourhood planning initiative', in S. Davoudi and A. Madanipour (eds) *Reconsidering localism*, London: Routledge, pp 147–67.

Lowndes, V. and Pratchett, L. (2012) 'Local governance under the Coalition government: austerity, localism and the "Big Society"', *Local Government Studies*, vol 38, no 1, pp 21–40.

Moore, G. (2015) 'New support for neighbourhood planning', 27 February. Available at: http://www.ourneighbourhoodplanning. org.uk/news/2015/02/27/New_Support_for_Neighbourhood_ Planning (accessed 14 September 2015).

Parker, G. (2008) 'Parish and community-led planning, local empowerment and local evidence bases', *Town Planning Review*, vol 79, no 1, pp 61–85.

Parker, G. (2012) 'Neighbourhood planning: precursors, lessons and prospects', *Journal of Planning and Environment Law*, vol 40: Occasional Paper #139.

Parker, G. (2014) 'Engaging neighbourhoods: experiences of transactive planning with communities in England', in N. Gallent and D. Ciaffi (eds) *Community action and planning*, Bristol: The Policy Press, pp 177–200.

Parker, G. and Murray, C. (2012) 'Beyond tokenism? Community-led planning and rational choices: findings from participants in local agenda-setting at the neighbourhood scale in England', *Town Planning Review*, vol 83, no 1, pp 1–28.

Parker, G., Lynn, T., Wargent, M. and Locality (2014) *User experience of neighbourhood planning in England*, October, London: Locality.

Parker, G., Lynn, T. and Wargent, M. (2015) 'Sticking to the script? The co-production of neighbourhood plans', *Town Planning Review*, vol 86, no 5, pp 519–36.

Parker, G. and Salter, K. (2016) 'Five years of neighbourhood planning. A review of take-up and distribution', *Town and Country Planning*, vol 85, no 5, pp 181–88.

PAS (Planning Advisory Service) (2015) 'Note on issues from emerging plans – some case studies', March. Available at: http:// www.pas.gov.uk/web/pas1/neighbourhood-planning/-/journal_ content/56/332612/7122302/ARTICLE (accessed 14 September 2015).

Prime Minister's Office (2015) 'The Queens Speech 2015. Technical notes on the Queens Speech', 27th May. Available at: https://www.gov.uk/government/uploads/system/uploads/attachment_data/file/430149/QS_lobby_pack_FINAL_NEW_2.pdf (accessed 14 September 2015).

RTPI (Royal Town Planning Institute) (2011) *Localism Bill: Existing tools for neighbourhood planning*, RTPI information note, 24 May, London: RTPI.

Smith, L. (2014) *Neighbourhood planning*, House of Commons Library Standard Note SN/SC/5838, July, London: House of Commons.

Turley (2014) *Neighbourhood planning: Plan and deliver?*, March, Bristol: Turley Planning Consultancy.

Weir, M. (1994) 'Urban poverty and defensive localism', *Dissent*, vol 41, no 3, pp 337–42.

Wilson, W. and Smith, L. (2015) *Housing and Planning Bill (Bill 75 of 2015–16)*, briefing paper, House of Commons Library No. 07331, October, London: House of Commons.

Part Two:
Experiences, contestations and debates

In Part Two, we explore the everyday practices of neighbourhood planning and the experiences of participants, and through these emerging histories, we investigate the key themes of power and empowerment, democratic renewal, and the remaking of planning and place. In the first three chapters, the emphasis is on the lived realities of neighbourhood planning, and the challenges, compromises and frustrations encountered in navigating the conflicting rationales of localism. These chapters introduce the range of actors engaged at the neighbourhood level and present divergent views and interpretations of the democratic practices of the locality, and the empowering potential of citizen planning. In the final two chapters in this section, we review these experiences to evaluate the extent to which power relations are changed through the constrained freedoms of localism, and how neighbourhood planning might impact on the purposes and democratic practices of planning.

In Chapter Six, David McGuinness and Carol Ludwig review the experiences of two of the earliest neighbourhood planning groups and chart the production of their neighbourhood plans, with a particular focus on the barriers to democratic practice in planning. Chapter Seven is innovative in introducing a range of voices from neighbourhood planning participants, each recounting their experiences in their own words. These accounts from neighbourhood planners, local authority planning officers, developers and consultants illuminate changing roles, a reshaping of planning knowledge and the frustrations of constructing an inclusive, local and democratic planning practice. These themes are investigated in a different context in Chapter Eight, as Claire Colomb challenges the possibilities of neighbourhood planning in the ethnic and socio-economic tensions of urban centres. Reviewing the practices of neighbourhood planning in London boroughs, she identifies the exclusionary dynamics evident in the construction of coherent localities and evidences the power claims made in the name of engaged communities. These questions of power and empowerment are explored further in Chapter Nine, as Sue Brownill reviews the impact of neighbourhood planning on the regulation of development and the expected outcomes of growth-dependent planning. Her chapter evidences changes in the topology of power relations as a result of neighbourhood planning and provides a clear analysis of their impact. The emotional attachments of neighbourhood planning are explored in the final chapter in this section (Chapter Ten), in which Quintin Bradley explores the mobilisation of place identity in collective neighbourhood action. He points to the feeling for place and emplacement that may be driving change in the social purposes of planning, as well as in its democratic practice.

SIX

Developing a neighbourhood plan: stories from 'community-led' planning pathfinders

David McGuinness and Carol Ludwig

Introduction

This chapter provides empirical data from two of the earliest neighbourhood planning pathfinders in England: Upper Eden in rural Cumbria and North Shields on the Tyneside coast. It critically explores how each neighbourhood navigated the plan-making process and provides first-hand insights into the challenges faced by the first wave of pathfinder neighbourhoods to embark on the neighbourhood planning process. The unfolding experiences of the two areas reveal some important questions about the impact of the initial lack of clear policy guidance about neighbourhood planning, whether *communities* have the capacity to develop robust neighbourhood plans without the *direct* assistance of professional planners and the *role* that professional planners should play in the neighbourhood plan development process. The chapter is organised into three sections: the first section analyses the North Shields case study; the second section analyses the Upper Eden case study; and the concluding section draws together key findings from the research. In doing so, the chapter unpacks some important lessons about the limitations and opportunities provided by 'community-led' planning.

Case study 1: North Shield Fish Quay Neighbourhood Plan

The fish quay lies within the metropolitan borough of North Tyneside, nine miles east of Newcastle in the North East of England. The North Shields Fish Quay Neighbourhood Plan (FQNP) was adopted by North Tyneside Council (NTC) on 8 April 2013. Although the final document is titled a 'neighbourhood plan', it is actually a Supplementary Planning Document (SPD) as it was not subjected to a referendum. Unlike most contemporary neighbourhood plans, the FQNP was proposed by the local authority (LA) to an existing resident group, and was deemed "the final piece in the regeneration jigsaw" (planning officer, NTC). The fish quay has experienced pockets of persistent blight due to the decline of traditional industries, a changing economic climate and the cessation of area-based regeneration funding initiatives. To attract new investors into the area, it was deemed essential to provide updated planning guidance relating to acceptable land uses on key derelict sites (which had formerly been designated for employment land). Such a case was presented by NTC in their bid to the Department of Communities and Local Government (DCLG) to become one of the pathfinders for neighbourhood planning. Following a successful application, NTC received £20,000 and the FQNP officially commenced in June 2011.

Planning stages

Formation of group

The Conservative Mayor of North Tyneside was keen to promote neighbourhood planning and support the government's localism agenda. As a metropolitan area with no parish councils, NTC approached an existing 'neighbourhood group' to gauge whether they wanted to produce a neighbourhood plan. While not organic, the formation of the group was nevertheless aided by the active citizen mobilisation in the area over the past decade. In 2002, a pressure group, Folk Interested in Shields Harbour (FISH), was established directly by citizens, and this group formed the basis of a more formalised 'Fish Quay Heritage Partnership', set up in 2005 with heritage lottery funding. In 2007, the partnership was involved in the preparation of a management strategy for the fish quay. Despite the natural morphing of FISH and the Fish Quay Heritage Partnership into the new FQNP group, new members were also encouraged to join. Following the formation of the neighbourhood group, a chairman was elected to lead the group, and an independent facilitator from the North of England Civic Trust was appointed to steer the project.

Guidance and support

When the FQNP group was confirmed, the first obstacle faced by the group was the lack of established support mechanisms and guidance to steer the process. The lack of information challenged not only the group, but also NTC and the facilitator: "Nobody really knew what a neighbourhood plan was…. The guidance came out about six months after we started" (independent facilitator). In particular, the interviewees involved with the FQNP all expressed confusion and frustration about the timing of the release of the guidance, which was further amplified by the absence of the expected two-way flow of information between the pathfinder group and central government.

Links to central government

The FQNP group expected some form of scaling-up or linking capital (Holman and Rydin, 2013), facilitating access to the higher tier of governance, which would enable them to genuinely influence the development of neighbourhood planning policy and guidance. The planning officer from NTC explained that they had a designated 'link officer' from DCLG but he only "met me once". This apparent indifference was deemed incomprehensible to the planning officer and the independent facilitator, both of whom considered that the pilot should be a tool for wider learning: "they brought out the regulations whilst we were still piloting … shouldn't we finish and you learn and then you pursue it?" (planning officer, NTC); "We had no reporting. DCLG weren't interested" (independent facilitator). In addition to these misconceptions, a further challenge at the outset was managing the range of expectations about neighbourhood planning that varied within the local actors.

Expectation management

Interviewees explained how the FQNP group initially envisaged a neighbourhood plan to be a tool to solve all existing problems in the area (eg traffic congestion) and a way to deliver new infrastructure, such as a new metro station. When the planning officer explained the constraints of the English planning system and the need to be in general conformity with the local plan, the group "were disappointed" (planning officer, NTC). This illustrated what the planning officer described as a severe "lack of understanding of the planning system". Indeed, she had to continually emphasise that "It's not a 'doing' document it's a 'guiding' document" (planning officer, NTC).

NTC was very clear about their expectations for the plan, as shown in the following extract: "We wanted a focus on those particular sites that were derelict and give them a proper … design brief" (planning officer, NTC). In terms of achieving this, NTC also had a preconceived idea about how the process would unfold:

> "we thought that they would write the document collaboratively amongst themselves, that we would point them towards the kind of information they should be looking for and they would go away and they would read it and digest it and put it into a document." (Planning officer, NTC)

This collaborative writing, the interviewees explained, did not materialise however; instead, "it ... did boil down to mostly just one guy writing it" (planning officer, NTC).

Indeed, while the notion of 'neighbourhood' planning, by virtue, carries with it an inherent expectation of democratic accountability and local representativeness, the reality of the process at the fish quay was that the resident chairman was solely responsible for writing the majority of the plan. This approach intensified the pressure on one individual and also increased the likelihood that the views of all sectors would not be adequately encompassed within the plan. This diminishing trend in collaboration was also evident in the falling rate of attendance and participation at meetings.

Process

Issues relating to attendance and participation

The FQNP group's fortnightly meetings commenced with high levels of attendance. The resident chair explained that there were "about 15 regular people turning up for the meetings and 40-odd people who could turn up to workshops". Despite the initial strength of participation, the number of people participating in FQNP meetings and contributing fell substantially over time. The planning officer identified key factors contributing to the dwindling input, including a sense of "fatigue" due to the length of the process and disillusionment with the ultimate level of power that the group wielded: "why are the council asking us to do this? We're working for free. It's not given as much power to us as we thought it would" (planning officer, NTC).

The resident chair, on the other hand, had a more cynical opinion about some of the motives within the group, suggesting: "what you get from the public is, 'We all have an opinion and we all want to be heard but none of us want to do anything'" (resident chair). One explanation for this reluctance of the wider FQNP group to write emerged as a severe skill deficit within the group.

Lack of skills within the community

All interviewees expressed concern that the group did not individually possess or have access to the skills required for effective governance of the neighbourhood plan: "[we] haven't got a clue how it works ... people don't have a lot of experience, and an extreme lack of skills" (resident chair). This created, in the planning officer's view, a self-perpetuating fear and lack of confidence to put their "head above the parapet" (planning officer, NTC). Moreover, this acknowledged skill deficit led to gross frustration about the unrealistic expectations placed on the group by the government: "they expect a group of amateurs who haven't got the facilities or the knowledge to suddenly do it" (resident chair).

In addition to such challenges, the chair explained that the logistical and administrative aspects of neighbourhood planning also often got overlooked. For example, many group members did not have access to a computer or email. These issues illustrate that despite a very competent chairman, the expectations placed on groups to govern themselves can be problematic. There are, however, important lessons to be learnt about the ways in which capacity building should be rolled out, as unpacked in the following.

Capacity building

At the beginning of the process, NTC organised a number of professional workshops, which were delivered by both civic institutions and professional planning organisations. Despite the capacity-building initiatives, the FQNP group expressed concern with the pressure placed upon them to rapidly learn how to become planners: "it takes god knows how many years to educate a planner ... and we're expected to be up to speed in four weeks" (resident chair). Consequently, the fast-paced capacity-building phase of the process not only risked information overload, but also did little to significantly reduce the group's wariness of the professionals and of the process. This trust was particularly tested with the independent facilitator, appointed from the North of England Civic Trust to help guide the group.

Issues with the 'facilitator'

The independent facilitator appointed to the group was a professional planner who had prior experience of working in the area and existing relationships with members of the FQNP. Despite these advantages, issues arose surrounding the role and responsibility of the facilitator in the process. From the outset, the facilitator took the decision to be *neutral* in guiding the group: "throughout the whole project ... I made sure that my opinion was completely impartial.... If I was asked for my opinion, I gave two opinions ... and allowed them to come to an informed conclusion" (independent facilitator). This neutrality was deemed unhelpful among the group and, indeed, was interpreted by some as obstructive: "If ... you don't know what you're doing, you want someone to tell you ... being told by a facilitator, 'Oh, I can't tell you that, I can't advise you', is then seen as you're trying to hide something" (resident chair).

The independent facilitator became increasingly uncomfortable with his role. While he strongly believed that the plan should come from the community (and thus not be professional-led), he nevertheless struggled with this neutral stance and felt it resulted in a weaker document:

> "[this] made me feel professionally castrated.... I felt that that was the wrong thing to be doing. There were policies [and] clauses in there that I don't agree with ... the decisions that the group came to on some things were bland ... they would have been far stronger decisions had there been ... *stronger guidance from professional planners.* (Independent facilitator, emphasis added)

The facilitator gave an example of one of the very large key development sites that was the impetus for the plan in the first place. He explained that the site needed design guidance but that the group decided to take a "laissez-faire approach". Instead of delivering the clarity of guidance that NTC expected, they left it open for developers to come forward with a proposal. The facilitator expressed his exasperation at this: "That's reactive planning; that's not forward planning" (independent facilitator).

In summing up what he had learnt from this experience, he maintained that "neighbourhood plans should be community-led", but he simultaneously argued that "they've *got* to be informed by professional planners" (independent facilitator, emphasis added). The absence of strong decision-making and robust guidance led to a comparatively weak plan. This is a concern because it has significant implications for the plan's operationalisation within the legal apparatus of the planning system, as discussed in the following.

Product: quality of the plan

The preceding issues have raised some serious questions about the quality of the final document and whether it is fit for purpose. As outlined at the beginning of this chapter, the FQNP was adopted as an SPD not a fully ratified neighbourhood plan. The reason for this was that the guidance emerged at a relatively late stage of plan preparation. The group were fatigued and therefore decided to pursue a less onerous route to providing their plan with some weight in planning decision-making. Cowie and Davoudi (2015) state that there were also concerns within the FQNP group over the lack of clarity (at the time) about who would be eligible to vote in a referendum.[1]

The planning officer described several characteristics of the final product (its length, the conversational tone in which it is written and the difficulty in identifying the key points) as prohibitive of its value as a planning tool: "I think it's definitely much longer than it needs to be, it's ... very sprawling ... very chatty" (planning officer, NTC). Directly linked to this was the concern shared by the planning officer and the independent facilitator that the document may not be defensible at appeal. The planning officer spent a lot of time balancing the need to edit the document to make it more robust, while appreciating that it was the community's document: "this has to be a sensible document ... justifiable, because I don't want my colleague to write a decision based on it and then as soon as someone appeals it, it's torn apart" (planning officer, NTC). The independent facilitator elaborated on this issue: "some of the neighbourhood plans are not robust enough in their wording ... there were many things in the plan which I don't think are clear enough ... a good barrister would destroy them" (independent facilitator).

This raises some important questions about the nature of neighbourhood planning and whether it is, indeed, fair and realistic to expect communities to write professional planning documents that are resilient to challenge and can withstand legal scrutiny. Nevertheless, despite the concerns about the quality of the final plan, the interviewees did all share some positive perspectives of the overall neighbourhood planning experience.

Positive aspects of local governance structures: development of networks

Interview data revealed an improved level of understanding of the multiple and disparate interests in the area. This knowledge exchange paved the way for better relationships within the group and created more outwardly oriented networks. The process undoubtedly developed a trust and rapport that had previously not existed. As the independent facilitator explained: "There was a lot more trust between many sectors of the group by the end of the project than there was at the beginning" (independent facilitator). Another major visible benefit was the improvement in the relationship between the wider community and the planning officers: "if I go out now to fish quay … there's a little bit of trust there, maybe that wasn't there before" (planning officer, NTC). This closer relationship had other benefits, such as a better understanding of the planning system, which the planning officer deemed would prove useful in the longer term. This was supplemented by a strengthened community capacity and skill set. As the resident chair stated: "I've learnt an awful lot in going through it". This evidence of learning within the community, together with the community mobilisation and outward-oriented networks that were formed during the process, presents some highly positive aspects of neighbourhood planning as a form of localised governance. Despite the ephemeral nature of the group (temporarily set up specifically to prepare a neighbourhood plan), the knowledge and skills gained by individuals will be lasting and can be applied to future participation in local plan-making. These positive side effects of the process, however, could arguably have been achieved through other means, for example, as part of more structured community work associated with NTC's local plan preparation. Indeed, what the fish quay case study has demonstrated is that the expedience of the *process* appears to have proven more useful and beneficial to all actors than the *product* (plan) itself.

Case study 2: Upper Eden Neighbourhood Plan

The Upper Eden Neighbourhood Development Plan (UENDP) was made by Eden District Council (EDC) on 11 April 2013. 'Upper Eden' is an administrative construct comprising 17 neighbouring parishes that came together in 2005 to develop a community/parish plan. Upper Eden is not a tightly bounded neighbourhood, but more an archipelago of dispersed rural settlements (circa 5,000 people) with an extremely sparsely populated rural district. As the first example of an adopted neighbourhood plan, the UENDP case study epitomises the importance of a professional planner as a 'facilitator' to codify the community's aspirations into 'planning speak' and to develop policies that are robust enough to withstand legal challenge.

Governance arrangements

Similar to North Tyneside, there had been a long history of partnership working in the small neighbouring rural parishes of Upper Eden prior to the preparation of the UENDP. The impetus for the UENDP (UECP, 2013) began under the parish/community planning regime of the Labour government. When the Planning and Compulsory Purchase Act 2004 stated that parish plans could be a material consideration in the planning process, this spurred the 17 rural parishes within Upper Eden to join together in 2005 to create the Upper Eden Community Plan (UECP) group. The central issue that drove the formation of the UECP was the lack of affordable housing for existing local residents. The community of Upper Eden had been pressing EDC to facilitate more specialist affordable housing in the Upper Eden valley (specifically, self-build and barn conversions on existing family farms) but their efforts to develop an area action plan to address their aspirations for housing policy had been continually frustrated. Many local residents resented the local authority's myopic focus on developing housing that was in close proximity to the main urban settlement of Penrith. The main reason articulated by the council for not pursuing a more dispersed pattern of development was the lack of sustainable transport within the outlying parishes of the district. This stance was deeply frustrating for Upper Eden residents, with many local residents feeling that planning policy had effectively left them in a "sustainability trap" (project officer, UECP).

In 2008, a community plan (UECP) was published, which represented the aspirations of the Upper Eden residents. The plan had a substantial list of action points (over 80), with not all the points directly relating to planning issues. The most significant planning element of the UECP was the proposal to build an average of 29 new homes per annum over the next decade in order to increase the number of residential households in Upper Eden by 10%. It was felt that this scale of development would go some way to ameliorate the lack of affordable housing in the area. Upper Eden communities, however, continued to lobby for a more formal planning outlet to strengthen their affordable housing aspirations. In 2010, the election of the Coalition government offered the community renewed hope via its localism initiative and the election of a new Conservative MP (Rory Stewart), who had a particular inclination to develop and drive the government's Big Society agenda.

Planning stages

Localism Act

Indeed, the MP for Upper Eden immediately approached both the UECP group and local politicians to enquire whether they had projects that they could develop through the government's Big Society agenda. His support for the neighbourhood plan was considered a crucial element in the successful progression of the plan; as the project officer responsible for developing the UENDP stated: "Rory Stewart got us to the table". Soon after the election, Upper Eden was visited by the government's Big Society czar (Nat Wei), which began a continual process of engagement between senior figures in the new government and Upper Eden.

Funding and resistance to neighbourhood planning

Despite the high-level political support, EDC officers had serious reservations about the implications of being a pathfinder authority trialling neighbourhood planning and initially maintained a thoroughly risk-averse approach to neighbourhood planning. Specifically, the EDC officers felt that the £20,000 of funding on offer was insufficient, particularly if there were a series of appeals related to the neighbourhood plan – an issue that was viewed as a live possibility due to a lack of clear guidance about the evolution of neighbourhood planning policy.

EDC took the proposals to develop a neighbourhood plan in Upper Eden to its cabinet but it was decided that the policy would be a financial risk and that the council would not support it. The policy officer describes this outcome as "a headache for the civil servants at DCLG" as they were eager for the pilot in Upper Eden to proceed. Subsequently, the civil servants arranged to fund the process from a community development (Big Society Vanguard) budget rather than through mainstream neighbourhood planning budgets in order to circumvent the unsupportive local authority by directing the funding straight to the community.

Guidance, support and links to central government

As reported in the North Tyneside case study, there was little effective policy guidance for the neighbourhood planning pathfinders. The policy area was rapidly evolving and the project officer describes a situation where:

> "There was no guidance and if you have ever read the Localism Act you will know it is completely impenetrable.... I was speaking to the guys at DCLG, they were helpful at saying that is what this is supposed to mean."

All the interviewees consulted in Eden gave the impression that at the micro-level, policy was being negotiated and clarified as it was being developed, with significant input from the Upper Eden pathfinder. The project officer drafting the plan stated: "DCLG were bouncing things off me and asking how things might work in practice. Everyone and their dog had a guide about how to do neighbourhood planning, they were rubbish because they either overcomplicated or oversimplified things" (policy officer, UECP).

Despite the absence of regulations, the project officer emphasised that "I have had massive help and support from the civil servants at DCLG". This 'hotline' to senior civil servants enjoyed by the UECP is atypical and was in complete contrast to the experience of the North Tyneside case study; it is perhaps attributable to Upper Eden possessing an influential MP from the party of government. The senior local politician from EDC adds weight to this view, stating: "this was done with the direct support of the MP and unusually we had a situation where members of the group ... developing this plan had direct access to officials and even ministers in Westminster".

There was a stark contrast in the early stage of plan development in Upper Eden between links with central government and links with EDC at the local level. While the relationship between the UECP group and the local authority improved markedly over time, at the outset of the process, there were clear tensions that were not helped by the delicate issue of managing expectations in the community.

Expectation management

EDC was acutely aware that localism had been launched by central government with emotive empowerment rhetoric that had significantly raised expectations. The senior politician stated at the outset that

"Eden [EDC] decided they would develop a neighbourhood planning protocol to manage the expectations of the communities and to set out in clear language 'what we can and can't do' in terms of neighbourhood planning", he stated:

> "I paraphrase it as, '*you can do what you want but not what you like*'; that encompasses the reconciling with national policy, local plans and SPDs. Sometimes, people want to get involved to stop development ... [neighbourhood planning] is to influence what happens not to stop it happening."

It took time for the expectations of the Upper Eden community to converge with the realities of developing a neighbourhood plan (which must be in conformity with existing planning policy). However, despite reservations about community expectations, both representatives from EDC were very clear that ownership of the plan must reside with the community: "it is extremely important the plans are owned by the communities they cover, it is not our plan, it is not the consultant's plan, it is their plan" (senior politician, EDC).

Process

Attendance and participation

Variants of community-led planning had been active in Upper Eden since the mid-2000s and much of the groundwork towards developing the UENDP had already been completed by the time the Localism Act proposed neighbourhood planning. Ultimately, the neighbourhood planning process in Upper Eden was driven by one particular individual who had been active in the area for a decade, initially as an employee of a local town council, then as a planning consultant (project officer) appointed to develop the neighbourhood plan by the UECP group. Throughout the interviews, the interviewer probed to explore if other individuals from the wider Upper Eden community had played significant roles in the neighbourhood plan development process. The project officer was evasive and stated: "The aims and objectives of the plan were set at the beginning; we had no reason to change them". It appears that the wider community (often rural farming families) played little part in the formal writing of the neighbourhood plan. The wider UECP group performed more of a ratifying role for the neighbourhood plan as it moved through the stages of drafting. The project officer confirmed this, stating: "We had a steering group that met to discuss the process as we went through, they relied on me to do most of the drafting". To be fair to the project officer, the bulk of the UENDP was a consolidation of previous iterations of the community-led planning process and much of the consultation work had already been completed when formulating the 2008 community plan. The project officer stated:

> "we knew what all the issues were ... we didn't need to go back through all the evidence gathering. We went straight to an issues and consultation paper ... basically a rough draft of the plan and a series of questions to focus the communities' responses and fine-tune your policy ideas."

Once at the formal draft stage, the UENDP went through a round of consultations that garnered 35 responses from a population of about 5,000. The project officer contrasted this response rate favourably to EDC's core strategy consultation, which he claimed received fewer responses from the whole of the district. After reflecting on the initial consultation responses, the project officer prepared a pre-submission draft, which received a further seven responses. A referendum was held on the UENDP on 7 March 2013, in which over 1,400 people voted (33.7% turnout); 90% of them (1,310) were in favour of the UENDP. As the UENDP was the first neighbourhood plan to go to referendum, it became a showpiece political event covered by national broadcasters. The senior politicians from EDC stated: "we had Rory Stewart MP, and two ministers of state [Nick Bowles and Don Foster] for the count in Brough Village Hall at 10.30 pm on a pouring Thursday night!".

Capacity building: lack of planning experience and skills

The practical approach to developing the neighbourhood plan in Upper Eden was in complete contrast to the process in North Tyneside, where the facilitator saw his role as restricted to *enabling* the local community to write the plan. In Upper Eden, the drafting of the neighbourhood plan was solely down to one planning professional (UECP project officer), who was entrusted to articulate the community's views into a robust planning document. The 'facilitator' in the Upper Eden example was an experienced planner who took an executive role in plan development. He describes his role in the following terms: "my role was to simply turn what they [the community] wanted into planning-speak".

The policy officer from EDC felt that, to some extent, the community in Upper Eden had taken a back seat in terms of the formal stages of preparing the neighbourhood plan because of their lack of planning knowledge and the time pressures involved in running rural farms and businesses, stating:

> "A lot of our interaction as a council seemed to be with him [project officer]. We should have had more interaction with the qualifying body and let them talk to him separately, to keep them in the loop on everything. I suspect it was because he was a professional and because he was local, there was a bit of a gap in knowledge."

The politician for EDC raised a wider concern about neighbourhood planning in isolated rural areas, stating that although there are people with skills and time on their hands, there is a problem that some "usual suspects" within communities get burnt out through constant engagement with community initiatives and "people don't do this kind of thing forever … to sustain community activities you need new blood for continuity and succession".

Role of the facilitator (project officer)

The approach to utilising a planning 'facilitator' in Upper Eden provides an interesting comparison between the two case studies. In North Tyneside, the facilitator took an extremely neutral and normative stance in terms of direct input into the plan, viewing his role purely as a facilitator and critical friend. In stark contrast, in Upper Eden, the planning consultant (appointed the project officer for the UECP group) was pivotally involved, taking an extremely 'hands-on' and pragmatic approach by personally writing the plan. Both interviewees from EDC were clear about the decisive role played by the UCEP project officer in developing the UENDP. The senior politician from EDC stated: "I would describe XXXX as the man with the mission" (name omitted). The policy officer from EDC concurred:

> "he was very central to the process. Talking to some of the people in the parish councils in the area, I don't get the feeling they had a grip on what was going on, they trusted him and relied on him to deliver. From our point of view as the council, he was very active and trusted to some extent."

Reflecting on his own role within the process, the UECP project officer felt that a planning practitioner working centrally in the neighbourhood planning process provided a crucial *knowledge brokerage* role between the community and the local authority:

> "You absolutely need someone with the planning knowledge. Communities are too easily bamboozled, ignored, obfuscated and generally put off ... if they approach the planning authority directly, they will be told about some new plan or some new consultation that will solve all their problems."

Product: quality of the plan

As the project officer (planning consultant) was centrally involved in the drafting of the UENDP, this meant less of a burden on EDC planning staff to support the drafting of the plan and greater confidence that the plan would be defensible at appeal. The senior politician from EDC stated: "The wording has to be sound and it has to be capable of consistent interpretation". Reflecting back on the whole process, the project officer felt in hindsight that the plan could have been more ambitious: "we have seven policies in the Upper Eden plan; I think only two policies have been used all the way through. I don't think we were bold enough". Like the FQNP, the final product of the UENDP process was therefore also a plan that may have failed to take some key decisions and provide sufficiently strong and meaningful planning guidance. Being pilots, insights can, however, be obtained from both case studies to inform future neighbourhood planning endeavours.

Conclusions: reflecting on the experiences of neighbourhood planning in North Shields and Upper Eden

As two of the earliest examples of neighbourhood planning in England, the FQNP and the UENDP processes provide useful insights into the intricacies of community mobilisation, self-regulation and the governance of neighbourhood planning. They pose a number of important questions: is neighbourhood planning truly an empowerment tool if the 'product' of the process is potentially not fit for purpose or fails to provide robust guidance? Or, is it more important that communities benefit and learn in some way from the *process*, for example, through enhanced knowledge about the planning system or better relationships with residents, local businesses and planners? Fundamentally, a key question to emerge from the two case studies is: to what extent do communities have the capacity to develop robust neighbourhood plans *without* the direct assistance of professional planners and what role professional planners should play in the neighbourhood plan development process?

From analysis of the two case studies, several points can be made to reflect on these questions. Both groups experienced similar problems in the early stages of the process. A lack of policy guidance was a key issue, although Upper Eden, via the project officer, benefitted from preferential engagement with central government (DCLG). Moreover, it took both groups significant time for their expectations to converge with the reality of what a neighbourhood plan could realistically achieve within the perceived constraints of general conformity. Significantly, there was existing active community mobilisation in both areas, which provided the foundations for the embryonic neighbourhood planning groups. In neither case, however, was the neighbourhood plan written through a process of true collaborative writing. In both examples, the drafting was completed by one individual. A key difference was that in Upper Eden, it was a professional planner (consultant) who prepared the plan.

In the FQNP, a series of capacity-building sessions were developed to try to 'upskill' the group; while welcomed, the skill set gained from this intensive, condensed training was still deemed by all to be insufficient to *produce* a meaningful plan robust enough to stand up to legal scrutiny. While Upper Eden contains significant community capital, the decision was still taken by the group to appoint the project officer (planning consultant) to independently prepare the plan. In contrast, the same role for the FQNP was filled by a professional planner who took a neutral approach, *facilitating* rather than contributing to writing the plan, which, in hindsight, he regretted. Throughout the process, both the 'facilitator' (FQNP) and the project officer (UENDP) turned away from the notion of 'community-led' planning and instead compromised by emphasising the importance of the community 'taking ownership' of the final plan. The project officer in Upper Eden effectively dominated the plan, viewing it as a personal commission.

From the preceding analysis, it can be concluded that while many areas engaged in neighbourhood planning will not hold the required skills to produce a robust and meaningful 'community-led' plan, such communities are undoubtedly disadvantaged if the lack of human capital is not compensated by direct and active civic institution/professional planning support *in addition to* an associated programme of capacity-building initiatives. Recently, limited central government support (via

Locality and Planning Aid) has been forthcoming for capacity building, but without sustained funding for *direct* professional involvement, the undeniable limits of neighbourhood planning, such as conformity with the local plan, the ultimate defensibility and operationalisation of the final plan, and the time invested by all involved, is unlikely to be worth the effort.

Note
1   Concerns were raised that local business-owners within the fish quay that lived outside the district would not be eligible to vote, whereas the majority of residents from the wider district who lived outside the fish quay boundary would be eligible to vote.

References
Cowie, P. and Davoudi, S. (2015) 'Is small really beautiful? The legitimacy of neighbourhood planning', in S. Davoudi and A. Madanipour (eds) *Reconsidering localism*, Abingdon: Routledge.

Holman, N. and Rydin, Y. (2013) 'What can social capital tell us about planning under localism', *Local Government Studies*, vol 39, no 1, pp 71–88.

UECP (Upper Eden Community Plan) (2013) *Upper Eden neighbourhood development plan*, Kirby Stephen: Upper Eden Community Plan.

SEVEN

Voices from the neighbourhood: stories from the participants in neighbourhood plans and the professionals working with them

Edited by Quintin Bradley and Sue Brownill

Introduction

In this chapter, we convey the everyday experiences of neighbourhood planning by bringing together the voices of a range of different actors involved in a variety of plans. We have presented these accounts as narratives without comment or interpretation as we believe they give a unique and powerful insight not only into the practical and emotional aspects of 'doing' neighbourhood planning, but also into the wider issues that this book is engaged with. Readers will be able to make connections between these accounts and the themes raised so far. The voices also give different perspectives reflecting the different interests engaged in neighbourhood development plans (NDPs): neighbourhood forum and parish/town council members; local authorities; developers; and consultants. They are, of course, not representative, but that was never the intention of this chapter. The accounts are drawn from a range of sources, including interviews and presentations to workshops. In some cases, the verbatim accounts have been slightly edited to clarify the meaning; however, we have remained as true to the original meaning as possible.

The neighbourhood

Voice 1

I'm the Chairman of the Neighbourhood Plan Steering Group in Linton, a small village of 270 houses north-east of Leeds. Like most communities, our neighbourhood plan was driven by fear of unwanted development. In 2012, we realised that there were quite a number of land sites that had been put forward for housing in our village. Nearly every resident within the village was going to be affected by one or more of these sites, and if all the sites were developed, it would double the size of the village, so there was great concern about this. We set out on the journey of producing our neighbourhood plan in May 2012 and, very naively, we thought it was going to be finished by December the same year. In 2015, we're nearly there. First, we needed to gather the information to prepare our plan. We organised a village survey and consultation meetings. We made a big mistake in the early part of the plan preparation by making it complicated. We set up the drafting committee, which carried out the research and organised all the consultation. However, as the village wanted to be involved in the whole process, we set up a steering group, of which every resident and key stakeholder could be a member. The drafting committee reported to the steering group, which effectively meant that the village needed to agree all the proposals that were put forward during the plan preparation. It was really cumbersome and time-consuming, but it did mean that we consulted with the village on every part of our plan. So, having gathered all the information, we started drafting the plan and we were able to obtain some help from Planning Aid England. At this time, we realised that there were a number of improvements that the villagers had identified that couldn't be handled through planning policy. These village improvements evolved into a list of 25 projects in our final plan, covering issues from highway safety through to just planting some bulbs to make the village look more attractive. These projects are something that the parish council can focus on during the coming years to develop the village and improve it, and if any Community Infrastructure Levy (CIL) becomes available from any future development, the parish council may decide to allocate some of this to the projects. Our plan was eventually ready for pre-submission consultation in June 2014, and we had a very good response from our residents and stakeholders. However, this was when the landowners and developers came out of the blocks, and if you look at any neighbourhood plan, the challenges are consistently coming from developers and landowners who feel that your plan is going to disadvantage them. The issues that we were challenged on were not just about what we had put into the plan, but also about how we put the plan together. The challenges included not being transparent, having a predetermined policy, not consulting sufficiently and even misappropriating government funding. So, I think it is very important that neighbourhood planning groups make sure that they keep a log right the way through their plan preparation process because you are in danger of forgetting what has happened in the early months of consultation and preparation.

After pre-submission consultation, we met with Leeds Planning Authority and worked very closely with them in editing the policies. Our final draft plan was submitted to Leeds City Council (LCC) in May 2015, who organised the statutory four weeks' consultation. They received positive responses from statutory consultees and a very large tome from some of the landowners, again challenging a number of issues about our plan preparation. LCC sent our plan for independent examination in August 2015. The general comments from the examiner were very positive on the whole. He commended the consultation and basic condition statements and the collaborative approach with LCC, as well as our exemplary approach to presenting policies. He also commended our transparent approach, which was one of the key challenges from two of the landowners. However, the examiner did delete five out of our original 14 policies; we were really quite disturbed when we heard this because we wondered whether we would be able to recommend the plan with these deletions to the village. However, having taken a step back and looked at what we were trying to achieve with our plan, we believed that we could still achieve our key objectives with the revised policies. We were absolutely delighted that our community involvement policy passed examination because it defines that any developer who submits an application for more than one house in Linton has to show how they have consulted with the village and the results of that consultation, so that is an amazing win for us. In Linton, over the last 10 years, a high proportion of five- or six-bedroom houses have been built, so we now have a policy which states that any development over one house has to include houses with less than four bedrooms to suit the needs of the ageing population in Linton, who may wish to downsize in the future. The village has taken on board all the deletions and changes to our final draft plan and LCC organised the referendum on 17 December. So, what are the main benefits for us? Obviously, it becomes part of Leeds' local plan. It's a statutory document that has more teeth and the council has to consider it when it is deciding future planning applications. Producing the plan has been a major benefit for our village not just because of the planning policies, but also in identifying various projects, which gives the community a focus for improving our village in the future. When there is any development in our village, we will also benefit from an increased percentage of CIL. However, above all, we now have a much stronger community spirit and this has been a direct result of preparing our plan.

(Note: Linton's referendum was held on 17 December 2015 and won a 96% 'yes' vote on a turnout of 49%. It was immediately challenged in an application for judicial review by a developer. The legal challenge was unsuccessful but the plan was put on hold while the developer appealed. The appeal was refused in October 2016.)

Voice 2

Really, the district council did no more than the statutory minimum on consultation. They didn't get out and about and talk to people, as a result of which, we began to feel that their plan was being imposed upon us. We started our plan in direct confrontation with them but they've since turned completely – the number of neighbourhood plans shows that they are very on board with neighbourhood planning. Our neighbourhood plan was made in 2013, but how to amend it is going to be an issue. It lasts until 2027 but the district's local plan, which is now being revised, will then become the latest plan and will take precedence. When we started our plan, there were no guidelines and all the way through the process the guidelines were still being written. It's never happened before that a higher plan is being prepared over a neighbourhood plan. We're a trailblazer again! There is no guidance on this. It looks like the smallest amendment needs to go back to a referendum, and you would think that there would be something in between. This is one of my concerns: that planning void, that time lapse, when their plan takes precedence over ours.

The plan is being compromised all the time by planning decisions. There are all sorts of examples where developers have tried and not got away with it and examples where they're nibbling at the edges of it. The pace of change is an issue given that planning permission has been given for most sites in the plan when, in fact, we wanted that stage to be in 10 years' time. However, they wanted to get under the wire before CIL (Community Infrastructure Levy) was introduced. Obviously, the possibility of CIL was one of the things that we sold the plan to the community on. The district council then dragged their feet and developers are canny, so most applications will have been decided before CIL comes in. CIL was meant to bring us £3 million – so we have had to get much more involved in Section 106 negotiations. Permitted development rights was the first one to sting us in the tail because within the first three to four months of the plan passing the referendum, we had a permitted development that added up to 10% of our 15-year site allocations; all of a sudden we got 72 more houses.

In the eyes of the community, these changes undermine the plan. At our level, we've become familiar with the process and if we can see that there is legality in it, then we have to accept it. However, from the community's point of view, it is 'I voted for the plan, why is this happening, why is that happening?' The community are still behind the plan where it fits with what they want. The plan was a model of how to do it – but not everyone was happy with it. There are still a few people denigrating the plan, saying that we didn't go through the right process. The arguments we have had since the plan was made proved to the community that the town council is defending the plan, so it has given people more confidence that there is something of value there.

There is a massive expectation on the town council to do a lot here because of the plan. I see that as a positive thing. Before the plan, the town council drifted along: people didn't engage with it, they didn't take notice of what was going on. Suddenly, we have a much higher profile. In May this year, we had a reasonable bunch of candidates put themselves up for council, so we had a decent election and fresh blood. We have the community holding the councillors more to account, which is how democracy should work. There are greater expectations, as, indeed, we have from the county, with devolution and localism and everything. However, I see all of those things as positive.

The relationship between us and the district council has improved. Perhaps because of the plan, there is more thinking done about what the town needs to know. If we retain that relationship, then the planning officers will generally come up with the right answer as they have to uphold the plan. That brings me on to what needs to be changed with neighbourhood planning moving forward. There needs to be a community right of appeal. At the moment, if a planning application is overturned, a developer can appeal against that decision, and if it is passed, then the community can't appeal against it. Particularly where there is an NDP, there should be a mechanism to allow that to happen.

From my point of view, we would do a neighbourhood plan again for two reasons. It's partly the way it has engaged the community and brought them together, and this has continued since the plan was finished. The other thing is that when you look at other places, we are much better off with a plan than without it – they have had a lot of development dumped on them. It gave us more control over development than we had in the past. Whether it is as much as we'd hoped for? Umm. In some ways, 'yes' because with any large development, the pre-application has to come to us first, and because we have an NDP, then what we have to say does carry a lot of weight. So, 'yes', definitely, it's put us on the map. If we want to speak to the

Photo 7.1: Doing neighbourhood planning: voices from a working group

Source: Hyde Park neighbourhood forum, Leeds: photograph Magdalena Szymanska

minister now, we'll get to speak to him, we won't get fobbed off. Our path to the decision-makers has been made a lot easier.

The planning authority

Voice 1

Previously, I had worked for Planning Aid Yorkshire, so I had an appreciation of what you can achieve when you get communities involved. I've also worked with all the major house-builders and know that when you offer communities some gain, it is much easier to plan and everyone wins. To my mind, neighbourhood planning marries these things together and helps give some responsibility back to communities – if only you can get it right and make it work. As a council, a lot of what we do is advice and assistance. What we try and do is not to get too involved, not too directive. One of the things we have to do is to guide the neighbourhood planning process without taking control. We have a community-led planning team supported by a rural community council doing parish plans. Where these are in place, the NDP just flows, and it provides a really solid basis for the planning officers to help. The policies are what drive change, and so it is important that communities are really clear about what it is that they are trying to achieve and what they want.

I always say to people thinking about doing a neighbourhood plan that the absolute bottom line is that it's a means of negotiating. It changes the dynamics from council and landowner, to council and town or parish council or neighbourhood forum and landowner. It goes from bipartite to tripartite. The decision is always with the council but the neighbourhood suddenly has much more say in what happens. Also, trust is absolutely essential. More often than not, they start the process because they do not trust the local planning authority. They feel that they are having development dumped on them, so turning that round is such a challenge. It is important to give flexibility to communities but the funding is fundamentally the problem. The grant drives behaviour, and that is to employ consultants, and I have not yet seen a consultant that doesn't try to work to a template. However, every community is different and there is no blueprint. Surprisingly, their pitches are all about the grant level, so they are targeting their offer on what they know the grant is and they can't afford to do that much in that budget. We are finding communities grabbing the grant and employing consultants as they think that is the easiest way of doing it, and then finding that key issues are left out. We do advise, but we know that the steering groups become determined that what they know is best. They are the experts, they are the locals and 'thank you very much, but we are going to go ahead and do it anyway'. We do recognise that local expertise is an asset to the local plan process if it can be evidenced and expressed clearly. We try to be a critical friend, stay at arm's length and try and review documents at the end of the process. When we get policies, we ask them where they got the policies from. Often, the response is 'the consultants wrote it'. They get policies from other plans that they know got through the examination process. We then say that as professional planners, we disagree that one size fits all. What may be relevant elsewhere may not reflect local needs or objectives. We are starting now to think about the quality of the policies. It's just starting to show in plans that are coming through. One plan allocated sites and wrote policies. The first application comes in broadly consistent with the plan but the planning officer says 'How do I make sense of this; how do I turn this policy into a decision against this application?' We are finding that we have to return written policies and put a lot more time and investment into getting these right at an earlier stage.

Keeping at arm's length is all very well but we are discovering that early engagement and collaboration is essential if we are not going to end up in dispute. If a community thinks that it has a policy that delivers a cricket pitch as part of a development but when the application comes in, they realise that the policy said only a provision, which means that all that has to be done is that a piece of land is set aside, both we and they lose faith in the process. So, the community said 'you passed these policies, you knew what we were trying to achieve'. The council can put itself in a position of disrepute and we realise now that we have been allowing, not guiding. So, this whole arm's-length approach is leading to some procedural problems. An internal review has identified that we need to be more hands-on, and we will have to change. We need to see neighbourhood planning as a single cross-cutting corporate project engaging all the professionals that can support it. It is projects that tend to drive our neighbourhood plans, with policies delivering these. The stronger plans are project-driven and help focus people's minds on how development can deliver these. We need to provide much more project planning up front so that these groups know what they want to achieve, where they may need specialist input and what the council can and can't do. We need to lead the process, not follow it, and to help groups focus the funding on where it is most needed. We can still do this without taking control but if neighbourhood plans are to have any bite, they have to be deliverable, and if they are to be deliverable, then we are going to have to invest more without compromising that trust.

Voice 2

We think that neighbourhood planning is a win–win situation for local communities and for the council – if it's done the right way. You could argue that one of the ways to try and make sure that happens is that you are part of it and you're involved properly, rather than sort of taking a little bit of interest and not getting overly involved, which is what some local authorities are doing. I really strongly believe that the neighbourhood planning process is all about building up relationships, building up trust, getting to know people. That's been my particular approach: it's not only thinking about the process, and, shall we say, the normal way of doing business; it's actually, quite frankly, about getting your hands dirty. The right support, at the right time, is the really critical thing.

It is about making neighbourhood planning easy and welcoming at the point of contact. I think that is so important because a lot of people can get turned off by the normal language; let's face it, actually, planning isn't rocket science. I mean it really isn't, you know. You speak to people and ask them what they want, and you don't need to ask them twice, they know exactly what they want. If you start to sort of scratch the surface sometimes and you say, 'Well, actually, this could be possible or that could be possible as well', quite often, you find people will say, 'Oh, I didn't realise that. Well in that case ...'. I think my experience is that people don't always know what's possible, and one of the key things for professionals to do is to actually say what's possible. I think that a real opportunity with neighbourhood planning is to actually do that, and you can only really do that if you've built up that relationship and trust. You can't just come in and go out again; it just won't work.

I think one of the things that applies to both parished and non-parished areas, whether they are affluent communities or deprived communities, is that the more they've got involved in the process and the more confidence and understanding and capacity they've built up over time, the more they want to do other things. That's one thing I've definitely observed over the past year or 18 months, and I think that's really healthy because, okay, the examiner is only going to be concerned with the basic conditions, but there's nothing to stop other things going into a neighbourhood plan. If you truly want to make an area more sustainable, then you can't only focus on planning issues, it's as simple as that. Planning shouldn't just be about land and buildings; planning should be about people as well. I think, in my opinion, neighbourhood planning is taking planning back to what it should be like, quite honestly.

In terms of planning support, a decision was made in Leeds that we don't want a two-tier planning system, where all the parishes have got their neighbourhood plans and everybody else has something else, whatever that may be. So, basically, the message to me was, you know, 'I'd like you to, without going overboard or going over the top, do something about it', basically. The way we've done it is that we've split communities into three different areas. One is those communities that are pretty highly engaged and they've got a high capacity to deliver a neighbourhood plan, and they are, generally speaking, the parish councils. So, to those areas, the level of help from the team is limited to the duty to support, but that's still providing a pretty high level of planning support. The next category are those areas that are not parish councils, but they are pretty well organised and they've got some sort of continuity, either through an existing community group that's perhaps sponsoring the neighbourhood plan or because of the particular skills that they have in that group. So, there, it's a bit of see what the particular needs are, you know, but not high priority. Then the third category is those areas where either it's a pilot area or it's a community that's deprived and we have been proactive in promoting neighbourhood planning, and they have a low capacity. In many cases, they don't have existing community groups; in some cases, there are trust issues with the council and with officers and members. In those areas, we're providing as much support as we realistically can with the resources that we've got, simple things like at the very least just letting those communities know that this is a new right that's open to them, going to local meetings and doing presentations, in a very different way to a presentation I would do to the council. That's been really successful. We've got a neighbourhood planning steering group and the purpose of that is to make sure, as far as we possibly can, that neighbourhood planning here is joined-up and complementary with the vision for Leeds. Within the council, the neighbourhood planning responsibilities are clearly not just about the planning service because there's no way that the council is going to achieve its aspirations without proper community engagement and empowerment. Also, there's no way that Leeds is going to be one of the best councils in the country if its staff haven't got the right skills to work with the people of the city. I think that's been a value of the steering group: doing things in a different way, in some cases, turning things on its head. Too often, you hear about people talking about the capacity of local communities to prepare a neighbourhood plan but, in actual fact, it's just as much about the capacity of council officers to support and guide the neighbourhood planning process. The real challenge is actually making it work.

The consultant

We started the business four years ago. We came out of a larger company anticipating that there would be opportunities through the Localism Act. We correctly surmised that our existing business and its ilk would not be interested in servicing that market because of fee rates and the fact that they work for developers – there would likely be conflicts of interest. We've just started supporting our 70th neighbourhood plan. It seems that the use of consultants is not widespread, but it's usually easy to spot those plans that haven't used them. Most of our clients have only come across consultants working for developers and that's not often been a good experience. So, there is a lot of baggage we have to overcome – not helped by the government's advice that communities can do it for themselves with online toolkits and enthusiasm. However, for most communities, the realities are somewhat different – as they soon discover after they've completed their initial surveys and need to undertake technical work and make policy choices.

Almost all of our projects are challenging: no up-to-date local plan; no five-year housing land supply; developers all over the place; and under-resourced planning authorities and parish councils that are not used to dealing with such major, high-profile projects. Our clients often need nurturing and their confidence building because it is just too complicated, too technical. They struggle with how the process works, what the purpose of policy is and how to scope their plans. There is also usually a significant information and experience gap between them and us. We do very little marketing; it is usually all word-of-mouth recommendations.

For example, we rarely have a brief from the client at the outset. So we say, 'this is what we did down the road, which is like your project, and we know it works because it passed its examination'; 25 plans in total now. We charge everyone the same day rate and don't negotiate. All our clients have used the Locality grant fund and topped it up from their own budgets. In our experience, a project will rarely need more than 25–30 days of our time and therefore usually costs about £12,000 in fees. If projects are spending more, then they are probably asking for work that is unnecessary. Clients should not over-rely on consultants and spend more. We use a standard process to avoid reinventing wheels and to keep costs down. Our clients welcome this as most want us to write their policies and produce their documents. They're not bothered if the village down the road has an identical policy; they want to know that it's fit for their purpose and will be used by the local planning authority. It also means we keep things simple and short.

We've had to change our approach over the last four years to meet client needs. We started with the conventional, linear process but soon discovered that it didn't work well. We realised that community expectations of their plans were being raised to undeliverable heights and the practical constraints of policy conformity and just the lie of the land were not being properly analysed. We now get into these issues with the client team straightaway, before they engage their communities in expressing opinions and preferences. We help them identify the 'policy space' that the plan may choose to occupy and advise them on how to go about examining that space in detail and to identify different ways in which it could be occupied. Crucially, there is a strong spatial planning dimension to this as we sketch out with them the 'jigsaw puzzle' that is their settlement and how assembling the puzzle in different ways leads to different outcomes – or town and country planning as it used to be known!

This work sets the action plan and timetable for the rest of the project, and it shapes their community engagement strategies so they focus on the things that the plan can manage and test the water on local preferences. It also helps focus them on examining the most helpful evidence and ignoring noisy data that are irrelevant for their purpose. It's amazing how much time is wasted by teams with scarce volunteer resources simply because they don't know how to do this. We know that most neighbourhood planning teams are not encouraged to think like that and, in my view, that is why most struggle. The toolkits take them in a different direction, treating projects just like local plans or community-led plans.

Neighbourhood plan policies should be designed to achieve a specific purpose by either lowering or increasing planning risk. Communities that need the planning system to fix local problems should therefore look to a neighbourhood plan. If a community is not looking to do a neighbourhood plan, it is almost always because a neighbourhood plan can't do anything for them. It's still not commonly known that a neighbourhood plan can only be useful if a planning application is required or being decided on. That's been tough because new permitted development rights and changes to how energy efficiency is managed, for example, have been taken out of the scope of neighbourhood plans, when many communities were keen to have something to say about them.

Even if sceptical at first, by the end of the project, our clients are always appreciative of our support. They always make all the policy choices but we go away and do all the difficult technical stuff because we know how to do it. Our job is to make their lives easier, and there's simply no substitute for professional support. I could put any number of our clients in front of you and they would say how crucial our help has been in getting them through this process. However, you know what we are like as planners: we don't assert ourselves and the value that we add.

The developer

I think there has been a misconception from the community groups about the role of the private sector in neighbourhood planning and I think this is multifaceted. One is that we are simply there for profit and that is our sole reason for existing, and we hold our hands up and say: 'Of course we are here to make a profit – we are a business – but that is not the only reason that we are here'. There is a misconception that we don't support neighbourhood planning, and we do support it, if it is done in the right way. I think it is a proper part of planning to get people involved in local issues, but it is about making local decisions, not about trying to find ways to avoid making big decisions, and I think that in some communities, this is how neighbourhood planning is being taking forward. Certainly, with some of the communities we've worked with, or tried to work with, that has been the case; they have been very anti-development.

There are several ways in which we get involved. We do try and get involved right at the start of the process in those areas where we have an interest or a land-holding. Very rarely are we taken up on that offer. We always say we are not there to promote our site; we want to be part of the process of getting a good neighbourhood plan in place. If our site doesn't get included through the process, then we will of course challenge that through the examination, but that is not the sole purpose of our involvement. If we are not involved in the early stages, then it becomes a little bit more confrontational. We respond to every consultation where we have an interest and quite often where we don't. Then, obviously, we engage in the examination process, and in a number of cases, we've unfortunately had to go down the legal route to ensure that neighbourhood plans are lawful.

We comment on many aspects within a neighbourhood plan but we are particularly concerned when a plan is seeking to stop growth or severely limit it to a handful of homes per year (say 10 to 20), which may not be what that community actually needs. A lot of communities know their problems and they'll admit them but the solution is harder to swallow. What a community should do is to identify the issues it's got and the facilities it needs, ascertain what level of growth is needed to deliver those facilities and address the problems, and then talk to developers and local landowners about how to deliver what they need. If they did it that way round, they would probably find that developers would be willing to fund significant improvements in the local area to help that community achieve its aims. A lot of the communities we speak to have an ageing population, they've lost the GP or the shop, and then when the answer is 'Well, what you need to support those is more development', the answer is 'No; that's not what we want'. It's local politics taking over. Everybody recognises there's a housing shortage but when it comes to granting permissions, they just want to say 'no'.

The system is working properly when the local plan is in place and a decision has been made through the local plan about where the growth is going to go. Then, the communities take that and work out if they accept it or if they want more growth to help them deliver their aspirations. We are completely happy with that. If our site gets picked, great; if our site doesn't get picked, we'll take it on the chin because it's gone through the proper process. We always thought that this was how the government's intention should have manifested itself through the guidance but, obviously, things have not quite developed in that way, although the government is still committed to progressing neighbourhood planning. Communities, in areas where there is no up-to-date local plan, have started to get wise to that and start bringing forward neighbourhood plans in order to take a lead and try to make decisions that should properly be made through the local plan. There are issues about how the guidance is drafted and a lot of people in the development industry thought that the legal system would solve these through the courts, but I don't think the decisions that have come out to date have done so. It's come down to the phrasing of the legislation, the way the guidance is written – both the legislation and guidance haven't been formulated in as robust a manner as they should have been. Case law isn't resolving these issues, so we need to see changes in the law, regulations and guidance to make it clear that local plans should come first and the neighbourhood plan should sit underneath that. I don't think you can do it the other way round because it causes too many problems, for the development industry, for communities, and for the local planning authority.

We hold our hands up to the fact that we are prepared to challenge neighbourhood plans but we've always said that we are like that because of how things are. We don't necessarily want to be that way; if we can get involved in a community, we will do, but sometimes if we are not let through the door, then we automatically become perceived as the bad guys. Where we can get involved, communities have overcome their misconceptions of developers. We've got to stop seeing each other as on different sides and we should work together as a partnership to deliver better neighbourhood plans that help achieve what the community wants while contributing to solving the country's housing crisis.

EIGHT

Participation and conflict in the formation of neighbourhood areas and forums in 'super-diverse' cities

Claire Colomb

Introduction

Political philosophies and practices of 'localism' can lead to both progressive and regressive outcomes (Davoudi and Madanipour, 2013; Madanipour and Davoudi, 2015). This chapter discusses whether neighbourhood planning has the potential to bring about more inclusive forms of public participation in, and engagement with, planning (and thus potentially more progressive and socially equitable forms of urban development), or, on the contrary, to stir up social conflict. The social and spatial imaginary that underpins parish and neighbourhood planning entails the idea of a relatively homogeneous, stable, identifiable and self-conscious 'local community' that possesses a sense of neighbourhood belonging and attachment and a set of common interests in relation to a defined place. It requires the capacity for local actors to mobilise collectively, to overcome individual and group differences, and to articulate a consensual vision for the future of that place. The innovation of neighbourhood planning is thus to 'vest plan-making in a notionally autonomous locally constituted body, and address residents as a collective identity rather than an amorphous and individually imagined public' (Bradley, 2015, p 103). Neighbourhood planning 'assumes a latent willingness and capacity within local communities to engage in plan-making and/or that these capacities can be developed' (Gunn et al, 2015, p 147). Yet, these assumptions cannot be taken for granted, in particular, in towns and cities with a very diverse population in ethnic, class and socio-economic terms.

The opportunity to engage in neighbourhood planning had been taken up by 1,500 groups across England between April 2012 and July 2015. Notwithstanding the Conservative ideological roots of neighbourhood planning in the English context, which have left many Left-leaning scholars sceptical and dismissive about its potential, neighbourhood planning is an innovation in public policy that potentially opens up new possibilities for public engagement in planning and thus warrants careful monitoring and evaluation. In theory, through the production of a neighbourhood plan, 'communities' are:

> able to choose where they want new homes, shops and offices to be built, have their say on what those new buildings should look like and what infrastructure should be provided, and grant planning permission for the new buildings they want to see go ahead. (DCLG, 2014a)

It certainly appears to go further than the existing mechanisms of public participation embedded in the English planning system (Baker et al, 2007; Brownill and Parker, 2010), which, like their counterparts in other countries (eg the USA), have been blamed by planning theorists for not achieving genuine participation, not satisfying participants that they are being heard, not improving policy decisions and not incorporating a broad spectrum of the public, or even discouraging or antagonising the members of the public who do try to work with them (Innes and Booher, 2004, p 419). Past research has shown that formal participatory channels often tend to be mobilised and dominated by articulate, educated and wealthy individuals and social groups, who may take a defensive attitude to urban development. It is therefore important to assess whether the composition of the groups involved in neighbourhood planning represents the socio-demographic diversity of their area and whether their outreach activities, their claims and their proposals cater for the interests of a broad section of the local population or, on the contrary, of narrow and powerful groups that dominate the process at the expense of others. The first studies of the implementation of neighbourhood planning in England showed that, so far, a majority of active groups have emerged in parished areas in rural, semi-rural or urban fringe locations, and that the uptake of neighbourhood planning has been (s)lower in urban areas (Parker, 2015). A number of commentators have hypothesised that this may be due to the challenges posed by the very diverse populations of large, heterogeneous urban areas (Bishop, 2010; Tribillon, 2014; Gunn et al, 2015). In London, the Planning and Housing Committee of the London Assembly, in its first review of the implementation of the Localism agenda in London, recognised that:

there is evidence to suggest that the legislation was designed for smaller, more homogenous areas than London. London's complex network of mixed communities with diverse interests seems to make even defining Neighbourhood Areas a difficult and time consuming process – and this is just the first stage of the process....

The underlying assumptions behind the push for Neighbourhood Planning [are] far more challenging in the capital than elsewhere. Indeed, we have heard views that the legislation is primarily aimed at rural communities and will not work in complex urban geographies. (London Assembly, 2014, pp 5, 9)

This chapter focuses on London – a highly unequal, fragmented and diverse city faced with rapid demographic growth and a high degree of population transience – and specifically discusses the first steps of the neighbourhood planning process: the formation of neighbourhood forums, their application for recognition by local planning authorities (in London, the borough councils) and, once formally designated, their initial outreach activities as part of the evidence-gathering process for the drafting of a neighbourhood plan. It addresses the following questions: who gets involved in neighbourhood planning processes, where and with what agenda (and who does not)? What specific tensions and politics emerge in the process of neighbourhood forum formation and application for recognition, and how do local authorities deal with these? Based on exploratory research in the London borough of Hackney, I argue that the assumption of a cohesive and articulate 'community' associated to a clearly recognised 'neighbourhood', capable of mobilising a broad cross-section of its population behind a common vision, is highly questionable. On the contrary, in some areas, there is mounting evidence that the opportunities offered by the neighbourhood planning process may stir up inter-group conflicts and, potentially, divide rather than unite the residents of an area.

The challenges of neighbourhood planning in London, the 'hyper-diverse' metropolis

London has been labelled a 'super-' or 'hyper-diverse' city (Vertovec, 2007; Raco et al, 2014), in particular, due to its considerable mix of nationalities and ethnic minority groups. According to the 2011 Census, 31% of the city's 8.17 million residents were born outside of the UK and 55% defined themselves as *other than White British*. Its population has been growing (projected to reach 8.8 million in 2021), and part of it is highly transient (eg students or international migrants at the bottom and top end of the occupational scale). London is also one of the most divided European cities in socio-economic terms. The richest 10% of London's residents have 273 times the income and assets of the poorest 10% (Dorling, 2011). In 2011, 28% of Londoners lived in households that were considered 'in poverty' after housing costs (Leeser, 2011). The acute shortage and unaffordability of housing in London compounds existing socio-economic inequalities, sharpening processes of socio-spatial segregation at various scales. Precisely because of its extreme diversity and stark socio-economic inequalities, London offers a salient lens through which to study the social tensions and conflicts potentially present in neighbourhood planning and the inclusionary or exclusionary nature of the process.

In London, the uptake of neighbourhood planning has been slow. As of September 2014, interest had been expressed by only 78 groups, of which 48 had been designated as neighbourhood forums (London Assembly, 2014). As of October 2015, only two neighbourhood plans had been approved following a referendum (Norland in Kensington and Chelsea; Fortune Green and West Hampstead in Camden). A map of neighbourhood planning initiatives in London in June 2015 (LCA, 2015) showed that there was a relative concentration of emerging neighbourhood forums in inner London boroughs, in particular, in West London, with comparatively little interest expressed in the outer boroughs. The boroughs of Westminster and Camden accounted for nearly half of the expressions of interest in establishing neighbourhood forums in London (London Assembly, 2014).

In relation to the question of who gets involved (and who does not) in neighbourhood planning, and in which areas, this cursory glance at the geography of emerging neighbourhood forums seems to indicate that they are being formed in relatively affluent neighbourhoods. In many cases, active members of existing local civic groups and established amenity societies – in particular, those focusing on the built environment and open space – are likely to form the backbone of emerging neighbourhood forums. These London findings match those observed in other parts of the country. The emerging literature on neighbourhood planning in England has focused on the *capacity* of communities to take the opportunities open to them (Holman and Rydin, 2013; Gunn et al, 2015; Sturzaker and Shaw, 2015) and on the *legitimacy* of the process (Davoudi and Cowie, 2013; Bradley, 2015; Cowie and Davoudi, 2015). Cowie and Davoudi (2015, p 185), in particular, discuss whether neighbourhood forums are democratically legitimate, and conclude that the self-selective nature of their formation tends to create 'an uneven geography of representation in favour of the more affluent, better-educated, and more vocal social groups who often have time, resources and know-how at their disposal'.

While there is, to date, no comprehensive study that would support this hypothesis with solid evidence for London as a whole, the pioneering work done by Tribillon (2014) lends support to it. Tribillon mapped the location and boundaries of emerging neighbourhood planning areas in London (as of September 2013) and compared their geographical coverage with three indicators of diversity: ethnic diversity (by ward), socio-economic diversity (measured through the proportion of different occupational groups by Lower Super Output Area), and which candidate received the most votes (by ward) in the 2010 mayoral election. His results showed, first, that neighbourhood areas tended to be located in the least ethnically diverse wards, but that a significant number of these neighbourhood areas had also been created within zones displaying a medium to high level of ethnic diversity. Second, most of the applications for designation as neighbourhood areas came from highly homogeneous areas in terms of occupational groups, where either 'managers' or 'elementary occupations' overwhelmingly dominated the others: 72% of the applications emanated from areas with a high to very high level of 'managers', while only 11% came from heterogeneous areas. Third, he showed a strong correlation between the political choices made by electors and the neighbourhood area boundaries, not in terms of the choice of party *per se*, but rather in terms of the level of political homogeneity within each of the neighbourhood areas.

Tribillon concludes that socio-economic homogeneity is the key factor in the formation of neighbourhood areas so far, a finding that matches the socio-spatial imaginary of neighbourhood planning evoked in the introduction. Tribillon consequently argues that in London, the neighbourhood planning process leads to a reinforcement of urban socio-economic divisions through a 'new parochialism', which reinforces 'the exclusionary trend already at work in socioeconomically homogeneous "neighbourhoods"' (Tribillon, 2014, p 1), as 'distinct homogeneous groups, mostly well-off, can now enact new administrative boundaries around their "neighbourhood", and gain more control over the planning of their environment' (Tribillon, 2014, p 8). He hypotheses that, by contrast, 'in the most socio-economically diverse neighbourhoods, the implementation of the Localism Act creates tensions and often results in failure' (Tribillon, 2014, p 8), a hypothesis to which we now turn.

The following section discusses the tensions and politics that have emerged in the process of neighbourhood forum formation and application for recognition in the inner London borough of Hackney. With 246,270 usual residents in 2011, it is a highly diverse borough in terms of nationalities, ethnic groups, educational and employment status, and income groups. It contains some of the poorest wards in England and retains some of the highest concentrations of social housing in London. Yet, several parts of the borough went through various waves of gentrification that have transformed the make-up of many neighbourhoods into relatively affluent areas. It is also home to a small number of highly concentrated communities defined along ethnic and/or religious lines, in particular, a large Haredi Jewish community around Stamford Hill in the northern part of the borough. As of September 2015, only one neighbourhood forum had been approved by Hackney Council and was actively preparing a neighbourhood plan for the Chatsworth Road area. Other applications for neighbourhood forum designation had been rejected, as discussed later.

The politics of neighbourhood area and forum designation in the London Borough of Hackney: 'what' and 'who' is the neighbourhood?

The London Assembly (2014, p 15) report on 'Localism in London' links the slow uptake of neighbourhood planning in London with 'the difficulties of satisfying the requirements for a commonly agreed geographical area when there are many distinctive communities living within the same part of the city':

> Self-defined communities often cross local authority boundaries, and may be fragmented or mobile. Residents may live and work in different parts of the city. In many parts of London – particularly central and inner London – transient and highly diverse communities live in and among areas of national and international significance. Communities in London exhibit wide variations in income levels, housing tenures, age ranges and occupations and there can be high population turnover. All of these factors can make it hard to develop a shared vision for a 'neighbourhood' in London. (London Assembly, 2014, pp 9–10)

The regulations on neighbourhood planning (HM Government, 2012) offer little guidance as to which criteria a local planning authority should use to designate a 'neighbourhood area' in response to an application by a relevant body – apart from the fact that such areas must not overlap with each other. The guidance provided by the Department for Communities and Local Government (DCLG) on what constitutes a neighbourhood area in non-parished contexts lists a number of considerations and criteria, which remain highly subjective and difficult to identify on the ground (DCLG, 2014b).

Neighbourhood forums have to 'establish a frontier and assemble a collective identity of place' (Bradley, 2015, p 102). As argued by Bradley (2015, p 103):

> the designation of a boundary has both practical and symbolic importance in not only setting the limit of a neighbourhood plan but in drawing a line between the planning authority and the neighbourhood, a political divide that constitutes collective identities and suggests the ever-present possibility of conflict.

A local planning authority can refuse to designate the area applied for by a constituted forum if it considers that the area is not appropriate, and must give reasons. In Hackney, as of September 2015, this had happened thrice. Two rounds of competing applications from two neighbourhood forums in the Stamford Hill area were rejected by the council in 2013 and 2014 (as detailed later). In 2015, the council rejected the application of the East Shoreditch Neighbourhood Forum, not because it took issue with its composition and representativeness (as was the case in Stamford Hill), but because it did not agree with the geographical boundaries of the area being proposed by the Forum, which it judged too large, not coherent and not appropriate for designation (for reasons of scale and character, explained in detail in LBH, 2015).

A neighbourhood forum has to include at least 21 people, have a written constitution and have an open membership, which should be drawn from different places in the neighbourhood area and from different sections of the community. Efforts must be made to include at least one person living in the area, one working in the area and one councillor (Locality, 2015). In terms of the requirements for the designation of a potential neighbourhood forum as a valid entity, the local authority must consider whether the prospective forum has taken reasonable steps to attempt to secure membership from different places and sections of the community in the area applied for, although legislation (HM Government, 2011, 2012) provides no further guidance on how local authorities should assess that. Given that only one neighbourhood forum can be designated for each neighbourhood area, this opens the ground for potentially competing applications covering a similar area, with different groups claiming to represent 'the neighbourhood'. This puts the local authority in a 'difficult and time consuming mediation role' (London Assembly, 2014, p 16). If a local planning authority receives more than one neighbourhood forum application for the same area or part thereof, official guidance states that it should encourage the applicants to consider working together as a single neighbourhood forum.

The case of the Stamford Hill area in the London borough of Hackney vividly illustrates the ambiguities, tensions and conflicts that can emerge in the process of defining *what* and *who* is the neighbourhood in a hyper-diverse city, and how neighbourhood planning can become contentious and divisive in an area marked by close proximity – but also strong micro socio-spatial segregation – between very different groups, and marred with a legacy of local conflict over planning issues. In 2013, two competing applications for neighbourhood area and neighbourhood forum status were submitted to the council for a large area of North Hackney. The first one, the Stamford Hill Neighbourhood Forum, was composed by a majority of Haredi Jewish residents, a Conservative ward councillor, alongside individuals from Polish, Muslim and African communities. The second, the North Hackney Neighbourhood Forum, was mainly composed of residents who were described by the media as a more secular group 'led by ... academics and trades unionists' (Booth, 2013; Geoghegan, 2013).

The tension between the two groups and their competing applications ran high and attracted attention from the local and national press. Both groups actively mobilised – via social media and other communication channels – to justify their representativeness and contest the legitimacy and intentions of the other group. The application of the Stamford Hill Neighbourhood Forum was, in particular, opposed by an existing residents' group founded in 1998 to campaign on planning and conservation issues, Hackney Planning Watch, some of whose members became actively involved in the rival North Hackney Neighbourhood Forum. The group argued that 'the proposed body has no history or tradition as a community organisation' and accused it of being 'an attempt by local Conservative and Liberal Democrat politicians to manipulate existing ethnic and religious divisions for their own short-term advantage and to the disadvantage of the wider community' (Barnett, 2013; Hackney Planning Watch, 2013a) in the context of a Labour-led borough council. These critiques were denied by the Stamford Hill Neighbourhood Forum, which stated, in turn, that it aimed to work for all communities in the area. Hackney Planning Watch nonetheless argued that the Forum sought to take political advantage of the needs of Stamford Hill's large Haredi Jewish population (one of the largest Haredi communities in the world), particularly the desire for more appropriate housing.[1]

The pressure for more and larger housing units (and associated social infrastructure like schools) has been a subject of contention in local planning and political debates for a number of years, as the Haredi Jewish population has larger than average family sizes and is expanding rapidly. Representatives of that community have campaigned for a relaxation of local planning regulations that would allow the construction of roof and house extensions on streets mainly composed of 19th-century low-rise family homes.[2] Members of Hackney Planning Watch feared that the Stamford Hill Neighbourhood Forum would support a plan advocating 'unsuitable extensions' to homes, while noting that the Haredi Jewish community does not form the majority of the population in Stamford Hill, is not a homogeneous group and that there are divisions within it over planning issues.[3] The rivalry between the two forums was reportedly described by a Jewish community leader who sought to broker cooperation between the two as a dispute between 'the yuppies and us' (Booth, 2013).

Hackney Planning Watch eventually launched a petition for the council *not* to recognise any neighbourhood forum in the Stamford Hill area, on the grounds of the tensions and rivalries triggered by the neighbourhood planning bidding process:

> We believe that devolving planning powers to either of these proposed forums would exacerbate pre-existing conflict over planning. Put simply, the issues of planning are too divisive in this area for a Neighbourhood Forum to work.... We are therefore petitioning the council and the relevant minister urging them not to grant a Neighbourhood Forum in this area. (Hackney Planning Watch, 2013b)

The group invoked the traditional function of local elected representatives as an appropriate mechanism to solve planning conflict and argued that 'functions like planning should remain with the council, not an unelected and unaccountable body like a Neighbourhood Forum' (Holden, quoted in Booth, 2013).

The council recognised that the two neighbourhood forum proposals raised major tensions in the local area and decided to reject both applications in July 2013, arguing that approving one or the other would 'not enhance community relations in this part of the borough' and that each application had not 'been universally supported by the wider community in North Hackney' (LBH, 2013b, 2013c). The council additionally rejected the very large areas covered by these applications (covering four and five wards), and instead designated a much smaller area deemed more appropriate and coherent for a neighbourhood area in Stamford Hill (LBH, 2013a).

The report prepared by the council's planning department to support the decision to reject both forums sets out the detailed rationale for that decision – one of the first cases in England and thus with little precedents to draw upon. The report acknowledged that both forum applications 'demonstrated how they have made best efforts to be both inclusive and representative of the Area' (LBH, 2013a).[4] However, it stressed that 'the scale of the opposition and support to both groups' submitted proposals would indicate that there are deep-seated divisions within the community in this part of Hackney on planning issues' (LBH, 2013a). The report concluded that 'it is very unlikely that the two applicants will resolve their differences and come forward with a joint forum application' (LBH, 2013a), and proposed, as a possible alternative, that the council could work together with the two groups to produce an area action plan (AAP) for Stamford Hill.

Two further applications for neighbourhood forum designation for the Central Stamford Hill Neighbourhood Area were presented to the council in 2014 and rejected, again, on the same grounds as the previous ones. The council decided instead to proceed with the preparation of an AAP for the area, a process that started in the spring of 2015. Contrary to the neighbourhood planning process, which is bottom-up, the preparation of the AAP is led by the council's planning department, in this instance, with the help of a planning consultancy commissioned to carry out preliminary studies and organise local consultation events (such as the planning workshop illustrated in Photo 8.1). The council's planning department has actively sought to build bridges between members of the previously rejected neighbourhood forums, and to engage with a broad range of stakeholders to overcome the conflict created by the failed neighbourhood planning process. A 'community panel' was set up to advise on the AAP process, composed of senior planning officers, councillors, local residents and community group representatives (representing, among others, the Jewish and Muslim communities living in the area). While it is too early to judge

Photo 8.1: Community planning workshop organised by Hackney Council for the preparation of the Stamford Hill Area Action Plan, October 2015

Source: Photograph: Claire Colomb

the outcomes of the AAP participation process in assuaging local social conflict over planning issues, the panel's meetings were attended by members of the formerly rival neighbourhood forums and have gradually re-established communication channels between previously opposed actors, although a degree of defiance still exist.[5]

This chapter has primarily focused on the very first step of the neighbourhood planning process. To further analyse whether neighbourhood planning can work towards more inclusionary and just forms of local planning, it is necessary to analyse in more depth what happens once a neighbourhood area and forum have been designated by the local planning authority. How do members of the forum reach out to a broader cross-section of the surrounding population in order to canvass views on key issues, needs and preferences as part of the evidence base to be prepared to underpin a draft neighbourhood plan? Forum members are confronted with the same challenges with so-called 'hard-to-reach' groups as professional planners have been in the context of formal public participation exercises.

How to include a wide range of individuals and groups is not specified in the legislation, and practices have varied. Across London, there is evidence of the deployment of a wide-ranging set of methods by neighbourhood forums to consult and engage with the residents and businesses of their area. Contrary to the hypothesis referred to in the first section of this chapter – that neighbourhood forums led by wealthy home-owning residents and traditional conservation and amenity societies are potentially driven by a rather protectionist agenda seeking to protect property values and resist new development – preliminary evidence from some London neighbourhood forums suggests otherwise (on the Highgate Neighbourhood Forum, where there was a genuine attempt at engaging a broad section of the local population beyond the social networks of the core active members of the neighbourhood forum, see Kesten et al, 2014).

In Hackney, the activities of the Chatsworth Road Neighbourhood Forum are illustrative of this. Chatsworth Road is a local high street in the Eastern part of the borough, located in a socially and ethnically mixed area that has undergone gentrification over the past decade, with the settlement of a 'new middle class' of young professionals with high cultural and social capital (Holland, 2012). The street has witnessed changes in its commercial fabric, in part, due to the renewal of its Sunday market in 2011 through the activities of the Chatsworth Road Traders and Residents Association. The association has been a key driver for the creation of a neighbourhood forum for the area, which was approved by Hackney Council in July 2013 and currently has more than 60 members. A cursory look at the composition and modes of action of this forum could lead us to hypothesise that it represents the mobilisation of a certain kind of 'pioneer gentrifiers', with high educational and cultural capital, in alliance with some long-standing residents and businesses, to protect a fragile social and functional mix threatened by rapid redevelopment and ongoing waves of gentrification. The rhetoric of the protection of social mix and diversity in the face of rapid change is very present in the communication materials prepared by the Forum, whose former chair, an urban designer, explained that 'gentrification has never been managed successfully before. We don't want people to feel victims of urban change, so we're taking a more proactive approach than elsewhere' (quoted in Holland, 2012). The Forum has sought to reach out to a broad public.

Various techniques were used, for example: a survey of 300 residents; a trader-focused survey filled in by 60% of local businesses; meetings with 14 representatives from religious groups, tenants organisations, elderly and youth clubs, local councillors, and the police; a project with pupils from a local school; and workshops attended by 200 people, making over 550 comments. This has culminated in the publication of a draft neighbourhood plan in the summer of 2015 (Chatsworth Road Neighbourhood Forum, 2015). There is no space here for a more thorough analysis of the role of (some) middle-class 'gentrifiers' with high degrees of cultural and social capital in processes of 'place making and place maintenance' (see Jackson and Benson, 2013), but it is worth reflecting on how, in an area like Chatsworth Road, the mobilisation of expertise, knowledge and social networks by these particular groups in the neighbourhood planning process may potentially benefit other groups in the context of an agenda that aims to be inclusive, at least rhetorically.

Conclusion: Neighbourhood planning in highly diverse urban areas – divisive or inclusionary?

The process of the formation of neighbourhood forums (Who gets involved, who does not?), and their designation by local authorities, is a crucial aspect of the neighbourhood planning process, which raises fundamental question of representation, voice, participation and exclusion. This chapter has focused on the first steps of the neighbourhood planning process and argued that in the context of a super-diverse and highly unequal city like London, neighbourhood planning can divide rather than unite individuals and social groups: it may be (mis)used in the complex politics of difference and fuel conflicts arising out of the juxtaposed micro-diversity of very heterogeneous areas. The local can become 'a contested site of the politics of identity' (Madanipour and Davoudi, 2015, p 277), as illustrated by the case of Stamford Hill. While the latter case may be seen as quite unique – due to the spatial concentration of a group defined primarily by its religious identity – there were other cases where a council was not satisfied that the proposed neighbourhood forum would be representative of the local community and thus rejected an application (eg Wapping in the London Borough of Tower Hamlets, or Hartlepool) (see Branson, 2014).

Dominant groups with common class, ethnic or religious characteristics can thus seek to use neighbourhood planning to further their interests in ways that are contested by others. There are clear difficulties in mobilising a wide cross-section of the local population in neighbourhood planning processes, in particular, disenfranchised or weakly organised groups (eg migrants, elderly, young people, etc). This leads some to a pessimistic conclusion: that many neighbourhood forums do not represent genuine diversity, but instead reinforce political and social inequalities and boundaries within the city (Tribillon, 2014; Bradley, 2015). However, there is also evidence that, in some cases, the individuals and groups who set a neighbourhood planning process into motion may genuinely seek to reach out to a wider section of the local population, out of political belief, pragmatic necessity or the search for consensus around the future of a 'place' that they care about. The agenda of existing interest groups that engage in the neighbourhood planning process can be self-serving, but it can also bridge across different groups to address broad issues that affect many. In London – a city where high land and house prices and rapid gentrification now threaten not only low-income groups, but middle-income groups too – neighbourhood planning could have the potential to bring together diverse groups and new coalitions, fostering more inclusive forms of urban development in a particular area. More empirical evidence will need to be gathered to further assess the impact of neighbourhood planning in terms of social equity in a city marked by stark social inequalities, housing shortages and socio-spatial segregation, where the power of real-estate and property-owning interests and the imperative of economic growth dominate the local and city-wide agenda.

Notes

[1] The five wards of the Northern part of the borough had just above 60,000 residents according to the 2011 Census, of which about 22% identified as Jewish, 13% as Muslim, 31% as Christian and 20% as having no religion.

[2] This illustrates Bradley's (2015) argument that groups can decide to get involved in neighbourhood planning on the basis of earlier grievances and competing claims of legitimacy.

[3] The identification of 'ethnic' or 'faith-based' communities as homogeneous groups in the context of public participation in planning is problematic (see Beebeejaun, 2006), although there is no space to discuss this here.

[4] Hackney Council has adopted its own procedure for assessing the representativeness of neighbourhood area and forum applications, through an equalities assessment form (see: http://www.hackney.gov.uk/central-stamford-hill-npf.htm#. VlrXjL9Fzsc) filled by applicants. It asks, among other things, for a description of the measures taken to ensure that the forum does not discriminate against the nine 'protected groups' defined by the Equality Act 2010.

[5] In the early stages of the process, part of the Haredi community was reported as perceiving the AAP process 'as not representative of their community or as an effective solution to its specific needs' (Rogers, 2015).

References

Baker, M., Coaffee, J. and Sherriff, G. (2007) 'Achieving successful participation in the new UK spatial planning system', *Planning Practice & Research*, vol 22, no 1, pp 79–93.

Barnett, A. (2013) 'Stamford Hill neighbourhood forum a front group for councillors, claim campaigners', *Hackney Citizen*, 19 January. Available at: http://hackneycitizen.co.uk/2013/01/19/stamford-hill-neighbourhood-hackney-planning-watch/ (accessed 15 November 2015).

Beebeejaun, Y. (2006) 'The participation trap: the limitations of participation for ethnic and racial groups', *International Planning Studies*, vol 11, no 1, pp 3–18.

Bishop, P. (2010) 'From parish plans to localism in England: straight track or long and winding road?', *Planning Practice and Research*, vol 25, no 5, pp 611–24.

Booth, R. (2013) 'Hackney planning row exposes faultlines in orthodox Jewish area', *The Guardian*, 8 March. Available at: http://www.theguardian.com/society/2013/mar/08/hackney-planning-row-orthdox-jewish (accessed 15 November 2015).

Bradley, Q. (2015) 'The political identities of neighbourhood planning in England', *Space and Polity*, vol 19, no 2, pp 97–109.

Branson, A. (2014) 'Hartlepool neighbourhood plan area designation blocked over consultation concerns', *Planning Resource*, 24 February. Available at: http://www.planningresource.co.uk/article/1282051/hartlepool-neighbourhood-plan-area-designation-blocked-consultation-concerns (accessed 15 November 2015).

Brownill, S. and Parker, G. (2010) 'Why bother with good works? The relevance of public participation(s) in planning in a post-collaborative era', *Planning Practice and Research*, vol 25, no 3, pp 275–82.

Chatsworth Road Neighbourhood Forum (2015) 'Chatsworth Road E5 neighbourhood plan'. Available at: https://chatsworthroadplan.wordpress.com/ (accessed 15 November 2015).

Cowie, P. and Davoudi, S. (2015) 'Is small really beautiful? The legitimacy of neighbourhood planning', in S. Davoudi and A. Madanipour (eds) *Reconsidering localism*, London: Routledge, pp 168–89.

Davoudi, S. and Cowie, P. (2013) 'Are English neighbourhood forums democratically legitimate?', *Planning Theory and Practice*, vol 14, no 4, pp 562–66.

Davoudi, S. and Madanipour, A. (2013) 'Localism and neo-liberal governmentality', *Town Planning Review*, vol 84, no 5, pp 551–62.

DCLG (Department for Communities and Local Government) (2014a) 'What is neighbourhood planning?'. Available at: http://planningguidance.planningportal.gov.uk/blog/guidance/neighbourhood-planning/what-is-neighbourhood-planning/ (accessed 15 November 2015).

DCLG (2014b) 'Designating a neighbourhood area'. Available at: http://planningguidance.communities.gov.uk/blog/guidance/neighbourhood-planning/designating-a-neighbourhood-area/ (accessed 15 November 2015).

Dorling, D. (2011) *Injustice. Why social inequality exists*, Bristol: The Policy Press.

Geoghegan, J. (2013) 'Hackney refuses neighbourhood plan bids over community tension fears', *Planning Resource*, 25 July. Available at: http://www.planningresource.co.uk/article/1192867/hackney-refuses-neighbourhood-plan-bids-community-tension-fears (accessed 15 November 2015).

Gunn, S., Brooks, E. and Vigar, G. (2015) 'The community's capacity to plan: the disproportionate requirements of the new English neighbourhood planning initiative', in S. Davoudi and A. Madanipour (eds) *Reconsidering localism*, London: Routledge, pp 147–67.

Hackney Planning Watch (2013a) 'Response to Hackney Council on the proposal for the establishment of a neighbourhood forum covering the wards of Springfield, New River, Lordship and Cazenove'. Available at: https://hackneyplanningwatch.files.wordpress.com/2013/01/hackney-planning-watch-response-to-proposed-neighbourhood-forum1.pdf (accessed 15 November 2015).

Hackney Planning Watch (2013b) 'Please reject both the Stamford Hill and North Hackney Neighbourhood Forums. Petition to Hackney Council'. Available at: https://www.change.org/p/hackney-council-please-reject-both-the-stamford-hill-and-north-hackney-neighbourhood-forums (accessed 15 November 2015).

HM Government (2011) 'The Localism Act. Schedule 9: neighbourhood planning'. Available at: http://www.legislation.gov.uk/ukpga/2011/20/schedule/9/enacted (accessed 15 November 2015).

HM Government (2012) 'The neighbourhood planning (general) regulations (2012)'. Available at: www.legislation.gov.uk/uksi/2012/637/contents/made (accessed 15 November 2015).

Holland, M. (2012) 'Chatsworth Road: the frontline of Hackney's gentrification', *The Guardian*, 7 July. Available at: http://www.theguardian.com/uk/2012/jul/07/chatsworth-road-frontline-hackney-gentrification (accessed 15 November 2015).

Holman, N. and Rydin, Y. (2013) 'What can social capital tell us about planning under localism?', *Local Government Studies*, vol 39, no 1, pp 71–88.

Innes, J. and Booher, D. (2004) 'Reframing public participation: strategies for the 21st century', *Planning Theory & Practice*, vol 5, no 4, pp 419–36.

Jackson, E. and Benson, M. (2013) 'Place-making and place maintenance: performativity, place and belonging among the middle classes', *Sociology*, vol 47, no 4, pp 793–809.

Kesten, J., Raco, M. and Colomb C. (2014) 'DIVERCITIES project, report 2f: governance arrangements and initiatives in London, UK'. Available at: http://www.urbandivercities.eu/wp-content/uploads/2013/05/UK_WP5_FinalReport.pdf (accessed 15 November 2015).

LBH (London Borough of Hackney) (2013a) 'Stamford Hill/North Hackney neighbourhood area/forum applications. Key decision no. LHR H14', Cabinet Meeting of 22 July. Available at: http://mginternet.hackney.gov.uk/documents/s31606/LHR%20H14%20 Stamford_Hill_and_North_hackney_Neighbourhood_Area_ Designation_Report.pdf (accessed 15 November 2015).

LBH (2013b) 'Neighbourhood forum refusal statement: Stamford Hill Forum'. Available at: http://www.hackney.gov.uk/Assets/ Documents/Stamford-hill-neighbourhood-forum-refusal-statement. pdf (accessed 15 November 2015).

LBH (2013c) 'Neighbourhood forum refusal statement: North Hackney Forum'. Available at: http://www.hackney.gov.uk/Assets/ Documents/North-hackney-Forum-refusal-statement.pdf (accessed 15 November 2015).

LBH (2015) 'East Shoreditch Neighbourhood Area and Forum. Key decision no. LHR K59', Cabinet Meeting of 23 February. Available at: http://mginternet.hackney.gov.uk/documents/s41422/ LHR%20K59_shoreditch_Cabinet_report_Dec_14_.pdf (accessed 15 November 2015).

LCA (London Communications Agency) (2015) 'London Neighbourhood Forums, June 2015'. Available at: http://www. londoncommunications.co.uk/wp-content/uploads/2015/06/ lnd_neighbourhood_forums_v3.15.05.19.pdf (accessed 15 November 2015).

Leeser, R. (2011) *Poverty: The hidden city*, London: Greater London Authority Intelligence Unit.

Locality (2015) 'Quick guide to neighbourhood plans'. Available at: http://mycommunity.org.uk/wp-content/uploads/2015/02/Neighbourhood-Planning-Quick-Guide.pdf (accessed 14 October 2016).

London Assembly (2014) 'Localism in London: what's the story'. Available at: https://www.london.gov.uk/LLDC/documents/s43257/15-01-22-Appendix%201-Final-Localism-Report.pdf (accessed 15 November 2015).

Madanipour, A. and Davoudi, S. (2015) 'Epilogue: promises and pitfalls of localism', in S. Davoudi and A. Madanipour (eds) *Reconsidering localism*, London: Routledge, pp 275–79.

Parker, G. (2015) 'The take-up of neighbourhood planning in England 2011–2015', Working Papers in Real Estate & Planning, 06/15, University of Reading, Reading. Available at: http://centaur.reading.ac.uk/43545/7/wp0615.pdf (accessed 15 November 2015).

Raco, M., Kesten, J. and Colomb, C. (2014) 'DIVERCITIES project. Assessment of urban policies in London, UK'. Available at: http://www.urbandivercities.eu/wp-content/uploads/2013/05/Urban-Policies-on-Diversity-in-London.pdf (accessed 15 November 2015).

Rogers, A. (2015) 'Hackney Planning Watch meeting boycotted over long-standing tensions on planning rights in community', *East London Lines*, 22 January. Available at: http://www.eastlondonlines.co.uk/2015/01/hackney-planning-watch-meeting-boycotted-over-long-standing-tensions-in-community/ (accessed 15 November 2015).

Sturzaker, J. and Shaw, D. (2015) 'Localism in practice: lessons from a pioneer neighbourhood plan in England', *Town Planning Review*, vol 86, no 5, pp 587–609.

Tribillon, J. (2014) 'The Localism Act in London: institutionalising urban divisions', *Metropolitiques*. Available at: http://www.metropolitiques.eu/spip.php?page=print&id_article=656 (accessed 15 November 2015).

Vertovec, S. (2007) 'Super-diversity and its implications', *Ethnic and Racial Studies*, vol 30, no 6, pp 1024–54.

NINE

Assembling neighbourhoods: topologies of power and the reshaping of planning

Sue Brownill

Introduction

The issue of power is central to neighbourhood planning, yet it is also one of its most contested and debated areas. Implicit (and often explicit) within these debates is the notion of scale. The spatial metaphors that accompany these debates often suggest the idea of power moving up or down a vertical scale between the neighbourhood and a variety of levels of governance (Bailey and Pill, 2014) or horizontally through networked power relations along the lines of collaborative planning (Healey, 1987; Gallant and Robinson, 2012). These relations are seen as either enabling or constraining the possibilities for neighbourhoods to determine their own futures and to craft the spatial practices of planning necessary to achieve them.

This chapter covers two issues in relation to these debates. First, it argues that the dynamics and relations of power in neighbourhood planning are, in reality, more complex than these spatial metaphors suggest. As such, it draws on notions of topologies of power (Allen and Cochrane, 2010; Allen, 2016), which suggest that it is the 'social relationships, exchanges and interactions involved' (Allen, 2016, p 3), rather than spatial metrics, which are of significance in understanding the complexities of the contemporary shifts in governance of which neighbourhood planning is part. Topological accounts replace distance with intensity and a focus on how different actors and interests are 'folded' into the emergent spaces of governance. Second, the chapter explores the ways in which such a perspective can enable an understanding of how 'the neighbourhood' is constructed through the dynamics of these assemblages of political actors, and the role of practices such as neighbourhood planning within this. The possibility that this can lead to 'spaces oriented to a variety of aims' (Clarke and Cochrane, 2013) is further explored in relation to debates about whether these spaces and practices reinforce the expected outcomes of growth-dependent planning or reshape, even replace, them.

The chapter begins by engaging with debates about the rescaling of governance, setting out the case for moving beyond existing topographical accounts to explore the topology of power. It then goes on to apply this lens to reveal the dynamics of the micro-politics of particular case studies and how a variety of 'localisms' are being assembled through the practices of neighbourhood planning.

Neighbourhoods, localism and topologies of power

Unlike generalised notions of participatory democracy, discussions of neighbourhood planning reinvent the local as the *place* where democracy is enacted and power is to be (re)located (Davoudi and Madanipour, 2015). Localism thus becomes one of the ways in which 'new state spaces' of power are being generated (Brenner, 2004). This can be envisaged and theorised in a number of different ways. Government rhetoric suggests the idea of devolving power to the smallest spatial level, often accompanied by metaphors of power cascading downwards. The history of community-led planning is similarly built on the idea of 'bottom-up' advocacy and 'ladders' of participation (Arnstein, 1969). These invite analogies with the 'Russian Doll' of a nested hierarchy of powers or plans (Bulkeley, 2005). Sitting alongside such understandings is a different spatial metaphor, that of networks, with power being seen on a more horizontal axis. In this way, neighbourhood planning could be seen as part of a move towards a more discursive form of planning where the neighbourhood is being recast as a place within democratic networked governance (Sorenson and Torfing, 2007; Gallant and Robinson, 2012).

However, these portrayals of a Euclidean spatial geometry of power have been criticised as oversimplifications. Accounts of 'collaborative' planning have been critiqued for their failure to fully account for the differences in power within such networks (Harris, 2002). Similarly, more nuanced analyses of the local as a relational nexus of territory, institutions and power have emerged (Davoudi and Madanipour, 2015), often within debates on neoliberal governmentality and the recasting of the local not as the site of devolution and empowerment, but as the site of 'governing through community'. The way that neighbourhood development plans (NDPs) have to 'conform' with national and local policies, and discussions of their role in ensuring the acceptance of growth, are given as evidence of the way in which such technologies and practices of governance are enacted in order to achieve particular outcomes. However, discussions of local interests 'jumping scale' to achieve influence suggest that this is not totally one-way.

While recognising the value of these approaches, Allen (2016) and Allen and Cochrane (2010) argue that they can still suggest notions of spatial hierarchies or 'governing at a distance' (Rose, 1999), which fail to capture the complexities of contemporary governance. Instead, borrowing from geometry, Allen (2016) argues for topological rather than topographical understandings of power. Such understandings focus not on fixed distances over a flat surface, or from a height, but on connections through which the distant can be made near and the near made distant. These connections and relations can stay the same while space is distorted; the Mobius strip is a classic example of topological thinking – where the two sides can be in a constant but ever-changing relationship (see Figure 9.1). As a result, the question is not whether power is devolved or spread, but how it reaches into or out of the local in an intensive rather than extensive manner. Elements of the central or local state and other actors do not therefore act 'above, below or alongside' the local, from a distance, but within it (Allen and Cochrane, 2010, p 1073). Therefore, rather than looking at how the state achieves its outcomes by cascading powers or governing from a distance, it is how different state actors become 'folded' into particular localities or how local actors can reach out to engage with others that should be the focus. In this way, it is not the relations between different *levels* of state and other power that is significant, but how they come together and play out in the same place.

Figure 9.1: The Mobius strip

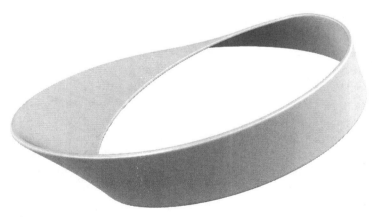

Source: Shutterstock

This, however, does not guarantee effectiveness in how power operates, nor does it erase geography as places are made and remade through these changing yet constant relationships. In this way, neighbourhoods come to be 'assembled' through these shifting and contentious relations. Developed from the work of Deleuze and Guattari (1988), 'assemblage' refers to the 'composition of diverse elements into some form of provisional socio-spatial formation' (Anderson and MacFarlane, 2011, p 124). Such diverse elements can encompass people, discourses, policies, objects, laws and the administrative measures that constitute them, and a variety of political actors. McCann and Ward (2011) have shown how through policy mobility, 'ideas from elsewhere' can be folded into these assemblages, and Sassen (2006) has stressed that they can change over time. The key issue, however, is that these elements can come together in different ways in different places and at different times, despite the constancy of the relations.

Brownill (2016) and Allen and Cochrane (2010) have used this understanding to explore how places are 'assembled' under localism. Thus, Allen and Cochrane (2010) showed how under the localism of New Labour, a region such as the south-east of England was 'made up' as a space oriented to growth through the bringing together of diverse public and private actors and institutions 'lodged' in particular places and the tensions, dynamics and negotiations between them. Brownill (2016) explored the practices of assemblage used in attempts to construct the 'Big Society' in Oxfordshire and the possibilities for challenge and reassembling spaces around alternative ideas that emerged through them. Such practices, including spatial practices, focus on the difficult task of bringing and holding together diverse and potentially contradictory elements that constitute assemblages and the ways in which actors seek to shape spaces suited to their own purposes. Both therefore echoed writers such as Newman and Clarke (2009) in seeing such attempts at assemblage as imperfect, with there being nothing inevitable about how the spaces of localism are constituted.

Debates on the usefulness of assemblage exist (for a fuller discussion of these, see Brownill, 2016), particularly the danger of overemphasising the processes of governance and the possibilities of challenge as opposed to outcomes (Stenson, 2008). Nevertheless, this approach is especially appropriate as a way of avoiding those easy and dichotomous readings of neighbourhood planning as either 'power to the people' or a new and unchallengeable form of state control. It also affords an exploration of how the neighbourhood can be made and remade through these processes and practices of assemblage. The chapter now turns to use this lens to explore neighbourhood planning in action.

Assembling the neighbourhood

In order to understand how the neighbourhood comes to be assembled under localism, it is necessary to explore how the different agencies, actors and elements come together in particular places and the relations between them. The following section will do this through exploring three aspects of these dynamics: the way interests 'reach' into and out of the neighbourhood in their efforts to exert influence; the 'power to' assemble the space of the neighbourhood around particular objectives and the role of planning within this; and, finally, the way assemblages can vary over time as well as space, and how possibilities can open up or close down as a result.

Reaching into and out of the neighbourhood

Localism and neighbourhood planning can be seen in the context of emerging forms of statecraft that aim to exert quieter forms of power. The framing of neighbourhood planning through government legislation and regulation, as set out in Chapter Two, has indicated how instead of *directing*, or, as was the case with New Labour, imposing top-down targets, neighbourhood planning *invited* communities to participate, setting up the possibility that different approaches could be taken in different areas. As such, while mindful of requirements for 'conformity' with existing plans, which will be returned to later, the government had to find different forms of persuading and exerting influence. At the same time, the neighbourhood forums and town and parish councils engaged in neighbourhood planning were also seeking to exert influence. It is here that the idea of reach can be useful in understanding how neighbourhood plans as a form of assemblage emerge.

An example of this can be seen in the 'origin narratives' of two contrasting NDPs: Thame, a market town in South Oxfordshire; and Somers Town, an inner-city area in Central London. The impetus for undertaking the plan in Thame was the town council's feeling that a distant local authority, South Oxfordshire District Council (SODC), was not listening to their needs. In particular, they objected to the inclusion in the draft local plan for an urban extension containing all the 775 houses required by the local plan on one site to the west of the town: "we began to feel that their plan was being imposed onto us", said one participant. However, this was not just a 'bottom-up' initiative as government policy reached into the locality and local actors reached out of the area. The plan started its life even before the Localism Bill was published. In interview, town councillors revealed they had been discussing the possibilities of an NDP with John Howell, the local MP and author of the policy document *Open source planning* (Conservative Party, 2010), which contributed to the rise of neighbourhood planning. Through this reaching out from the neighbourhood, they were therefore 'ahead of the game'. At the inquiry into the plan in November 2011, the town council successfully made representations to the inspector to be allowed to use the new neighbourhood planning powers to decide where the allocated housing numbers should go. Subsequent frequent visits by successive planning ministers to the town contrasted with town councillors' perceptions that "we have hardly seen a district council officer here", implying that the more 'distant' Whitehall had more of a presence in the emerging assemblage than the local authority.

In Somers Town, national policy entered into a different form of assemblage. Voluntary Action Camden organised a workshop in 2011 on the opportunities presented by the Localism Act to address the threats to low-income neighbourhoods posed by development pressures and Camden Council's Community Investment Programme, which sought to redevelop council assets to fill public sector funding gaps. A 'Camden blueprint' emerged from this, which stated that 'neighbourhood planning is a potential gift to all those concerned to secure real evidence of sustainable social development and the promotion of community cohesion and community development' (Voluntary Action Camden, 2012, p 3), and Somers Town Community Association expressed its interest in addressing local priorities through a neighbourhood plan.

While the regulations may have been flexible enough to allow these different forms of localism to emerge, the fact that national and local planning policy are also elements of the neighbourhood plan assemblage suggests that the room to manoeuvre for local areas would be circumscribed. However, in practice, that did not prove such a deterministic factor as might be expected, as in 2012, 56% of local planning authorities (LPAs) had no approved local plan (Dunton, 2014), resulting in a very different policy space. While, in these situations, the National Planning Policy framework (NPPF) takes precedence, there was no guidance on what weight to give an emergent neighbourhood plan. It was a common theme in many of our interviews that the regulations governing neighbourhood planning when they were first published did not cover many key issues such as this. In interview, a Department for Communities and Local Government (DCLG) official said that that was partly due to their (erroneous) expectation that most groups would opt for a Neighbourhood Development Order and not a neighbourhood plan, and the regulations were written accordingly. This fluid situation meant that processes of negotiation, conflict and reach came to the fore.

An example of this happened just down the road from Thame in Aylesbury Vale, an authority with no agreed local plan at the time. During a planning meeting that was discussing an application for 130 homes, which went against the emerging Buckingham Neighbourhood Plan, a phone call from then Planning Minister Greg Clark directed the council not to approve the proposals: 'The committee could not make a decision on this application as the secretary of state has instructed the council to not grant permission without specific authorization' (Pitcher, 2015). In effect, the secretary of state had 'reached into' the neighbourhood to support the NDP, underlining Allen's attention to the intensity rather than the spread of state influence. In a further indication of the twisted and complex web of cross-cutting relations of power, the officer report had recommended approval on the basis of conformity with national planning policy promoting sustainable development, showing how the government was caught between promoting growth and localism.

Even where plans exist, 'conformity' can be flexible. In a number of interviews, planning officers from different LPAs expressed their opinion that some neighbourhood plans in their areas were not 'in conformity' with their plans, but that the LPA had supported them on the basis of 'being seen to' encourage neighbourhood planning and, for frontrunners, not wanting to go against central government. Nevertheless, groups in areas with a robust local plan, for example, Oxford, commented that "we are finding it hard to write our own policies, for example on housing, as key issues such as affordable provision and containing concentrations of private rented housing are covered in the local plan".

Other non-local interests can be folded into assemblages, consultants being a case in point, given that many communities often lack the skills required to complete a statutory plan and grants are available. This can take a variety of forms, including major private sector agencies, 'niche' smaller consultancies, 'technical aid' from Planning Aid or Locality, and even students working with neighbourhood planning groups as part of their courses. Whether they have a determining role is open to question but such actors play a role in bringing 'ideas from elsewhere' into the locality, to the point where some interviewees expressed concerns that 'flat-pack Ikea' neighbourhood plans were emerging as a result of the templates followed by consultants. Relationships can be difficult: Thame employed a national consultant at a 'six figure cost' but felt that they lacked the skills and experience initially to properly manage the situation to their advantage. As well as consultants, the plethora of sites spreading 'good practice' is another non-local element that enters the neighbourhood arena. An example of the way such ideas can spread is the distinction between land-use policies and community projects first included in the Exeter St James plan and now widely adopted.

Further key elements in any assemblage are landowners and developers. Interestingly, this does not always equate with the image of a rapacious/distant private sector. In Thame, the owner of the original site for the extension was a local farmer and previous town councillor, who was convinced that his development was best for the town. Instead, the plan favoured sites promoted by more 'distant' national developers. However, in other places, the role of landowners and developers has been more combatant. Some developers have led a string of legal challenges against NDPs where their sites were not allocated for housing or were allocated reduced numbers, partly using such actions to set precedents for other areas and to fill the regulatory grey space.

'Power to' and the reshaping of planning

The previous section has outlined how neighbourhood plans can be seen as assemblages of a range of different forces and actors steering, negotiating and shaping the neighbourhood as it emerges. The dynamics surrounding the 'power to' orientate neighbourhoods towards particular purposes can be seen in relation to arguments about the nature of planning and the emerging spatial practices of neighbourhood planning.

In Thame, it is clear that one reason for all those ministerial trips was to reinforce the government's objective to remake the neighbourhood as a place that accepts growth. This was typified by the DCLG press release when the plan was passed, stating 'Thame says "yes" to housing' (DCLG, 2013), when, in reality, the town had reluctantly accepted the allocation set out in the local plan. In this sense, central government was reaching into the neighbourhood as a way of reconfiguring space in a way they hoped would set a trend for other places within the overall aspiration that NDPs would unlock growth (see also Chapter Four). However, the rationale for the town council was not housing numbers, but to take 'a once in a lifetime opportunity to ensure the character and identity of the town' (TTC, 2013, p 2), even if this meant merely 'tweaking' pre-existing plans through determining where development should go.

It is possible to see other purposes of planning emerging through NDPs, as indicated by Somers Town. Sandwiched between Kings Cross and Euston stations and a possible High Speed 2 (HS2) site, the Forum hoped to use the plan to enable a working-class community to 'stay put and get a slice of the action' through the neighbourhood plan (see Figure 9.2). The draft plan seeks to 'help local people out of disadvantage' through affordable housing and access to other services (STNF, 2015). This reassertion of the social purposes of planning puts it in direct conflict with the growth pressures in the area and also the austerity-driven strategies of the local council, which is seeking to commercially redevelop sites currently used for community assets in the area in order to fund social and educational provision; 'the Community Investment Programme (CIP) is our answer to government spending

Figure 9.2: Somers Town neighbourhood development plan

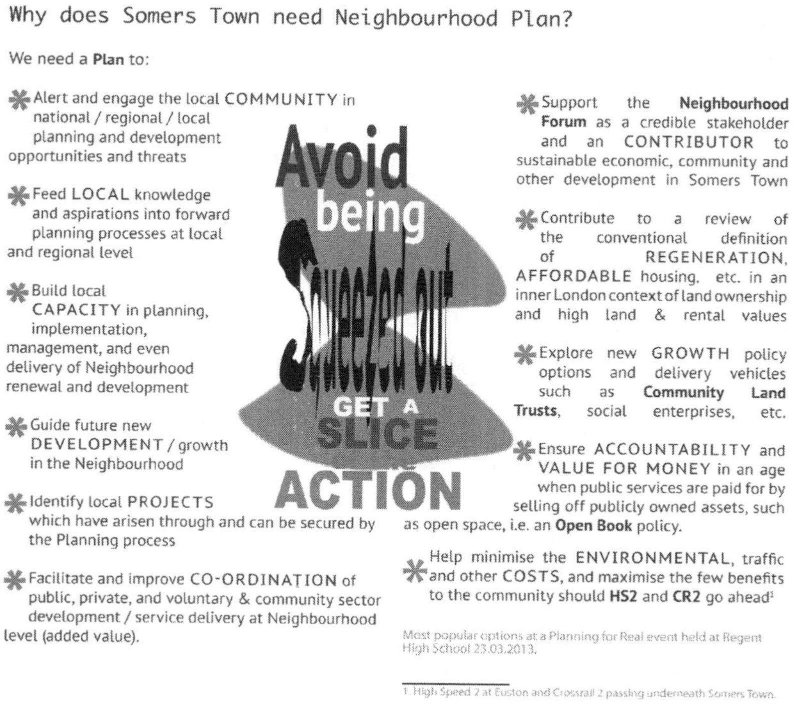

Why does Somers Town need Neighbourhood Plan?

We need a **Plan** to:

* Alert and engage the local COMMUNITY in national / regional / local planning and development opportunities and threats

* Feed LOCAL knowledge and aspirations into forward planning processes at local and regional level

* Build local CAPACITY in planning, implementation, management, and even delivery of Neighbourhood renewal and development

* Guide future new DEVELOPMENT / growth in the Neighbourhood

* Identify local PROJECTS which have arisen through and can be secured by the Planning process

* Facilitate and improve CO-ORDINATION of public, private, and voluntary & community sector development / service delivery at Neighbourhood level (added value).

* Support the **Neighbourhood Forum** as a credible stakeholder and an CONTRIBUTOR to sustainable economic, community and other development in Somers Town

* Contribute to a review of the conventional definition of REGENERATION, AFFORDABLE housing, etc. in an inner London context of land ownership and high land & rental values

* Explore new GROWTH policy options and delivery vehicles such as **Community Land Trusts**, social enterprises, etc.

* Ensure ACCOUNTABILITY and VALUE FOR MONEY in an age when public services are paid for by selling off publicly owned assets, such as open space, i.e. an **Open Book** policy.

* Help minimise the ENVIRONMENTAL, traffic and other COSTS, and maximise the few benefits to the community should **HS2** and **CR2** go ahead[1]

Most popular options at a Planning for Real event held at Regent High School 23.03.2013.

1. High Speed 2 at Euston and Crossrail 2 passing underneath Somers Town.

Source: STNF (2015).

cuts whilst simultaneously ensuring we continue to invest in schools, homes and community facilities in Camden' (LBC, no date).

These contrasting examples show how neighbourhoods come to be assembled around a variety of purposes. The question then arises as to whether, in these spaces, alternative purposes of planning can re-emerge or reassert themselves, and, more to the point, which interests will have the 'power to' assert their vision and purposes. Chapter Four further indicates the potential for the spatial practices of neighbourhood planning to challenge the growth agenda through promoting regeneration (Inner East Preston, Spring Boroughs, Lawrence Weston, Holbeck and Heathfield Park), challenging speculative housing (Woodcote) and promoting community-owned land and assets (West Ferring).

However, there is a danger of falling into the localist trap (Mohan and Stokke, 2000) which assumes that local policies are 'right' when they may be exclusionary and pre-empt or avoid strategic solutions. One area that has proved contentious is the extent to which NDPs can contain policies to restrict the allocation of affordable housing. Woodcote's plan, for example, contains a policy that 20% of affordable homes should go to people with a 'local connection'. Attempts to put similar policies into a plan in Laurence Weston, an inner-city area of Bristol, came up against claims of potential breaches of equalities policies and denying the ability of those in housing need across the city to access affordable housing. There are also limitations to the extent to which policies in neighbourhood plans can intervene in wider socio-spatial processes, a point made eloquently by one of the Somers Town group:

> "It is a ludicrous example of how enormous a challenge for a local community an NDP is. Many of the issues we are dealing with should be addressed at the London Plan level. Somers Town is dealing in microcosm with planning issues which are regional."

This balancing of local and strategic policies and the extent to which NDPs can or should determine policy is therefore not clear-cut.

Temporal shifts

According to Sassen (2006), a key feature of assemblages is how they shift over time. Temporality is therefore an important aspect to take into consideration when looking at NDPs. In particular, the process of shaping the neighbourhood does not stop at the referendum and, as one planning officer put it, an NDP is really a "negotiating tool" for neighbourhoods rather than a blueprint that will determine the future of the area. As a result, after a plan is 'made' or adopted, the dynamics of power relations continue to impact on how the space of 'the neighbourhood' is shaped.

This is illustrated clearly by the history of the Thame plan. In 2013, the Thame neighbourhood plan became the second plan in England to be adopted and the first to allocate housing sites and include an extensive range of policies (64 in total). Since then, it is possible to see the way in which government policies continued to reach into the neighbourhood, reshaping the ground of neighbourhood planning in the process. After the Localism Act, the government introduced permitted development rights (PDRs), which allow for the change of use from land zoned for office use in plans to residential without the need for planning permission. In Thame, this resulted in three developments not included in the plan, one of which was for more than 70 housing units, to go ahead (TTC, 2015). While the government was being consistent in its quest to promote growth, this undermined some of its own commitments to promoting local control over development.

Such changes in the room to manoeuvre for neighbourhood plans is also shown through legal cases over the extent to which neighbourhood plans can take precedence in the 'hierarchy' of local plans. In one such case in Devises, the refusal of an application for 350 homes by then Secretary of State Eric Pickles was successfully challenged in the courts by the developer (Carpenter, 2015). Similar cases appeared to establish a principle that only those plans close to completion (such as Buckingham, quoted earlier) could be material considerations in refusing planning applications, thereby potentially closing some of the windows of opportunity that NDPs had to shape development. Many of these cases have been brought by developers with interests across a number of neighbourhood plan areas, once again, underlining how neighbourhood planning is constantly being reinterpreted and remade through the interplay between the range of different interests and elements within the neighbourhood planning assemblage. The Planning Inspectorate and the judiciary therefore become further significant non-local elements folded into the neighbourhood.

Another such example from Thame is what happens when the plans NDPs have to be in conformity with change. Two years after the plan was published, SODC began reviewing its local plan in the light of a county-wide housing needs assessment that showed the need for up to 100,000 additional units. This meant that the Thame plan would also have to be revised to accept increased numbers. The lack of regulations left the Thame plan in limbo as, according to members of the town council, "it would be nice to have some government guidance on what weight it has rather than leave it to the discretion of an inspector". In order to get clarity, more reaching out occurred (Thame.net, 2016), with councillors lobbying ministers on the grounds that as the plan's housing targets had already been exceeded as a result of PDRs, any increases should be slight. At the time of writing, the outcome of this is still unclear. Clarity was not provided by changes to neighbourhood planning regulations covered by the 2015 Housing and Planning Bill, which were restricted to putting greater requirements on LPAs to speedily accredit neighbourhood plan forums and areas and review drafts, once again, indicating that government is seeking to align with neighbourhoods to restrict and control the role of LPAs.

A further issue is how far the 'sweeteners' attached to NDPs devolve to the community in the form of planning obligations (Community Infrastructure Levy [CIL] and Section 106). In Thame, most of the major applications were determined before the council set its CIL level, meaning that Thame Town Council missed out on the £3 million that they thought would come to them and forcing them into protracted Section 106 negotiations. The situation for neighbourhood forums, who cannot act as 'accountable' bodies to hold money, is more uncertain as the local authority has to hold the money for them. This inevitably sets up tensions. One planning officer overheard at a meeting said that his authority "would never allow" neighbourhood forums to receive and determine CIL spending. However, some NDPs, for example, Sudbury Town in Brent, have tried to influence this through including extensive 'shopping lists' for planning obligation spending as NDP policies.

For Somers Town, the space for their NDP was dramatically altered with the submission by Camden Council of a planning application to itself for proposals linked to the CIP just after the draft neighbourhood plan was published. These covered a major part of the neighbourhood area and included the replacement of a local school funded by a 25-storey (largely private) residential tower on remodelled open space in the area. The proposal contravened many of the policies in the draft plan, particularly for affordable housing, but the council approved the application in June 2016.

It has to be remembered that the decisions on planning applications in the NDP area are made by the local authority, not the neighbourhood plan group. As one Thame Town Council representative said: "the NDP is being amended all the time by planning decisions". This puts the onus on groups working with their local authorities. In Thame, this has largely been a positive experience, although they have also trained a member of staff to comment on all planning committee papers relating to Thame. Indeed, one of the outcomes of the NDP process in Thame has been an increase in trust between the different levels of local government. SODC has also promoted NDPs throughout its area.

In other areas, some groups are finding that the policies that they thought would lead to specific outcomes are not doing so. Cringleford was hailed by the government as accepting higher housing numbers than in the local plan. However, to some extent, this was because the housing density policy that the community thought would keep housing numbers at the level in the plan was not robust. In part, this was due to the wording of the policy being changed by the inspector to add 'approximately' to the limit of 25 dwellings per hectare, meaning a development of 28 (leading to higher numbers) could be interpreted as falling within it (Dunton, 2015).

The wording of the referendum sums up the potentially ambiguous status of NDP policies: 'Do you want XXX council to take the XXX Neighbourhood Plan into consideration when it makes decisions on planning applications?'. An overheard vociferous exchange between a resident and a councillor outside Thame Town Hall during an open event to get support for the 'yes' vote at the referendum highlights the contradictions here. The furious resident was refusing to vote 'yes' as the plan still meant SODC would take the decisions.

This further illustrates the work needed to build and hold together the assemblage around a plan. In Thame, this was made difficult by parts of the community feeling that they had been excluded from key decisions on the siting of housing developments. In interview, opponents expressed the view that the process to decide on the housing sites had been taken behind closed doors by a working party in which the majority of residents came from areas adjacent to the rejected extension site. Objections were made at the hearing, letters were written to the local press and calls were also made to reopen the referendum in attempts to overturn these allocations: 'I feel angry that citizens are being manipulated' (Thame.net, 2013). Thame may have voted 'yes' to housing but the majority in favour at the referendum was one of the lowest recorded. Keeping the plan a 'living document not just sitting on a shelf' was also seen as important in keeping residents on board. However, plans for a green living plan had to wait two years to be started and suggestions for a monitoring committee involving residents, not just councillors, were rejected.

Photo 9.1: Reaching in: reshaping planning in the neighbourhood

Source: Hyde Park neighbourhood forum, Leeds: photograph Magdalena Szymanska

Despite this, for Thame, the feeling was that it had changed the power dynamics with councillors engaged in pre-application discussions with developers, and had created an improved relationship with SODC: "If we want to speak to Greg Clark [the then planning minister] now we'll get to speak to him and we won't be fobbed off. Our path to the decision-makers has been made a lot easier". Reach and intensity will therefore continue to shape the neighbourhood dynamics.

Conclusions

As Clark and Cochrane (2013, p 10) argue, 'localism is not straightforwardly local', but neither is it determined by the national or other levels of power. A focus on the topologies of power can reveal the way that neighbourhoods are being made across time and space through the negotiations, conflicts and relationships between the diverse elements within local assemblages. This points to fuzzy power relations that cannot be read off in terms of power moving up or down nested hierarchies. The reach of, and 'folding' in of, various actors and elements presents different perspectives on notions of 'governance at a distance' and suggests an alternative to a scalar view of power. In a similar way, neighbourhood actors reach out to forge alliances and secure their objectives, underlining how localism should be seen, as Davoudi and Madanipour (2015, p 18) suggest, as a 'relational territorial nexus'. The experience of neighbourhood planning shows the potential for working these spaces of power, that there is nothing inevitable about the outcomes and that the possibility for assembling localities around progressive elements exists.

However, it would be wrong to suggest that this implies a horizontal or 'collaborative' landscape of power. It is clear that the 'freedoms' of localism offered to neighbourhoods are constrained. This means that there is a need to avoid the dangers that critics of assemblage point to of becoming empirically descriptive and overoptimistic about possibilities rather than critical of relations and outcomes. For example, Allen and Cochrane (2010) conclude that these processes of assemblage and negotiation are a way for governments to operate within neoliberalisation; however, neoliberalism becomes part of the assemblage rather than determining it. Similarly, it is unlikely that neighbourhood planning will be 'disassembled', unlike its predecessor, the Big Society, although it could be reassembled as an activity of local authorities. However, at the very least, exploring the dynamics of neighbourhood planning shows that governments have to negotiate for the changes they want to see, they have to incentivise to create neighbourhoods oriented to growth, and this can, in itself, open up room for manoeuvre.

Already within these spaces, it is possible to see different approaches to planning emerging that are reasserting some of those purposes of social equity and environmental justice constrained by the 'growth-dependent paradigm'. There is therefore a need to have the conceptual and methodological tools that can highlight the dynamics and contradictions in contemporary practices of the remaking of publics and places. In this way, it becomes possible to move beyond binaries and to open up the spaces for a more progressive form of localism, even in an age of austerity.

References

Allen, J. (2016) *Topologies of power*, Abingdon: Routledge.

Allen, J. and Cochrane, A. (2010) 'Assemblages of state power: topological shifts in the organization of government and politics', *Antipode*, vol 42, no 5, pp 1071–89.

Anderson, B. and McFarlane, C. (2011) 'Assemblage and geography', *Area*, vol 42, no 2, pp 124–7.

Arnstein, S. (1969) 'A ladder of citizen participation', *Journal of the American Institution of Planning*, vol 35, no 4, pp 216–24.

Bailey, N. and Pill, M. (2014) 'Can the state empower communities through localism? An evaluation of recent approaches to neighbourhood governance in England', *Environment and Planning C: Government and Policy*, vol 33, pp 289–304.

Brenner, N. (2004) *New state spaces, urban governance and the rescaling of statehood*, Oxford: OUP.

Brownill, S. (2016) 'Assembling localism: practices of assemblage and building localism and the 'Big Society' in Oxfordshire, England', in Y. Rydin and L. Tate (eds) *Actor network theory and planning*, Abingdon: Routledge.

Bulkeley, H. (2005) 'Reconfiguring environmental governance: towards a politics of scales and networks', *Political Geography*, vol 2, pp 875–902.

Carpenter, J. (2015) 'Pickles suffers third neighbourhood plan legal setback', *Planning* Resource, 7 May. Available at: http://www.planningresource.co.uk/article/1346198/pickles-suffers-third-neighbourhood-plan-legal-setback

Clark, N. and Cochrane, A. (2013) 'Geographies and politics of localism, the localism of the UKs Coalition government', *Political Geography*, vol 34, pp 10–23.

Conservative Party (2010) *Open source planning*, London: Conservative party.

Davoudi, S. and Madanipour, A. (2015) 'Localism and the post-social governmentality', in S. Davoudi and A. Madanipour (eds) *Reconsidering localism*, London: Routledge, pp 77–102.

DCLG (Department for Communities and Local Government) (2013) 'Communities say yes to locally led housebuilding'. Available at: https://www.gov.uk/government/news/communities-say-yes-to-locally-led-housebuilding

Deleuze, G. and Guattari, F. (1988) *A thousand plateaus: Capitalism and schizophrenia*, London: The Athlone Press.

Dunton, J. (2014) 'Just one in seven local authorities have local plan that complies with the NPPF'. Available at: http://www.planningresource.co.uk/article/1299337/just-one-seven-authorities-local-plan-complies-nppf

Dunton, J. (2015) 'Why pioneering parish council believes neighbourhood planning rhetoric not matched in reality', *Planning Resource*, 6 March. Available at: http://www.planningresource.co.uk/article/1337020/why-pioneering-parish-council-believes-neighbourhood-planning-rhetoric-not-matched-reality

Gallant, N. and Robinson, S. (2012) *Neighbourhood planning*, Bristol: The Policy Press.

Harris, N. (2002) 'Collaborative planning: from critical foundations to practice forms', in P. Allmendinger and M. Tewdwr-Jones (eds) *Planning futures: New directions in planning theory*, Abingdon: Routledge, pp 21–43.

Healey, P. (1987) *Collaborative planning*, London: Macmillan.

LBC (London Borough of Camden) (no date) 'The Community Investment Programme'. Available at: http://www.camden.gov. uk/ccm/content/environment/planning-and-built-environment/ two/placeshaping/twocolumn/community-investment- programme/?page=2#section-2

McCann, E. and Ward, K. (2011) *Mobile urbanism. Cities and policy making in an age of globalisation*, Minnesota: University of Minnesota Press.

Mohan, G. and Stokke, K., (2000) 'Participatory development and empowerment: the dangers of localism', *Third World Quarterly*, vol 21, no 2, pp 247–68.

Newman, J. and Clarke, J. (2009) *Publics, politics and power: Remaking the public in public services*, London: Sage.

Pitcher, G. (2015) 'Clark steps in to halt decision on Buckinghamshire homes', 4 September. Available at: http://www.planningresource. co.uk/article/1362887/clark-steps-halt-decision-buckinghamshire- homes

Rose, N. (1999) *Powers of freedom: Reframing political thought*, Cambridge: Cambridge University Press.

Sassen, S. (2006) *Territory, authority, rights: From mediaeval to global assemblages*, Princeton: Princeton University Press.

Sorensen, E. and Torfing, J. (eds) (2007) *Theories of democratic network governance*, London: Palgrave Macmillan.

Stenson, K. (2008) 'Sovereignty, social governance and community safety', *Social Work and Society*, vol 6, no 1, pp 1–14.

STNF (Somers Town Neighbourhood Forum) (2015) *Somers Town neighbourhood plan*, London: Somers Town Neighbourhood Forum.

Thame.net (2013) 'Thame neighbourhood plan'. Available at: http:// www.thame.net/archives/8053

Thame.net (2016) 'Allow us to update our neighbourhood plan'. Available at: http://www.thame.net/archives/23568

TTC (Thame Town Council) (2013) *Thame neighbourhood plan*, Thame: Thame Town Council.

TTC (2015) 'Thame neighbourhood plan monitoring and delivery plan'. Available at: http://www.thametowncouncil.gov.uk/index. php?option=com_jdownloads&Itemid=148&view=finish&cid=12 925&catid=3

Voluntary Action Camden (2012) *The Camden blueprint*, London: VAC.

TEN

A passion for place: the emotional identifications and empowerment of neighbourhood planning

Quintin Bradley

Introduction

The relationship between people and place possesses a powerful fascination for governments. The belief that people feel an emotional bond with the place in which they live has motivated state strategies of localism, with their promise to devolve policymaking to neighbourhoods. Localism has been understood as a technology of spatial governmentality that uses place and place relationships to influence the behaviour and subjectivity of citizens (Gibson, 2001; Davoudi and Madanipour, 2015). The same bond between people and place is mobilised by community organisations and citizen groups to inspire participants and foster their ability to bring about change (Somerville, 2016). A political analysis of 'emplacement', therefore, can help us interpret government technologies of localism and decode the way in which they are acted out by communities.

This chapter explores the passion for place that can be expressed in localism and its planning initiatives. Planning scholarship tends to shy away from the emotional realm and planners, in practice, assert their distance from attachment (Umemoto, 2012). The policy of neighbourhood planning in England is unusual in that it addresses people's emotional commitment to place (Clarke, 2011). An exploration of its passions has much to offer our understanding of localism and community planning. The chapter reviews the literature on place and place attachment and draws on social movement studies to understand how place is invoked in neighbourhood plans and how place attachment can mobilise collective action. The first part of the chapter introduces emplacement as an issue of social policy and a topic of academic and philosophical study. I then move on to discuss the connections between place attachment and community action and to introduce the concept of place identity framing as a tool of analysis. Research with neighbourhood plans is then explored to understand how a convincing narrative of place attachment and place identity can be assembled, and how it can be used to mobilise community support.

Place and emplacement

The appeal to place is a recurring theme in strategies of 'governing through community' (Rose, 1999, p 176). Feelings for place and belonging have become biopolitical indicators of well-being, civic engagement and public order in a political rationality that turns loving attachment into a terrain of governance (Cruikshank, 1999). The subjective, contingent and largely unconscious phenomena of place-based relationships has been deeded with the authority of rational purpose and captured in an instrumental definition. Place attachment describes 'the bonding that occurs between people and their meaningful environments' (Scannell and Gifford, 2010a, p 1) and is recognised as a multidimensional concept combining emotional, cognitive and behavioural processes. These processes have been enumerated, respectively, as place affect or place bonding, place identity, and place dependence (Jorgensen and Stedman, 2001; Ramkissoon et al, 2013). The concept of place attachment originated in the environmental psychology literature and evolved through a wide range of positivist research studies. It is used to convey negative as well as positive feelings, and has been studied at different spatial scales, though most popularly at the neighbourhood level (Lewicka, 2011; Manzo and Devine-Wright, 2014). Place attachment refers to associations with physical or natural landscapes, and there is a separate but complementary literature on sense of community and neighbourhood belonging that studies the social relationships of place (Trenttelman, 2009). The distinction is problematic since the definition of place as meaningful environment implies the shaping role of human interaction. There is now a substantial body of work that attempts to bring the different literatures together so that they express a 'spectrum of complementary experiences' of attachment to place and community (Seamon, 2014, p 11).

Human geographers would argue that the relationship with place is largely unconscious and is felt 'in the bones' (Tuan, 1975, p 165). Place is not a backdrop or a setting from which we stand distinct; instead, 'people and their worlds are integrally intertwined' (Seamon, 2014, p 11). Emplacement, like embodiment, is a condition of being. Phenomenological philosophers regard place as an aspect of human agency, as the capacity for human action or the power to act as one's

Photo 10.1: A place for memory and emotion

Source: Hyde Park neighbourhood forum, Leeds: photograph Magdalena Szymanska

self. In *Being and time*, Martin Heidegger (1962) originated the term 'Dasein' – literally translated as 'There Being' – to designate what it is to be human. Dasein is Heidegger's name for humanity and for the type of emplaced being that humans have, a being-in-the-world, where space and spatiality are conditions of personal and social identity (Gorner, 2007). Place identity vies with place attachment in environmental psychology as the dominant descriptor of place relations and expresses some of the sense of interrelatedness conveyed in the phenomenological understanding of emplacement (Proshansky et al, 1983; Trigger-Ross and Uzzell, 1996). Place identity has been incorporated into social identity and identity process theories to signify the continuing and dynamic role of place in the regulation of the self (Manzo, 2005; Hauge, 2007). Places are an essential component in the identity projects of self-coherence, self-worth and self-expression (Korpela, 1989). They acquire symbolic meaning as a social category, bestow status and distinction, act as stable reference points or anchors of identity (Hay, 1998), and contribute to the identity processes of continuity, distinctiveness, efficacy and self-esteem, and the articulation of a coherent sense of self (Uzzell et al, 2002). 'Places can heal, provide nurturance and opportunities for emotional development and self-understanding' (Manzo, 2005, p 82). Equally, places can be badges of stigma and deprivation that transmit moral, economic and political judgements and mark the gradients of belonging and exclusion (Jupp, 2008; Jupp, 2013).

Although individuals are confronted with a reality of place 'out there', which they may invest in meaning for themselves, they are socialised as unitary beings-in-place, where place is largely defined by the norms and values of socio-spatial positioning and grounds the experience of power relations and social inequalities (Dixon and Durrheim, 2004; Manzo and Perkins, 2006). Emplacement is rule-bound and its prescriptions are learned through embodiment. The body has a front and a back, and the sense of personal space is integral to the notion of individual autonomy, to the behavioural norms and codes of particular societies and their power relations (Goffman, 1971). Physical and social settings are imbued with characteristic meanings that govern expected behaviour and social interaction, and are associated with particular cognitive and emotional responses (Goffman, 1969; Jenkins, 2008). They 'create a social terrain, as well as a physical terrain, that must be navigated in order to preserve or alter one's identity' (Wright, 1997, p 4). It is through place that the authorised roles and categories that define social identity are learned and internalised (Proshansky et al, 1983, p 64).

The functional properties of place in socialisation, as well as in the construction of subjectivity, are important to identify in any analysis of the production of space. Place is both a state of being and a fixed point in a formative political and economic process. It is a spatialised moment in the global flow of commodities, money, labour and capital (Merrifield, 1993, p 522), and it is where the rules of everyday life under capitalism are inscribed and contested in human activity. Place can be understood as coded by the social relations of the capitalist mode of production and place identity can be theorised as the performative enactment of that code. In *The production of space*, Lefebvre (1991 [1974], p 17) argued that subjectivity is materialised through the citation of a spatial code and that subjects accede to 'their space and to their status as subjects' by means of this code. Lefebvre understood subjectivity and subject formation as emplaced citations of regulatory norms. Space, he argued, is a process of signification in which places indicate and authorise specific social practices. Lefebvre explained this coding of place as a dialectical relationship in which the signification of social practices and the citation of social norms operate through the relationship between subjects and their surroundings (Lefebvre, 1991 [1974], pp 38–9; Merrifield, 1993). The meanings attached to place convey messages about the structure of society and the positions, roles and behaviours expected of subjects. Places can be understood as positions that people can locate themselves in, or be pushed into, displaced from or refused access to. These positions are clusters of rights, duties and prohibitions that define the possibilities of action (Harre and Moghaddam, 2003). The conscious mobilisation of place as a source of identification, then, is a more political act than the phenomenological and environmental psychology literature would suggest. State programmes that are predicated on a bond between people and place address a fundamental source of socialisation and may seek to enlist it in the governance of behaviour. Similarly, those strategies of localism that promise opportunities to influence place may carry alluring messages of personal and collective empowerment for citizens and community groups. In changing places, status and social identity are also made malleable (Bradley, 2014).

Place attachment and collective action

Place-based values and processes are 'the very stuff' of participatory community planning', and multiple studies confirm place attachment and identity as factors driving environmental activism and community engagement (Manzo and Perkins, 2006, p 343). The complex interconnections between people and place mean that plans to change a particular environment can be perceived as a threat to personal autonomy or identity, while residential displacement often manifests itself as a deep sense of personal loss (Dixon and Durrheim, 2004; Long and Perkins, 2007; Hernandez et al, 2010; Scannell and Gifford, 2010b). A mass of data from survey responses to researcher-defined questions demonstrate connections between place attachment and acts of neighbourly concern and civic volunteering, and link it to a reduction in crime and nuisance (Devine-Wright, 2009; Mihaylov and Perkins, 2014).

The incursion of new symbolic meanings and associations that change the social construction of place, or threaten a sense of self or a social identity that is vested in place, have been divined as the motivation behind many place-based campaigns against planning decisions (Lalli, 1992). However, strong attachments to or identifications with place are not necessarily linked to public objections, particularly where development is perceived to enhance rather than threaten the symbolic meanings ascribed to a place or its social connections (Devine-Wright, 2012). Places acquire their meanings through social interaction and are therefore constantly in negotiation, and as places change, so do the emotions, cognitions and behaviours associated with them (Tuan, 1975). The same place will inspire conflicting and competing interpretations, so one of the primary tasks of any community or environmental group is to promote a convincing social construction of place identity that can secure universal acceptance (Wiles, 2005). This has been described as a process of place definition and proposed as an additional dimension of place attachment since boundaries and attributes need to be defined before place can achieve a distinctive identity (Mihaylov and Perkinsm 2015). Local activists must attempt to synthesise the multiple and contradictory values that residents ascribe to place and integrate them into a definition that can be packaged and promoted (Larsen, 2008). In doing so, they privilege one location in the fluid and mobile geography of human experience, badge it as a place of shared significance and promote it as a collective identity more salient than other personal and social identifications. The construction of shared place meanings by community organisations has been theorised through the concept of place framing (Martin, 2003). Martin drew on the social movement concept of collective action frames to explain how organisational discourses are assembled to inspire and legitimise place-protective action (Snow et al, 1986; Snow and Benford, 1988; Benford and Snow, 2000). She argued that place framing by neighbourhood organisations is motivational in its construction of a shared community identity, diagnostic in identifying threats to the community and prognostic in setting out a strategy for local action (Martin, 2003). How place attachment or identity features in Martin's model is not fully elaborated and further analysis is required to understand how the place definition work of community activists mobilises the emotions and cognitions of place attachment to generate the collective efficacy required to inspire place-based action. One approach to this analysis is through the social movement concept of collective identity (Melucci, 1995). Alberto Melucci argued that collective identities are framed by groups in a discursive assemblage of shared narratives, rituals and meaningful signs. Collective identity frames are emotional and often passionate constructs that are negotiated, elaborated and developed in group relationships, and acquire their resonance through storytelling and symbolic action (Polletta and Jasper, 2001). Applied to the place-based work of community organisations, the theory of collective identity broadens Martin's structure of place framing to include the emotional connections between place and personal and collective efficacy. The concept of *place identity frames* enables connections to be drawn between place attachment and the practices of identity work diagnosed by social movement theorists. Place identity frames attach symbolic meanings to places and, in Lefebvre's (1991 [1974]) terms, attempt to change the spatial code of place in a bid to impact on the spatial practices associated with it. Community organisations seek to challenge the dominant spatial codes upon which social relationships are founded and this conflict takes place on symbolic grounds (Melucci, 1988). In place identity frames, community groups attempt to inspire feelings of collective efficacy by addressing the correspondence between place and emplacement.

Place identity frames can be understood as an assemblage of three collective identity processes: the demarcation of boundaries; the production of a repertoire of shared values; and the promotion of collective efficacy or belief in the ability to bring about change (Gamson, 1992; Taylor and Whittier, 1995). Drawing on the literature of place attachment, these processes comprise the boundary work of place definition, the construction of meaning through place dependence and place affect, and the mobilisation of place social bonding or sense of community as the basis for feelings of efficacy (Kingston et al, 1999). Place definition entails a characterisation of place as distinct and meaningful (Mihaylov and Perkins, 2015). Place dependence and place affect attribute value to place and identify it as serving particular needs. Place social bonding forges connections between people and place, and posits a connection to place as community (Manzo and Perkins, 2006). Understood as a set of interlocking identity work processes, place identity frames are integrative social constructions that provide a recognisable structure to place-related emotions and cognitions. They can be analysed in the written and spoken word of community groups as patterns of 'identity talk' (Snow and Anderson, 1987, p 1348). These patterns draw on generic place identity discourses and place associations to assemble their frame of resonance. They can appropriate a positive generic place identity, embrace an already-established identity in order to amplify it, distance a place from stigmatised associations or seek a new identity altogether (Snow and McAdam, 2000).

In the next section, this framework of identity talk is applied as a tool of analysis to the production of neighbourhood plans by community groups. It involves an examination of draft and final plans, applications for designation, minutes of meetings, and consultation strategies, bolstered by interviews with the chairs and secretaries of neighbourhood planning committees or forums, observation at meetings, and separate interviews with the relevant officers from the planning authority. The aim of the analysis is to reveal the discursive production of place identity frames and to explore how community groups mobilise a passion for place in neighbourhood planning.

Place identity in neighbourhood plans

Sense of place and sense of identity are phrases that leap out of the pages of almost every neighbourhood plan produced in England from 2011 onward. The government guide to neighbourhood planning explained:

> People around the country value and love the places they live in. To make sure that you and your neighbour have the community you aspire to, the government has given you new legal powers and new opportunities to preserve what you like and change what you don't like about the city, town or village you live in. (DCLG, 2013, p 4)

The policy of neighbourhood planning deployed the emotions of place attachment as a lever to engage communities in support of development. It promised new powers to protect and enhance place attachment and established a planning policy around which distinctive place identity frames might be articulated.

Neighbourhood plans are assembled around a social construction of place characteristics and values. This place identity frame begins with the negotiation of an agreed place definition that locates the neighbourhood within a meaningful structure of positive and negative characteristics. Place characteristics and definitions are pieced together from a wide range of local contributions but they draw on an existing symbolic range and conform to particular patterns. The task of the frame is not just to assert a common identification of place, but to invite participants to see themselves as acquiring value through place membership. In defining a neighbourhood, those leading the neighbourhood plan seek to forge a connection between the characteristics of place and a positive social identity. Linking place identity with a sense of community is an essential task in distilling a coherent vision of place from potentially discordant views and securing the interest and commitment of participants to the plan.

Those leading a neighbourhood plan in the London borough of Hackney seized on the symbolic attributes of 'one of London's last real high streets' to give a positive definition to an otherwise amorphous neighbourhood (Vane, 2013). In launching the Chatsworth Road neighbourhood plan, they assembled a unifying frame around the symbol of a bustling high street with its neighbourly encounters – an idea inspired by Jane Jacobs's vision of urban design, more recently popularised in English popular culture by Mary Portas (2011). The area of Lower Clapton was symbolically transformed in this new definition by its proximity to Chatsworth Road high street. This was place framing by 'identity appropriation' (Snow and McAdam, 2000, p 47); a reassuring image of neighbourliness was seized on to provide a unifying symbol for a locality undergoing rapid change and disruption as 'the frontline of gentrification' (Holland, 2012). The Chatsworth Road neighbourhood forum used the familiar identification of the high street to portray a 'neighbourhood where we recognise people who use the same shops … where we often bump into people we know' (Chatsworth Road E5, 2013). Chatsworth Road itself was becoming a place where designer boutiques and art galleries crowded out the cheaper food stores, and where the existing low-waged population felt threatened by displacement. The appropriation of the high street as a unifying image allowed the neighbourhood forum to promote initiatives associated with the incursion of a more affluent population, like the Sunday food and vintage clothing markets, as a contribution to diversity and, at the same time, to portray themselves as champions of those marginalised residents who wrote 'we just want our community back' on the comments page of the forum website (Chatsworth Road E5, 2013). The neighbourhood forum deployed its place identity frame to symbolically neutralise a disruptive process of rapid change and gentrification by defining the area around a reordered diversity of the shopping cultures of middle-class bohemians (Holland, 2012; Tissot, 2015).

An appropriated identity can stamp a disparate neighbourhood with a recognisable brand and mobilise a population around a resonant symbol in the face of tensions and divisions. In more distinct neighbourhoods, the neighbourhood plan can embrace an existing positive place identity and seek to amplify it so that it acquires greater resonance as a motivational force (Snow and McAdam, 2000). In formulating their neighbourhood plan, the town council of Thame in South Oxfordshire embraced the identity of the English market town and used this symbol to solicit the support of the population in the face of divisive new house-building. The front cover of the neighbourhood plan, passed at referendum in 2012, depicted the high street market with the flag of the UK, the Union Flag, flying overhead. This image fixed the identity of the town firmly in a world of tradition, heritage and institutional order. In the neighbourhood plan vision statement, Thame's market town character is amplified into a set of principles that structure the proposals for development. A market town is defined as compact and surrounded by countryside; it is an attraction for visitors and an amenity for its residents. A market town is 'highly walkable', so nowhere should be more than 15 minutes' walk away from the market or from the countryside at the edge of the town (Thame Town Council, 2012, p 6). This identity frame provided the rationale for the location of the controversial housing development forced on Thame by the South Oxfordshire core strategy. It defined Thame around the human relationships of the street market and the trust and responsibility associated with commercial exchange. It affirmed a sense of community purpose and belonging and asserted a relationship to the local rural economy. The place identity frame of a market town provided a narrative that gave spatial order to the development of the town and asserted the moral authority of its imagined community.

The policy discourse of neighbourhood planning assumes that every neighbourhood inspires passionate attachment and that place identity is distinct and easily recognised. However, macroeconomic change can transform the fortunes of a particular neighbourhood and erode the coherence of a sense of place. Another task of place framing that can be discerned in the neighbourhood planning process is identity seeking, where the plan becomes an attempt to forge a new identity for a locality and to reconstruct a convincing narrative of community. The parish of Allendale in the North Pennines was one of the first rural areas to submit a neighbourhood plan and was distinctive in its attempt to express a new place identity that would acknowledge the changes to its economy. Situated in the wild hill country of Northumberland, Allendale owed its early fortunes to the lead-mining industry and depended for its continued viability on declining incomes from upland sheep farming. The chair of the parish council explained:

> "What we have here is a post-industrial landscape, but it is also post-agricultural, and that's the hard bit for people to hear. Most of the stock in this valley was wiped out by foot and mouth and a lot of farmers have not restocked, or have restocked at a much lower level." (Interview, 2013)

The neighbourhood plan proved an opportunity to acknowledge the changing economic rationale for the parish and to redefine Allendale around a new reference point. The lack of industry and the decline of farming were reframed as a narrative of open spaces and wild countryside: 'the landscape character, appearance, tranquillity and dark skies of the North Pennine Area of Outstanding Natural Beauty' (Allendale Parish Council, 2014, p 10). The plan gave approval for the conversion and reuse of abandoned and derelict buildings, and provided an enabling framework that would support new housing and economic development within environmental limits. It provided a blueprint for rural sustainability that was in keeping with its remote and open location. The parish of Allendale was defined by its lack; its place identity became one of adaption to the silence of a sparse landscape.

The concept of place attachment can convey negative associations as well as the affection it suggests. The framing work of neighbourhood plans addressed lost and altered place identities and provided an opportunity to transform unattractive environments. The frame of 'identity distancing' was adopted by the Cheshire town of Winsford, whose neighbourhood plan went to successful referendum in 2014 (Snow and McAdam, 2000, p 47). An overspill town built around an 'unattractive' shopping centre, Winsford was perceived to have a poor reputation and its neighbourhood plan unsparingly confessed that its identity needed to be improved and the place transformed (Winsford Town Council, 2014, p 9). The proposals included in the neighbourhood plan mapped out new growth areas and the location of 3,300 more homes but asserted a claim to place identity in the capabilities of its population, promising 'a place full of community spirit and an active community life, set around a lively programme of town events' (Winsford Town Council, 2014, p 11). Urging a 'yes' vote in the referendum, the Town Council called on the power of positive thinking, casting the neighbourhood ballot as a test of faith in the possibility of a better Winsford: 'the only town you'll ever need'.

Place identity frames are a negotiation rather than a defined agreement. The four examples outlined earlier suggest that narratives of place identity in neighbourhood planning can be assembled from established traditions, appropriated from a symbolic register and rebirthed as expressions of hope and explorations into the unknown. The project of undertaking a neighbourhood plan becomes a journey into the subjectivity of place that uncovers new vistas. The neighbourhood forum in Holbeck, in the northern city of Leeds, felt that their area had lost much of its identity. It was "surrounded by exits and access roads to the motorways, the inner, the outer ring road, the slip road to the M61", as the secretary of the neighbourhood forum said (Interview, 2014). Many houses and flats had been demolished and the population was becoming increasingly transient. Encouraged by the local planning authority to widen their neighbourhood boundary to include an area of industry, the forum members began a voyage of discovery into the history of their neighbourhood. They explored converted factories, and semi-derelict mills dating from the 1800s, and marvelled at the wonders of Victorian design. Devising their plan, the forum members negotiated an extension to the local conservation area, hatched a scheme to bring an old railway viaduct back into use as a high-level cycle route and worked voluntarily to save an 1877 workingmen's hall from financial collapse. The logo of the neighbourhood forum was inspired by this discovered Victorian heritage and depicts the viaduct, the church spire and the terracotta brick of the houses. The chair of the neighbourhood forum explained:

> "Holbeck was world famous for its locomotives and engineering. It was the most influential and internationally known area during the Industrial Revolution. And so it is a heritage that we shouldn't forget, and it's that kind of image that we want to project to the people and to businesses through the neighbourhood plan; that Holbeck is still a national company, an international area that kind of deals worldwide."

The recovery of a lost place identity, referenced to commercial empire and industrial enterprise, has boosted the confidence of the forum members in dealing with the municipal authority and developers. Their discovery of the once-global primacy of the neighbourhood has awarded them a new status too. As the secretary of the neighbourhood forum said:

> "I think we are now more confident to challenge, or query, things. We are not intimidated by people saying 'Oh, we are not going to consider that', like. And if you, like, get people by the shoulders, sit them down and say 'Just listen to what we are saying please'. It's brought about, I won't say U-turns, but bodies and organisations and council have become quite amenable."

There is a complex interrelation between social status and place and this appears to extend far beyond dominant spatial permissions and norms. The assemblage of new place meanings can suggest greater liberty or enhanced capability. Similarly, a resolute belief in a sense of community may illuminate the potential resonance of place. Symbols of place identification can be mobilised to suture conflict, denote civic belonging, invite new beginnings and inspire a sense of collective efficacy.

Conclusion

Neighbourhood planning in England provided a statutory process of plan-making and popular referendum through which place identity frames could be assembled and assented to by communities. These neighbourhood identities had to be appropriated and enhanced from a value-laden register of place characteristics, and new place identities were adopted and negative associations discarded. A recurring theme in neighbourhood plans was an address to the social identity of place. Neighbourhood characteristics were defined to encourage feelings of enhanced self-worth, and an appeal to the efficacy of community action was fundamental to these place identity frames. In shaping the look and feel of place, neighbourhood planning attempted to change socio-spatial positions and fashion emplacement into a source of collective empowerment.

References

Allendale Parish Council (2014) 'Allendale neighbourhood development plan'. Available at: http://www.northumberland.gov. uk (accessed 24 July 2015).

Benford, R. and Snow, D. (2000) 'Framing processes & social movements: an overview and assessment', *Annual Review of Sociology*, vol 26, pp 611–31.

Bradley, Q. (2014) 'Bringing democracy back home: community localism and the domestication of political space', *Environment & Planning D: Society & Space*, vol 32, no 4, pp 642–57.

Chatsworth Road E5 (2013) 'Neighbourhood plan'. Available at: http://www.chatsworthrde5.co.uk (accessed 24 July 2015).

Clarke, G. (2011) 'Local planning for sustainable development', speech to Campaign to Protect Rural England, 10 February, Department of Communities and Local Government, London.

Cruikshank, B. (1999) *The will to empower*, London: Cornell University Press.

Davoudi, S. and Madanipour, A. (2015) *Reconsidering localism*, London: Routledge.

DCLG (Department of Communities and Local Government) (2013) *You've got the power: A quick and simple guide to community rights*, London: Department of Communities and Local Government.

Devine-Wright, P. (2009) 'Rethinking NIMBYism: the role of place attachment and place identity in explaining place-protective action', *Journal of Community & Applied Social Psychology*, vol 19, pp 426–41.

Devine-Wright, P. (2012) 'Explaining NIMBY objections to a power line', *Environment and Behaviour*, vol 45, no 6, 761–81.

Dixon, J. and Durrheim, K. (2004) 'Dislocating identity: desegregation and the transformation of place', *Journal of Environmental Psychology*, vol 24, pp 455–73.

Gamson, W. (1992) *Talking politics*, Cambridge: Cambridge University Press.

Gibson, K. (2001) 'Regional subjections & becoming', *Environment & Planning D: Society & Space*, vol 19, no 6, pp 639–67.

Goffman, E. (1969) *The presentation of the self in everyday life*, Harmondsworth: Penguin Books.

Goffman, E. (1971) *Relations in public*, London and Allen Lane: The Penguin Press.

Gorner, P. (2007) *Heidegger's being and time. An introduction*, Cambridge: Cambridge University Press.

Harre, R. and Moghaddam, F. (2003) *The self and others*, London: Praeger Publishers.

Hauge, A.L. (2007) 'Identity and place: a critical comparison of three identity theories', *Architectural Science Review*, vol 50, no 1, pp 44–51.

Hay, R. (1998) 'Sense of place in developmental context', *Journal of Environmental Psychology*, vol 18, pp 5–29.

Heidegger, M. (1962) *Being and time* (translated from the German by Macquarrie, J. and Robinson, E.), Oxford: Blackwell.

Hernandez, B., Martin, A., Ruiz, C. and Del Carmen Hidalgo, M. (2010) 'The role of place identity and place attachment in breaking environmental protection laws', *Journal of Environmental Psychology*, vol 30, pp 281–8.

Holland, M. (2012) 'Chatsworth Road: the frontline of Hackney's gentrification', *The Guardian*, 7 July. Available at: http://www.theguardian.co.uk (accessed 24 July 2015).

Jenkins, R. (2008) *Social identity*, London: Routledge.

Jorgensen, B. and Stedman, R. (2001) 'Sense of place as an attitude: lakeshore owners' attitudes towards their properties', *Journal of Environmental Psychology*, vol 21, pp 233–48.

Jupp, E. (2008) 'The feeling of participation: everyday spaces and urban change', *Geoforum*, vol 39, pp 331–43.

Jupp, E. (2013) '"I feel more at home here than in my own community": Approaching the emotional geographies of neighbourhood policy', *Critical Social Policy*, vol 33, no 3, pp 532–53.

Kingston, S., Mitchell, R., Florin, P. and Stevenson, J. (1999) 'Sense of community in neighbourhoods as a multi-level construct', *Journal of Community Psychology*, vol 27, no 6, pp 681–94.

Korpela, K. (1989) 'Place-identity as a product of environmental self-regulation', *Journal of Environmental Psychology*, vol 9, pp 241–56.

Lalli, M. (1992) 'Urban-related identity: theory, measurement and empirical findings', *Journal of Environmental Psychology*, vol 12, pp 285–303.

Larsen, S. (2008) 'Place making, grassroots organising and rural protest: a case study of Anahom Lake, B.C.', *Journal of Rural Studies*, vol 24, pp 172–81.

Lefebvre, H. (1991 [1974]) *The production of space* (trans Nicholson-Smith, D.), Oxford: Blackwell.

Lewicka, M. (2011) 'Place attachment: how far have we come in the last 40 years?', *Journal of Environmental Psychology*, vol 31, pp 207–30.

Long, D.A. and Perkins, D. (2007) 'Community social and place predictors of sense of community: a longitudinal analysis', *Journal of Community Psychology*, vol 35, no 5, pp 563–81.

Manzo, L. (2005) 'For better or worse: exploring multiple dimensions of place meaning', *Journal of Environmental Psychology*, vol 25, pp 67–86.

Manzo, L. and Devine-Wright, P. (2014) *Place attachment: Advances in theory, methods and applications*, London: Routledge.

Manzo, L. and Perkins, D. (2006) 'Finding common ground: the importance of place attachment to community participation and planning', *Journal of Planning Literature*, vol 20, no 4, pp 335–50.

Martin, D. (2003) 'Place-framing as place making: constituting a neighbourhood for organising and activism', *Annals of the Association of American Geographers*, vol 93, no 3, pp 730–50.

Melucci, A. (1988) 'Getting involved: identity and mobilisation in social movements', in B. Klandermans, H. Kriesi and S. Tarrow (eds) *From structure to action: Comparing social movement research across cultures*, London: JAI.

Melucci, A. (1995) 'The process of collective identity', in H. Johnston and B. Klandermans (eds) *Social movements & culture*, London: UCL Press.

Merrifield, A. (1993) 'Place and space: a Lefebvrian reconciliation', *Transactions of the Institute of British Geographers*, vol 18, no 4, pp 516–31.

Mihaylov, N. and Perkins, D. (2014) 'Community place attachment and its role in social capital development', in L. Manzo and P. Devine-Wright (eds) *Place attachment: Advances in theory, methods and applications*, London: Routledge, pp 61–74.

Mihaylov, N. and Perkins, D. (2015) 'Local environmental grassroots activism: contributions from environmental psychology, sociology and politics', *Behavioural Sciences*, vol 5, pp 121–53.

Polletta, F. and Jasper, J. (2001) 'Collective identity and social movements', *Annual Review of Sociology*, vol 27, pp 283–305.

Portas, M. (2011) *The Portas Review: An independent review into the future of our high streets*, London: Department of Business, Innovation and Skills.

Proshansky, H., Fabian, A. and Kaminoff, R. (1983) 'Place identity: physical world socialisation of the self', *Journal of Environmental Psychology*, vol 3, pp 57–83.

Ramkissoon, H., Smith, L.D. and Weiler, B. (2013) 'Relationships between place attachment, place satisfaction and pro-environmental behaviour in an Australian national park', *Journal of Sustainable Tourism*, vol 21, no 3, pp 434 –57.

Rose, N. (1999) *Powers of freedom*, Cambridge: Cambridge University Press.

Scannell, L. and Gifford, R. (2010a) 'Defining place attachment: a tripartite organising framework', *Journal of Environmental Psychology*, vol 30, pp 1–10.

Scannell, L. and Gifford, R. (2010b) 'The relations between natural and civic place attachment and pro-environmental behaviour', *Journal of Environmental Psychology*, vol 30, pp 289–97.

Seamon, D. (2014) 'Place attachment and phenomenology: the synergistic dynamism of place', in L. Manzo and P. Devine-Wright (eds) *Place attachment: Advances in theory, methods and applications*, London: Routledge, pp 11–20.

Snow, D. and Anderson, L. (1987) 'Identity work among the homeless: the verbal construction and avowal of personal identities', *Annual Journal of Sociology*, vol 92, no 6, pp 1336–71.

Snow, D. and Benford, R. (1988) 'Ideology, frame resonance and participant mobilisation', in B. Klandermans, H. Kriesi and S. Tarrow (eds) *From structure to action: Comparing social movement research across cultures*, London: JAI.

Snow, D. and McAdam, D. (2000) 'Identity work processes in the context of social movements: clarifying the identity/movement nexus', in S. Stryker, T. Owens and R. White (eds) *Self, identity & social movements*, London: University of Minnesota Press.

Snow, D., Rochford, E.B., Jr, Worden, S. and Benford, R. (1986) 'Frame alignment processes, micromobilisation and movement participation', *American Sociological Review*, vol 51, no 4, pp 464–81.

Somerville, P. (2016) *Understanding community* (2nd edn), Bristol: The Policy Press.

Taylor, V. and Whittier, N. (1995) 'Analytical approaches to social movement culture: the culture of the women's movement', in: H. Johnstone and B. Klandermans (eds) *Social movements and culture*, London: UCL Press, pp 163–87.

Thame Town Council (2012) 'Thame neighbourhood plan'. Available at: http://www.southoxon.gov.uk (accessed 24 July 2015).

Tissot, S. (2015) *Good neighbours: Gentrifying diversity in Boston's South End*, New York, NY: Verso.

Trenttelman, C. (2009) 'Place attachment and community attachment: a primer grounded in the lived experience of a community sociologist', *Society and Natural Resources*, vol 22, pp 191–210.

Trigger-Ross, C. and Uzzell, D. (1996) 'Place and identity processes', *Journal of Environmental Psychology*, vol 16, pp 205–20.

Tuan, Y. (1975) 'Place: an experiential perspective', *The Geographical Review*, vol 65, no 2, pp 151–65.

Umemoto, K. (2012) 'Seeking the value of loving attachment in planning research', in L. Porter, L. Sandercock and K. Umemoto (eds) 'What's love got to do with it? Illuminations on loving attachment in planning', *Planning Theory & Practice*, vol 13, no 4, pp 594–8.

Uzzell, D., Pol, E. and Badenas, D. (2002) 'Place identification, social cohesion and environmental sustainability', *Environment and Behaviour*, vol 34, no 1, pp 26–53.

Vane, H. (2013) 'Residents ponder the future of one of London's last real high streets', *The Hackney Post*, 16 March. Available at: http://www.hackneypost.co.uk (accessed 24 July 2015).

Wiles, J. (2005) 'Conceptualising place in the care of older people: the contributions of geographical gerontology', *International Journal of Older People Nursing*, vol 14, no 8b, pp 100–8.

Winsford Town Council (2014) 'Winsford neighbourhood plan: a vision for Winsford up to 2030'. Available at: http://www.winsford.gov.uk (accessed 24 July 2015).

Wright, T. (1997) *Out of place: Homeless mobilisations, subcities, and contested landscapes*, Albany, NY: State University of New York Press.

Part Three:
International comparisons in
community planning

Part three provides an international perspective on the English experience of neighbourhood planning to amplify its themes and to place it in the context of debates about global shifts in the spatial scale of governance and empowerment. It discusses the concept of locality, identifies the further potential of community planning beyond land use and explores the impact of different state and governance structures on ideas of localism and devolution. This section reminds us that planning at the neighbourhood level can be assembled differently in different places and at different times. The need to avoid easy readings of universalised shifts towards a generic form of localism in Western democratic countries therefore becomes clear. This section also offers some differing conclusions on the possibilities for the emergence of a more progressive localism and provides further insights into the scope and scale of planning at the neighbourhood level

Simon Pemberton begins this section in Chapter Eleven, exploring neighbourhood planning in the context of a wider notion of community planning, and of a broader range of meanings of localism across the devolved nations of the UK. The chapter serves to highlight the restrictive scope of neighbourhood planning in the English context and returns to the debates about the purposes of planning highlighted in the introduction. The focus on state strategy situates neighbourhood planning firmly within the liberal governance model and its promotion of an entrepreneurial public, while also suggesting that alternative strategies are being followed in different parts of the UK. In Chapter Twelve, Camille Gardesse and Jodelle Zetlaoui-Léger isolate the market dynamics and localist discourses that are central to the theory and practice of neighbourhood planning in England, in contrast to the French tradition of a centralised and republican state. They show how the concept of the central state as the custodian of the public good and the exclusion of the idea of community from the construction of republican citizenship created a 'French exception' to the liberal norms of participation in planning. These differing spatial scales of governance direct attention to the role of the central state as opposed to neighbourhoods in safeguarding the principles of equality and redistributive social justice in the uneven outcomes of participatory democratic practice, and highlight, once again, the market logics underpinning the English experience of localism and neighbourhood planning. Chapters Thirteen and Fourteen provide further contrast by examining localism in federal state systems. First, in Chapter Thirteen, Paul Burton discusses the operation of 'localism' in the territories and state authorities of Australia, questioning whether it can even be said to exist in practice. In doing so, he directs attention to the complexities of multilevel governance, and the significance of the power relations between state actors that determine the meanings of localism, the locality and democratic participation in planning. In Chapter Fourteen, Larry Bennett points to the technical and managerial rationalities of governance at work in the adoption of diverse practices of participatory planning in the US. His account of the evolution of the 'many lives' of community planning shows the value of exploring policy trajectories over time as well as space. The chapter reinforces the need to question what impact these initiatives of localism may have on state relations of power, as well as on the deepening of democratic practice and spatial justice.

ELEVEN

Community-based planning and localism in the devolved UK

Simon Pemberton

Introduction

This chapter explores how community-based planning and localism are evolving differentially in the devolved UK. Devolution in the UK has been seen as integral to the government's attempts to modernise the ways in which the public sector is organised and managed (Peel and Lloyd, 2007). However, it has been introduced in a relatively piecemeal manner, with reforms addressed to different purposes in separate parts of the UK, and with a subsequent differentiation in institutional governance arrangements (and associated executive, legislative and financial powers) that drew upon distinctive administrative practices that had previously accumulated in each territory (Pemberton and Lloyd, 2008). In this context, the chapter initially sets out a framework to understand the differing nature of community-based planning arrangements evolving in the UK. In particular, it places such changes within a broader context of the rescaling of the state and the importance of the changing institutions and geography of the state in shaping the governance and policy arrangements for community-based planning. Subsequently, a comparative analysis is undertaken of the arrangements emerging, and the implications for wider debates concerned with planning and governance are discussed.

Community-based planning and the rescaling of the state

Given that the UK model of devolution is permissive of divergence in policy design and implementation (Jeffrey, 2007), it is perhaps unsurprising that community-based planning has been socially constructed and implemented differently across the devolved UK (Gallent, 2013). Indeed, while there have been convergent paths towards community-based planning, divergent forms have subsequently emerged. For example, in terms of convergence, there have been ongoing and long-standing concerns across the UK with securing the effective engagement and participation of local communities in planning processes or planning at the local level (Skeffington Committee, 1969; Sarkissian et al, 2010), as well as the involvement of communities in designing, developing and implementing local plans focused on reshaping the local environment (Kelly, 2009). However, divergent forms of community-based planning can be identified.

Of particular note in this respect has been the emergence of neighbourhood planning in England. The Localism Act 2011 provided the opportunity for local communities/neighbourhoods to develop neighbourhood plans, as well as to take responsibility for designing, developing and delivering local services (DCLG, 2011). Hence, community-based planning in England has increasingly focused on land use and economic development issues. This is in contrast to the situation in other parts of the UK, where a broader conception of community-based planning has held sway. This has involved community-based planning being viewed as a response to fragmented delivery and institutional arrangements for public services in local communities. In various iterations, it has been developed both as a process and a strategy for the integrated delivery of local public services by securing greater coordination across and within organisational boundaries (Pemberton and Lloyd, 2008).

Nevertheless, to begin to understand how and why different forms of community-based planning have emerged in a devolved UK, a number of different theoretical and/or conceptual approaches can be drawn upon. First, the work of Jessop (1990, 2008) has been used to highlight how devolution may be reflective of the 'hollowing out' of national state functions under a neoliberal market-led regime to other scales of governance (Goodwin et al, 2005). Nevertheless, Goodwin et al (2005) move on to argue that devolution is also an expression of the 'filling in' of the state by social and political forces – and with new structures and sub-national scales of governance emerging. This can be explored further in respect of community-based planning arrangements in the devolved UK.

Linked to discussions of filling in are the concepts of 'structural' and 'relational' filling in (Shaw and Mackinnon, 2011). Structural filling in refers to the establishment of new organisational forms of governance and engagement (eg neighbourhood planning and/or other forms of community-based planning) and the reconfiguration of those already in existence. On the other hand, relational filling in highlights how such new or reconfigured arrangements may be reflective (or not) of relations and links with institutions/organisations, communities and/

or individuals elsewhere. Again, this needs to be explored in relation to community-based planning arrangements.

Third, the work of Shaw et al (2009) is also of relevance to understanding the differential nature of community-based planning arrangements. Shaw et al (2009) argue that there has been – to varying degrees – evidence of institutional, policy and strategy isomorphism since devolution was introduced in the UK in 1998 with the creation of the Scottish Parliament, the National Assembly for Wales and the Northern Ireland Assembly. This describes the tendency of key actors to make governance and policy arrangements increasingly similar while attempting to change them (DiMaggio and Powell, 1983). Such issues also warrant exploration.

These different approaches suggest that there is a lack of a coherent body of theoretical work on UK devolution. However, in response, Goodwin et al (2013) suggest that a modified strategic–relational approach (SRA) may help to bring some of the strands highlighted earlier together. Indeed, the SRA can help to examine 'the interactions between the processes of hollowing out and filling in ... in each of its constituent territories' (Goodwin et al, 2013, p 161).

Consequently, a key objective of this chapter is to illustrate the value of adopting and applying the SRA – including related approaches outlined earlier – to community-based planning. The SRA helps to draw our attention to how the changing institutions and geography of the state can influence the nature of political strategies and how these may subsequently influence the new forms, structures and scales emerging for community-based planning arrangements. However, equally, it also draws our attention to the dialectical relationship that exists in respect of how local political strategies can themselves inform the changing institutions and geography of the state (Pemberton and Goodwin, 2010). What this means is that it becomes possible to locate new forms and scales of community-based planning – for example, the shift to promoting neighbourhood planning and new forms of localism in England – within wider sets of social and political forces that may mediate or influence the reconfiguration of state power.

The SRA has been identified as 'perhaps the most theoretically sophisticated discussion of the state currently available' (Kelly, 1999, p 109). There are three key points in relation to the modified SRA. First, the state needs to be viewed in relational terms: the power of the state is the power of the social and political forces acting in and through the state, such as state managers and other interests at a variety of scales (Jessop, 1990, pp 269–70). However, the state is more permeable to certain social and political forces (and operating at different scales) than others. The forces that can gain access to new institutions associated with the governance of community-based planning will vary depending on the scale and nature of such arrangements.

Second, a relational view of the state does not guarantee that it will deliver a particular set of activities. Rather, its coherence is created through particular (hegemonic) projects and activities. These may be promoted by different actors and interests. They are then able to implement a series of political strategies at the local level. Consequently, as structures for governing community-based planning change, so, too, will the dominant social and political forces and the political strategies that are pursued. Those who are able to act 'in and through' the state will seek to develop a range of political strategies that are then used by civil servants and politicians to 'harness state institutions towards particular socio-economic projects' (Brenner, 2004, p 87).

Third, the state may be 'strategically' and 'spatially' selective: certain types of political strategy are favoured by the state over others. As a result, particularly powerful (hegemonic) groups may exert more power than others and the state may therefore privilege their strategies, interests, coalitions, spatial scales of action and time horizons over others (Jessop, 1997).

The framework can therefore be utilised to explore the changing structures and practices of community-based planning. However, in order to understand some of the influences of relevance, there is first a need to consider how the very nature of community-based planning in the devolved UK may have both a spatial and temporal dimension.

Temporal, structural and spatial variations in community-based planning arrangements in the devolved UK

With regards to processes of the hollowing out and filling in of the state, and associated processes of structural and relational filling in for community-based planning arrangements, what we see in a devolved UK are both temporal, structural and spatial variations emerging both within and between each of the devolved territories. This is despite an initial common interest in developing community-based planning within each area of the UK: (1) to address an increasingly 'congested state' (Sullivan and Skelcher, 2002); (2) to secure the integration of activity, responsibility and expenditure across different scales of working (Morphet, 2004); (3) to align the disparate cultures, aims, responsibilities, management systems and planning frameworks of organisations towards shared and negotiated public goals and to secure financial savings (Richards et al, 1999); and (4) to promote greater democratic engagement in local communities (Stoker, 2003).

In England and Wales, the Local Government Act 2000 placed a duty on local authorities to produce community strategies as part of an agenda for the modernisation of public services and a new role of community leadership for local government. In England, local strategic partnerships (LSPs) – non-statutory bodies bringing together public, voluntary, community and private sector organisations to coordinate the contribution that each can make to improve localities – were initially responsible for community-based planning (DCLG, 2007a). Similar arrangements developed in Wales through community strategy partnerships (CSPs) to support the pooling of budgets, policy integration, joint collaboration and consultation (Williams et al, 2006).

However, it was not until 2003 that similar powers were introduced in Scotland, with the Local Government (Scotland) Act (Carley, 2006). In Scotland, there was a historical continuity to such forms of intervention and policy management (Lloyd, 1997). As a result, community-based planning gradually emerged and both drew upon and reflected distinctive features of established Scottish public administrative practice, including an emphasis on partnership working (Illsley and Lloyd, 2001). Nevertheless, while broadly similar arrangements have continued to evolve and mutate in Scotland and Wales, in England, the focus has changed markedly over time from an initial focus on strategy development to one now concerned with active community engagement at the neighbourhood level.

Northern Ireland has lagged further behind as a consequence of devolution being linked to the peace process and the suspension of the Northern Ireland Executive and Assembly on a number of occasions. Thus, it is only with the implementation of the Review of Public Administration (RPA) in 2015 that community planning has become a statutory function for local government (Pemberton et al, 2015).

Second, in relation to structural and spatial variation, a degree of relational filling in can be witnessed in respect of community-based planning. Initially, there was a degree of 'tracking' of English governance and policy structures for community-based planning in Wales (Laffin, 2007), but in Scotland, although 32 community planning partnerships (CPPs) were set up and had equivalent functions to LSPs in England and CSPs in Wales, there was much more of an emphasis on locating community planning within broader regeneration agendas (Scottish Executive, 2006). This took place at a later date in England and Wales. Indeed, in England, the 2004 Egan Review highlighted that community strategies needed to become more strategic and take a greater cross-disciplinary and integrated approach to social, economic and environmental issues. Consequently, they were reshaped through 2005 and beyond into 'sustainable community strategies' (SCSs) (Allmendinger and Haughton, 2007).

In addition, it was recognised in England that, in similarity to Scotland's emphasis on aligning local and national priorities for action through specified single outcome agreements (SOAs), there needed to be a delivery plan for the SCS for it to be meaningful. Hence, local area agreements (LAAs) were established in England that set out priority outcomes for a local area as agreed between central government and a local area represented by a local authority and LSP, and through linking the SCS to the LAA (DCLG, 2007b). Such changes in community-based planning were also reflected in Wales, with local service boards (LSBs) replacing CSPs in 2009 in order to develop local service agreements (LSAs) to link community and area priorities and to effectively integrate and deliver services that were responsive to citizens' needs (Welsh Assembly Government, 2007).

With regards to Northern Ireland, traditional processes of community-based planning generally took the form of 'development plans', which guided development decisions in a local area. These were managed centrally (Northern Ireland Assembly, 2008). However, following the RPA, there is now a statutory obligation for a variety of partners to work with local authorities through a community planning partnership (CPP) in developing and delivering the community plan. Therefore, the use of the CPP term illustrates processes of relational filling in at work both spatially and temporally, as well as both structural and strategic isomorphism in evidence; as such, models of provision have been informed by practice from elsewhere (Pemberton et al, 2015).

The arrangements for community-based planning in the devolved UK now involve a clear dichotomy (see Table 11.1). On the one hand, in Northern Ireland, Scotland and Wales, there is a degree of consistency in respect of community-based planning – both in terms of strategy and governance. Concerns with the modernisation of the public sector and improving performance are evident, along – to varying degrees – with concerns around fairness, local responsiveness and closer engagement with communities. In Wales, the Well-being of Future Generations (Wales) Act 2015 has led to public service boards (PSBs) with responsibility for well-being plans replacing the previous LSBs (and their respective single integrated plans). This reflects ambitions to move the LSBs to a more statutory footing and to link the local activity of PSBs and their respective partners to seven high-level goals set out in the Act, concerned with long-term sustainability,

Table 11.1: Summary of community-based planning initiatives under UK devolution

	England	Wales	Scotland	Northern Ireland
Rationale	Initial emphasis on promoting the well-being of local areas to address fragmented delivery. With Localism Act 2011, there has been a shift to a concern with securing economic prosperity, housing growth and active community engagement.	Modernisation of the public sector and the promotion of citizen-centred public services.	Securing equality, fairness and social justice; community empowerment; local discretion and mediating social-democratic values.	Review of Public Administration; local government reform and decentralisation/devolution of powers to local government and local communities.
Policy and governance arrangements	Community strategies and sustainable community strategies (SCSs) and local area agreements (LAAs) (delivery plan) of non-statutory local strategic partnerships (LSPs). Localism Act removes requirement for LSPs; 2014 requirement for local authorities to prepare the SCS removed. Some work of SCS picked up by health and well-being boards and community safety partnerships. New 'rights' under Localism Act – emphasis on statutory neighbourhood development plans through neighbourhood planning partnerships/neighbourhood development forums.	Community strategies, community strategy partnerships. Later replaced by local service boards (LSBs) and single integrated plans (SIPs). Well-being of Future Generations Act 2015 – new public service boards (PSBs) and well-being plans created. Planning Act 2015 Wales – 'place plans' as supplementary planning guidance (SPG) produced by town and community councils in conjunction with local authorities.	32 community planning partnerships (CPPs) –involve public agencies working together with the community to plan and deliver better services; a coordinating and rationalisation mechanism; pooling of budgets across different service providers. Single outcome agreements to manage centre–local relations and align local priorities with national priorities for public service reform. Some areas now engaging in neighbourhood community action plans to identify local priorities for CPPs.	Community planning partnerships set up following Review of Public Administration (RPA) and creation of 11 new local authorities. Local authority implementing community planning processes (in conjunction with other partners) and production of community plans that are aligned with existing community development.

Source: Pemberton et al (2015).

prosperity, health and so on. This closely resonates with the Scottish model. It also highlights how the extent of institutional and policy isomorphism can wax and wane over time between the different devolved administrations of the UK.

Applying the strategic-relational approach to understand the changing nature of community-based planning arrangements

Having charted and described the ways in which both governance and policy arrangements have developed for community-based planning in the devolved UK, there is a need to consider some of the key influences that have shaped such arrangements. Empirically, we can therefore apply the SRA approach to help develop a number of new insights of relevance.

Due to the way in which the UK state continues to govern England in a highly centralised way (compared to the devolution of authority elsewhere; see Pike and Tomaney, 2009), as well as the particular nature of community-based planning arrangements focused around neighbourhood planning, the application of the SRA is particularly focused on England. Nevertheless, reference is initially made to other parts of the UK in order to provide a suitable counterpoint.

The SRA's stress on political strategies and state projects draws attention to their respective importance in shaping different 'objects of governance' for community-based planning. These may be underpinned by new political strategies and state projects that emerge, and that are promoted by the dominant social and political forces operating at different scales. They will also be shaped by the specific historical and contemporary socio-political arrangements that exist.

Thus, in Northern Ireland, political and constitutional factors have combined with economic efficiency concerns to inform the development of a state project concerned with modernising public services and securing institutional and service integration (Pemberton et al, 2015). In turn, the application of the SRA framework highlights how new structures and scales of governance have been created to deliver such an agenda. For example, the RPA reduced the number of local authorities in Northern Ireland from 26 to 11 from April 2015 onwards. However, new responsibilities and functions were devolved to local government, including community planning. In this respect, there are concerns with linking community planning with statutory land-use planning to facilitate new processes of place shaping that move beyond land use *per se*.

Such an approach has therefore led to an increase in the importance of social and political forces at the local (rather than national) level given that, historically, planning has been centralised (McNeill et al, 2006). A wider set of partners (eg planners, community organisations and interest groups) are now involved in community planning processes. However, the application of the SRA highlights that as well as new objects of governance for community planning being developed around social well-being and economic development, long-standing political and religious tensions have also resulted in such objects of governance being aligned with existing processes and structures of community development and the wider peace agenda. Hence, they are focused on securing an 'edge-to-edge' approach that attempts to address the needs of all businesses and residents, rather than specific locations or groups.

Turning attention to Scotland, using the SRA framework helps to identify how the ruling Scottish National Party have – through various commissions – reiterated a national centre-left-focused state project around securing equality, fairness and social justice, rather than a singular focus on economic growth. Coupled to this has been the Christie Commission's (2011) work on improving the coordination and integration of public services to secure economic efficiencies. In the context of community-based planning arrangements, such rationales around local democracy and resource efficiencies have therefore informed the development of new multi-scalar arrangements for CPPs in Scotland. As such, there has been a reiteration of how CPPs need to work at a national level to agree a clear plan with the Scottish government for how local partner organisations will work together to achieve outcomes specified in an SOA. However, with the new Community Empowerment (Scotland) Act 2015, there is also a statutory requirement for all community planning partners to develop and extend arrangements at a local level to facilitate public participation in shaping priorities, as well as in the design and delivery of services to improve local outcomes.

Hence, the SRA's emphasis on exploring the dominant forces operating at different scales highlights how new objects of governance for CPPs are being shaped both nationally and locally, with a particular focus on the pooling of budgets to secure financial savings as well as concerns with addressing local needs and priorities more flexibly. In this respect, it is important to note how the Community Empowerment (Scotland) Act has also introduced other new community 'rights' of relevance to community-based planning, such as extending the 'community right to buy' to the whole of Scotland, rather than just in areas with a population of 10,000 or less. Nevertheless, while this change is aimed at making it easier for a wider range of local social and political actors to register an interest and exercise the right to buy land or property from (traditionally powerful) landowners, concerns remain over whether this will result in new forms of community empowerment and the extent to which community-based planning arrangements are broadly reflective of all local actors and interests.

In Wales, a national state project concerned with securing integration and resource efficiencies has informed the basis of public sector reform, with the SRA framework drawing attention to the importance of new structures and scales of working for community-based planning to deliver such ambitions. For example, the Williams Commission's *Review of public services in Wales* has led to proposals to reduce the numbers of local authorities by at least 50% in an attempt to create economies of scale and financial savings (Commission on Public Service, Governance and Delivery, 2014). Alongside the proposed restructuring and rescaling of local government, new community-based planning arrangements have emerged in the form of PSBs.

Indeed, the Well-being of Future Generations (Wales) Act 2015 sets out seven overarching national goals that the new PSBs have to address locally. However, this leads to questions as to which actors will be more or less dominant or privileged in respect of the new arrangements, including the wider involvement of local communities and other local actors. For example, the role of planners and planning itself is unclear and this may compound the extent to which a 'bottom-up' approach is adopted involving local groups and those most marginalised. This is important given that the Planning (Wales) Act 2015 removed proposals for statutory 'place plans' at a local level. Arguably, such place plans would have strengthened the links between physical land-use planning and the more strategic approach of the PSB focused on integrated service delivery at the community level. Consequently, objects of governance for community-based planning in Wales are increasingly reflective of technocratic national concerns around efficient local service delivery rather than democratic engagement.

However, it is in England that the SRA most obviously highlights how new objects of governance for community-based planning have emerged, underpinned by new national political strategies and state projects. With the Localism Act 2011, there has been a move away from earlier community-based planning approaches synonymous with institutional and service integration, as expressed through SCSs. New concerns with securing economic and housing growth have predominated, and these have also been informed by the new structures, strategies and scales of working that have emerged. The regional apparatus has disappeared – for example, there has been the abolition of regional development agencies (RDAs) and regional assemblies (RAs) – and at a sub-regional level, new local enterprise partnerships (LEPs) – with a primary economic function – have emerged.

With regards to the evolving nature of community-based planning arrangements at a local level, the SRA draws attention to how the election of a new national Coalition government in 2010 led to a new hegemonic project focused around re-stimulating the private sector and community-self-help. Ellis et al (2013) define this as 'pro-development localism', which involves aligning localism with economic development (Cowell, 2013). However, the emphasis on reduced state involvement has meant that the opportunity for divergence in respect of housing and economic growth across England (and, indeed, the UK) may persist and, indeed, become further uneven. Indeed, the emphasis within neighbourhood plans of allocating more – not less – land for housing development in overall terms suggests the strategic privileging of private sector interests over and above other actors.

Relating to this latter point, the SRA can also be used to explore the ways in which the actions of new structures and political actors that emerge in the context of community-based planning may lead to the development of new governance arrangements that have a different territorial and relational expression. In turn, associated questions arise over which actors are the dominant forces, and how such dominance is expressed. A less-heralded feature of the Localism Act was that it removed the requirement for LSPs and local authorities to prepare SCSs. Hence, those involved in neighbourhood planning arrangements are now different from those who were previously involved in broader efforts to promote the well-being of local areas, as expressed through LSPs and SCSs. More specifically, while local authorities still have a major role to play in ensuring that any neighbourhood plan is in general conformity with existing plans, the new arrangements facilitate central government's growth objectives in the context of community-based planning, as well as those of private developers.

Implications for planning and governance

Based upon the aforementioned framework, as well as previous research (see Pemberton and Lloyd, 2008, 2011; Pemberton et al, 2015), a number of further implications can be drawn out in the final section of this chapter. Of particular interest are issues concerned with the geographies and spatiality of governance for community-based planning and associated outcomes. The path dependency and historical context for community-based planning can affect the nature and effectiveness of any new arrangements. For example, in England, there have been problems, on the one hand, in ensuring the coterminosity of new structures of neighbourhood planning with pre-existing structures and scales of working. Indeed, the history of urban regeneration activity and intervention in many UK cities (and, indeed, rural areas) has meant that there is a legacy of both active and (now) defunct programmes operating at the local level (Tallon, 2010). Similarly, in Wales, embryonic city-regional arrangements overlay the new PSBs with responsibility for community-based planning.

In addition, concerns over path dependency can also work from the 'outside in': the previous restructuring and rescaling of the state can differentially impact on the extent to which organisations or institutions are suitably placed to engage with the new community-based planning structures that are set up. In essence, existing actors may find this more or less problematic given their scales of working and territorial remit, as well as the extent to which existing networks or relationships exist with those involved in any new community-based planning arrangements that emerge.

However, on the other hand, there may also be difficulties in securing horizontal and vertical integration in governance for community-based planning where there is little evidence of any previous intervention. For example, in terms of the development of neighbourhood planning in non-parish areas of England, the chronology of boundary drawing for neighbourhood planning partnerships may be problematic. In some instances, those areas engaging in the process later have found that proposed territorial scales of working cut across or challenge the rationality of existing boundary designations. This raises interesting questions over the extent to which both a temporal and relational – as well as territorial – approach to community-based planning approaches is required. As such, a porous, dynamic and non-bounded view is required for such processes, which, at the local level, reflects the relationship between place, mobility and identity (Adey, 2010).

One further key issue concerns the nature of centre–local relations and the extent to which community-based planning arrangements are being used to 'look up' or to 'look down'. This can be referred to as 'the balcony analogy': the extent to which such processes are being driven from below (at the neighbourhood level) or from above (by central government). In England, the need to link neighbourhood planning to other policy areas and structures is important, and especially with the dissolution of many LSP structures. The other 'rights' of neighbourhood planning – such as new models of service delivery –

and their respective integration with each other may also be crucial. However, in Wales, the ways in which the PSBs engage with local neighbourhoods will also be of relevance. Consequently, there is a need to critically consider how the national and local are connected, the degree of formality and/or flexibility in such arrangements, and the implications for local discretion. Again, the value of the locally flexible – yet vertically linked – model of community-based planning in Scotland may be instructive to consider, as well as its implications for securing a more 'progressive' localism.

Conclusion

This chapter has highlighted the complexity of community-based planning arrangements in the devolved UK. A first salient point is that the institutional structure that has emerged for such arrangements has promoted a different understanding of its role and function, as well as its intended outcomes. Through a focus on the processes of both hollowing out and filling in, it was noted that there has been a degree of structural and strategic isomorphism – operating in different directions and at different times – between each area of the devolved UK. For example, in England, while there has been an abandonment of traditional approaches to community-based planning, new structures and policies also emerged, which have an economic rationality associated with them. Moreover, filling in with respect to the emergence of new governance structures has additionally continued in other areas – for example, in Wales and Northern Ireland, while community-based planning arrangements in Scotland have also continued to evolve.

Second, from a theoretical and empirical perspective, the use of the SRA highlights how future forms of community-based planning – in terms of governance, policy and practice – can be understood in the context of the changing nature of state institutions, as well as national and local political strategy. It then becomes possible to understand how new objects of governance for community-based planning may emerge in particular places, at particular times and across varying territorial scales according to the predominant social and political forces at work.

Finally, and more broadly, a third contribution of the chapter is that it also provides a concrete example of the scale differentiation and rescaling of a particular state activity – in this instance, community-based planning – as well as how such structures and processes have evolved over time (see Brenner, 2009). However, through a focus on issues of governance, it also highlights the difficulties in developing arrangements that are integrated, inclusive and empowering. To conclude, over 15 years on from initial devolution in the UK, the search for the most 'appropriate' forms of community-based planning continue.

References

Adey, P. (2010) *Mobility*, Abingdon: Routledge.

Allmendinger, P. and Haughton, G. (2007) 'The fluid scales and scope of UK spatial planning', *Environment and Planning A*, vol 39, no 6, pp 1478–96.

Brenner, N. (2004) *New state spaces: Urban governance and the rescaling of statehood*, Oxford: Oxford University Press.

Brenner, N. (2009) 'Open questions of state rescaling', *Cambridge Journal of Regions, Economy and Society*, vol 2, no 1, pp 123–139.

Carley, M. (2006) 'Partnership and statutory local governance in a devolved Scotland', *International Journal of Public Sector Management*, vol 19, no 3, pp 250–60.

Christie Commission (2011) *Commission on the future delivery of public services*, Edinburgh: HMSO.

Commission on Public Service, Governance and Delivery (2014) 'Full report'. Available at: http://wales.gov.uk/topics/improvingservices/public-service-governance-and-delivery/report/?lang=en (accessed 10 August 2015).

Cowell, R. (2013) 'The greenest government ever? Planning and sustainability in England after the May 2010 elections', *Planning Practice and Research*, vol 28, no 1, pp 27–44.

DCLG (Department of Communities and Local Government) (2007a) *Local strategic partnerships (LSPs) and spatial planning – a practical guide*, London: DCLG.

DCLG (2007b) *Developing the future arrangements for local area agreements*, London: DCLG.

DCLG (2011) *Neighbourhood planning in England: A guide*, London: DCLG.

DiMaggio, P. and Powell, W. (1983) 'The iron cage revisited: institutional isomorphism and collective rationality in organizational fields', *American Sociological Review*, vol 23, pp 111–36.

Ellis, G., Cowell, R., Sherry-Brennan, F., Strachan, P. and Toke, D. (2013) 'Planning, energy and devolution in the UK', *Town Planning Review*, vol 84, no 3, pp 397–410.

Gallent, N. (2013) 'Reconnecting people and planning: parish plans and the English localism agenda', *Town Planning Review*, vol 84, no 3, pp 371–96.

Goodwin, M., Jones, M. and Jones, P. (2005) 'Devolution, constitutional change and economic development: explaining and understanding the new institutional geographies of the British state', *Regional Studies*, vol 39, pp 421–36.

Goodwin, M., Jones, M. and Jones, R. (2013) *Rescaling the state*, Manchester: Manchester University Press.

Illsley, B. and Lloyd, M.G. (2001) 'A community leadership initiative for Scotland?', *Politics*, vol 21, no 2, pp 124–9.

Jeffery, C. (2007) 'The unfinished business of devolution: seven open questions', *Public Policy and Administration*, vol 22, no 1, pp 92–108.

Jessop, B. (1990) *State theory: Putting the capitalist state in its place*, Cambridge: Polity Press.

Jessop, B. (1997) 'A neo-Gramscian approach to the regulation of urban regimes', in M. Lauria (ed) *Reconstructing urban regime theory: Regulating urban politics in a global economy*, London: Sage, pp 51–73.

Jessop, B. (2008) *State power: A strategic relational approach*, Cambridge: Polity Press.

Kelly, D. (1999) 'The strategic-relational view of the state', *Politics*, vol 19, no 2, pp 109–15.

Kelly, E. (2009) *Community planning: An introduction to the comprehensive plan*, Washington, DC: Island Press.

Laffin, M. (2007) 'Comparative British central – local relations: regional centralism, governance and intergovernmental relations', *Public Policy and Administration*, vol 22, no 1, pp 74–91.

Lloyd, M.G. (1997) 'Regional reports and strategic planning innovation: lessons from Scotland', *European Planning Studies*, vol 5, no 6, pp 731–9.

McNeill, L., Rafferty, G. and Sterret, K. (2006) *Community planning in Belfast*, Belfast: Queens University.

Morphet, J. (2004) *RTPI: Scoping paper on integrated planning*, London: Royal Town Planning Institute Research and Knowledge Committee.

Northern Ireland Assembly (2008) *Local Government (Boundaries) Act (Northern Ireland) 2008, Chapter 7*. Available at: http://legislation.data. gov.uk/cy/nia/2008/7/enacted/data.htm?wrap=true (accessed10 August 2015).

Peel, D. and Lloyd, M.G. (2007) 'Neo-traditional planning. Towards a new ethos for land use planning?', *Land Use Policy*, vol 24, no 2, pp 396–403.

Pemberton, S. and Goodwin, M. (2010) 'State power, local government reorganisation and accumulation and hegemony in the countryside', *Journal of Rural Studies*, vol 26, no 3, pp 272–83.

Pemberton, S. and Lloyd, M.G. (2008) 'Devolution, community planning and institutional de-congestion?', *Local Government Studies*, vol 34, no 4, pp 437–51.

Pemberton, S. and Lloyd, M.G. (2011) 'Facilitating institutional reform in the UK: reconciling city-regions and community planning for efficiency gains?', *European Planning Studies*, vol 19, no 3, pp 501–17.

Pemberton, S., Peel, D. and Lloyd, G. (2015) 'The "filling in" of community-based planning in the devolved UK?', *The Geographical Journal*, vol 181, pp 6–15.

Pike, A. and Tomaney, J. (2009) 'The state and uneven development: the governance of economic development in England in the post-devolution UK', *Cambridge Journal of Regions, Economy and Society*, vol 2, no 1, pp 13–34.

Richards, S., Barnes, M., Coulson, A., Gaister, L., Leach, S. and Sullivan, H. (1999) *Cross-cutting issues in public policy and public services*, London: Department of the Environment, Transport and the Regions.

Sarkissian, W., Hurford, D. and Henman, C. (2010) *Creative community planning*, London: Earthscan.

Scottish Executive (2006) *People and place: Regeneration policy statement*, Edinburgh: Scottish Executive.

Shaw, J. and MacKinnon, D. (2011) 'Moving on with "filling in"? Some thoughts on state restructuring after devolution', *Area*, vol 43, no 1, pp 23–30.

Shaw, J., MacKinnon, D. and Docherty, I. (2009) 'Divergence or convergence? Devolution and transport policy in the United Kingdom', *Environment and Planning C*, vol 27, pp 546–67.

Skeffington Committee (1969) *People and planning: Report of the Skeffington Committee on Public Participation in Planning*, London: HMSO.

Stoker, G. (2003) *Transforming local governance: From Thatcherism to New Labour*, Basingstoke: Palgrave Macmillan.

Sullivan, H. and Skelcher, C. (2002) *Working across boundaries: Collaboration in public services*, London: Palgrave MacMillan.

Tallon, A. (2010) *Urban regeneration in the UK*, London: Routledge.

Welsh Assembly Government (2007) *Making the connections – local service boards in Wales: A prospectus for the first phase 2007–08*, Cardiff: Welsh Assembly Government.

Williams, P., Rogers, S., Sullivan, H., Evans, L. and Crow, A. (2006) *People, plans and partnerships: A national evaluation of community strategies in Wales*, Cardiff: Welsh Assembly Government.

TWELVE

Citizen participation: an essential lever for urban transformation in France?

Camille Gardesse and Jodelle Zetlaoui-Léger

Introduction

Planning in France has always been a state affair. In the 17th century, a territorial administration was created to implement the rational organisation of space through centralised infrastructure as the cornerstone of the new-born nation state and, from the late 18th century, a vector for republican values (Foucault, 1975). In the late 20th century, despite a shift towards decentralisation that saw private actors taking a central role in urban planning, things remained fundamentally unchanged. By defining and implementing urban laws, including the process for the declaration of public utility, national and local government remain responsible for orchestrating spatial planning.[1] This hierarchical system continues to deeply structure the mechanisms governing urban development despite the changing 'rules of the urban game' (Bourdin et al, 2006). According to professionals and researchers, the changes occurring include: the need for greater horizontal cooperation between all actors; the growing importance of public–private partnerships in project organisation; and the necessary promotion of the principle of citizen participation in urban design and infrastructure projects. Another change under way is the fledgling role accorded to residents[2] during specific phases of urban planning process phases. Without calling into question the fundamentals of representative democracy, where the final decision-making power is accorded to elected administrators, new political forms are emerging in which citizen participation is integrated into public action in the field of urban development.

These transformations call into question the French notion of *l'intérêt collectif* (the collective interest), which has its roots in the concept of *l'intérêt général* (the general interest). This relationship to the collective interest largely distinguishes French and Anglo-Saxon approaches to citizen participation in urban planning. The expression *l'intérêt général* is more generic and impersonal than *l'intérêt collectif*, a term derived from the *substantialiste* approach of the Jacobin state during the French Revolution and that better captures the notion of a group of individuals. In the 18th century, the notion of the 'general interest' became current, replacing the 'common good', with its religious and moral connotations. For the following two centuries, the legitimacy of state intervention was entirely based on this concept, and in certain domains, the only legitimate actors were public authorities. Yet, as the nature of public action evolved, this vision of the state's role became increasingly contested and new regulatory modes emerged involving different types of actors, including members of civil society endowed with a certain form of legitimacy.

In France, the notion of 'the general interest' implies a stable condition defined by a centralised, devolved state or by its local representatives. In comparison, the Anglo-Saxon conception of 'the collective interest' is more related to the *bien commun* (common good), an expression whose etymology suggests negotiation, shared responsibilities and interdependence. This 'common good' is identified through debate and through the expression of different interests and points of view (Bacqué and Gauthier, 2011). In comparison, French public officials, elected by universal suffrage, consider themselves to be the custodians of the 'general interest' (Rosanvallon, 2008). Intrinsically linked to republican ideals, these constitutive elements of the French nation-state become apparent in different forms during urban and infrastructure projects.

In this way, a deep hierarchical gap has evolved between elected officials and their constituents, as well as between publicly mandated planning experts and residents. This gap reinforces the effects of the *positiviste* vision of the construction of scientific and technical knowledge. With its roots in the Enlightenment and consolidated through the prism of national histories, positivism spread throughout the world and across disciplines, including that of urban planning (Allemendinger, 2002). In France, this led to the attribution of highly distinct roles for elected officials and residents in the production of the lived environment, de facto excluding 'ordinary citizens' from any possible recognition of political or technical competences and thus the capacity to act. The elitist exercise of power has contributed to a growing distrust between the elected and their electors, an issue at the heart of citizen participation policies of recent years.

Another principle at the heart of French political culture provides the key to understanding the attitude of elected officials and professionals towards citizen participation, and the approach to the democratisation of public action on a local level. This principle considers citizenship as being based on equal rights and obligations in a republican system that does not recognise the idea of 'community', considered to potentially associate an ethnic or religious minority to a geographical space. These two principles have led to major differences between France and Anglo-Saxon countries, where *communautaire* and 'empowerment' practices have structured social and urban policy for the last 40 years, in particular, in poor neighbourhoods (Bacqué et al, 2005). Despite these differences, the concepts of 'common good' and *capacitation citoyenne* (the French version of the Anglo-Saxon term 'empowerment') have entered into the urban planning vocabulary in France since the end of the 2000s. Imported by associations working in underprivileged neighbourhoods and by citizen participation activists and researchers aware of international experiences, these terms have been slowly picked up by elected officials and planning professionals. How are these intentions expressed in the definition and implementation of urban projects? What are the challenges to citizen participation if it is to gain scope and momentum in France today?

In considering these questions, this chapter will situate the contemporary period within a broader, dynamic context of the evolution of resident involvement in urban planning in France. It argues that the history of French citizen participation since the 1960s can be understood through three key periods that correspond to fundamental shifts in the attitudes of public authorities and citizen organisations towards its objectives and methods.

From 'urban struggle' to the attempted control by public authorities of resident participation

The regulatory framework for citizen participation: concertation rather than 'participation'

As in many countries around the world at this time, the incursion by residents into French urban planning occurred in the 1960s and took the form of local protests to productivist economic objectives and to a rational global planning model. Against a backdrop of rapid urban growth and concern for egalitarian territorial treatment, the scope and urgency of post-war housing and infrastructure problems resulted in particularly centralised modes of planning and standardised constructions. Led by an alliance of the state, developers and architects, this approach tended to overlook local specificities, the history of places and the different ways in which existing spaces had been appropriated (Lefebvre, 1968). In the 1970s, Marxist sociologists labelled resistance to this model of urban design *luttes urbaines* (urban struggle), a movement essentially led in France by middle-class individuals belonging to either newly created 'revolutionary' groups or more structured associations, unaligned to any political parties but in the tradition of left-wing or Christian activism through popular education (Castells, 1973).

These 'urban struggles' and other participative experiences carried out in the momentum of May 1968 faltered and became rare in the 1980s. This period was marked by several new phenomena, including the departure of the middle class from the popular neighbourhoods that had fostered these movements, the upward mobility of key association leaders who were drawn into the political sphere and the progressive implementation of a legal and institutional framework for resident participation that channelled it towards bodies with only limited power. In this slippage, the 'bottom-up' activist movement became a 'top-down' movement organised and normalised by the state through ambiguous structures created for mediation between associations and regulatory entities. Incentive-based legislation emerged in the domain of urban planning with the directive that citizens should be involved in every step of the development of projects concerning their living environment. In this framework, the creation of local democratic structures, as well as mediation channels between institutional actors and members of civil society (such as *conseils consultation locative* [local housing, neighbourhood and development committees]), were encouraged or made obligatory depending on the size of the town. During this period, while most countries used the term 'participation' to refer to resident involvement in public projects, in France, the term *'concertation'* was adopted. Far-left activists considered the term 'participation' to be a tool used by 'the dominant' over 'the dominated', and local and national political elites feared its potential as a counter-resistance instrument that would undermine their authority and revive social tensions. While they could not radically object to its underlying principles (for to do so would be contrary to the French Constitution), local officials argued for the creation of an administrative framework to structure residents' involvement in urban projects.

The term *'concertation'* has no direct equivalent in English and was preferred by French legislators in the drawing up of urban planning texts. Introduced within economic planning à la *française*, the notion of *concertation* bears an institutional connotation. From the 1950s, it referred to a working relationship established between bureaucrats and key economic players to fix growth objectives, a term then broadened to include territorial and infrastructural development policy. From the 1970s onwards, '*concertation*' replaced 'participation' in the vocabulary of elected officials and development professionals, with a broader meaning that included dialogue with residents and, most of all, associations. This development was not innocuous, for it expressed the public authorities' desire to organise and control forms of dialogue, as well as a preference for dealing with intermediary actors. It reflects a politico-administrative culture anchored in a top-down vision of the organisation of state actions. However, whereas '*concertation*' in its original vocabulary of economic planning referred to negotiations between stakeholders with a shared goal, this was not the case when residents were to be involved. Over the following years, the term was gradually emptied of any substance in terms of both legislation and practice. In 1992, the French *Conseil d'Etat* (Council of State) decreed that, in reference to the urban code, the minimal and acceptable level for *concertation* was the publication of project information and the gathering of public commentary and observations.

Participative experiences limited in scope and visibility

While the political and legislative context seemed favourable to the development of resident participation, no serious thought was given to the right to be informed and to participate, no concrete objectives were identified, and there was no consideration of the means required to implement these rights (Blondiaux, 2005). Thus, from the 1990s onwards, with due respect for their legal obligations, public project contractors did not hesitate to highlight the element of *concertation* in their operations. However, at a closer inspection, it quickly became apparent that the processes in question rarely went beyond a consultative phase.[3]

To explain their reticence towards including residents at the early, diagnostic phase of urban projects, local authorities cited the fear of appearing before residents without the financial or technical guarantees to ensure a particular project or outcome. Urban project management methods also contributed to this reticence; technical managers, used to simply recording needs and formulating recommendations, dreaded facing endless, impossible requests from inhabitants and preferred to present them with already well-advanced projects. Furthermore, a high level of resident involvement was rarely considered important; in a fatalistic way, contractors would express regret over certain populations' lack of interest in urban projects, thus explaining the low diversity of participating groups. However, in general, contractors were perfectly satisfied for their main interlocutor to be concerned resident associations as, though often vociferous and likely to slow down a project's advancement, they could be channelled and controlled. Finally, citizen *concertation* was generally perceived to be politically risky due to the level of transparency and debate required for it to be effective (Dimeglio and Zetlaoui-Léger, 2007; Gardesse, 2011). With all of these factors combined, certain parts of the population – typically, the young, working class, underprivileged and recent immigrants – were the least represented and any *concertation citoyenne* occurred in a very closed circuit (Carrel, 2014).

From the 1980s, some more ambitious processes were nonetheless tried out, for example, in the development of the 'generative programming' method concerning social housing rehabilitation and public facility projects, based on a collaborative process between political, technical and civic bodies (Conan, 1997 ; Zetlaoui-Léger, 2015). In the 1990s, English agency John Thomson and Partners applied its urban planning approach to several French cities, in collaboration with French urban designer Eléonore Hauptmann. Despite the quality of the results obtained and the steps taken to sustain them, these experimental projects required difficult paradigm shifts, and urban project management habits did not evolve much in France until the middle of the 2000s.

Added to this institutional reluctance, citizen mobilisation appeared to be difficult to muster, a situation further complicated by France's fundamental rejection of any form of communitarianism. In Anglo-Saxon countries, community planning techniques are based on the identification of shared-interest groups (age, profession, culture, leisure) and can also include other 'life communities' (eg ethnic or religious), with the involvement of these groups in the collective elaboration of projects (Wates, 2000). However, in France, these practices are difficult to envisage, for they refer to social groups who have no legal definition or rights, and it is easier to involve populations who are already involved in well-identified associative structures. The issue of the scope and representative nature of resident participation in France is often used to undermine its effectiveness. The problem is hard to resolve and citizen participation can be discouraged and even discredited by its excessive institutionalisation.

From 2000: inhabitants' role in urban planning reconsidered?

The preceding developments confirm the general perception of a highly bureaucratic French democracy. They also show how political initiatives to regulate resident involvement in urban development were more concerned by potential risk to the representative French democratic system than a real political desire to change the decision-making process. These initiatives did not convey any conviction about the renewal of political authority or the role and effect of citizen participation on the quality of decision-making. Nevertheless, change was occurring at the heart of the French administration. With a growing awareness that conflict was increasingly complicating the preparation of major projects, fostering public debate over major infrastructure and urban design projects became an 'obligation for public action' (Bacqué and Gauthier, 2011). Centralised rules were no longer politically relevant or socially efficient, thereby opening up the decision-making process to residents. The institutionalisation of resident participation in French urban projects in the last quarter of the 20th century could be seen as a response to what Pierre Müller (1992) called the 'crisis in the French public policy model', or, in other words, the operational failure of a certain number of fundamental principles, frameworks and tools. The change in attitude in the French state to resident participation in urban planning was also due to external pressure, in particular, the growing concerns about sustainable development in the international community, as announced by the International Conference on Environment and Development organised in Rio in 1992.

The influence of environmental discourses

With its global, holistic vision of local development issues (Berke, 2002) and of the interdependence between those who produce urban space and those who live in it, sustainable development originated a profound renewal of citizen participation approaches and the organisation of projects, in particular, on a neighbourhood scale. In the 1990s, and against a backdrop of decentralisation, 'the neighbourhood' emerged as the pivotal entity for engaging local democratic renewal in France. Confronted with deep social crisis in the *banlieues* (underprivileged suburbs), the *Politique de la Ville* placed the neighbourhood at the centre of an urban policy aimed at renewing and anchoring citizenship in a territorial framework (Bacqué et al, 2005). From the mid-2000s, public authorities considered the neighbourhood as a pertinent and perfectly scaled lever for testing and disseminating new sustainable urban practices.[4] The first ecodistrict projects raised pointed questions about the processes and reception of change in people's everyday habitat and habits.

With growing awareness about global environmental issues, such as climate change or biodiversity conservation, sustainable development created a new roadmap, with a discourse about the need to change living habits. Urban project managers now actively sought to accompany residents in these changes, contrary to their behaviour during the modernisation period in the 1950s and 1970s. In particular, communication with residents was greatly intensified during the first ecodistrict projects, with the aim of informing, explaining and encouraging 'more virtuous' living habits (according to expert definitions). These information channels are still the most frequent 'participative' modes adopted by urban project managers, their main objective generally being to establish that citizens' daily lives conform to standardised buildings designed to meet an idealised eco-resident typology (Renauld, 2014). However, ecodistrict projects were also a chance for almost a quarter of French local authorities to attempt more ambitious participative approaches, such as the collaborative design of partial or entire projects. These experiences were possible when urban contractors, in particular, local authorities, closely linked environmental issues with socio-economic and political issues in a process of re-democratisation that transformed residents into active citizens.

In developing these actions, and by observing how residents expressed their point of view on quality of life and urban use practices, it became clear that instead of being occasionally consulted and/or generally dissociated from decision-making, residents needed to be integrated throughout the entire project process (Zetlaoui-Léger et al, 2015).

Political, cultural and professional codes under stress

In terms of the organisation of urban projects, the changes at Paris City Hall since the early 2000s are an interesting reflection of the overall changes in the practice and representation of public action but also of how institutional inertia acts as a brake on citizen participation in France. For example, the organisation and implementation of the Paris Rive Gauche (13th arrondissement) and Pajol (18th arrondissement) in the mid-1990s, as well as the 2002 launch of the Les Halles forum and garden renovations, revealed changed attitudes by certain political and technical actors towards citizen *concertation*. These changes not only expressed the desire to break with previous ways of operating, but were also the result of committed resident groups who used *concertation* regulations to communicate their claims and propositions on the subject. While the movement was initially one of protest (against a lack of information about City Hall's intentions and the fact that residents had not been seriously involved in the projects), it was accompanied by proposals for the neighbourhood's future, as well as ideas about how to genuinely conduct a 'concerted' approach. These experiences were instructive for public authorities and professionals working on the projects (Schön, 1983), and as a result, training sessions were developed to encourage project leaders to change methods during these and future operations. Many public officials and urban professionals recognised the need for a collective cultural adaptation to citizen participation. They stopped invoking the often-impossible requirement that only residents with a full understanding of citizenship, architectural and urban regulatory codes could take part in participative urban projects. Today, the city of Paris – as well as other cities such as Bordeaux and Strasbourg – offers training and guidelines on this subject for political, technical and administrative staff to help them with their projects and practice. Several City Hall departments are now obliged to integrate participation into their actions. Participation is no longer systematically perceived as a communications process for convincing residents to adhere to a project envisioned by an elected official. Instead, it is now an indispensable mechanism in urban projects.

Despite these transformations, one cannot speak of a radical about-turn in urban project practice and the local management of public affairs. Urban affairs in France are largely organised through a double-delegation power model that gives priority to technical thinking. On the one hand is the representative democratic system, considered to be the only legitimate political system; on the other hand is the designer-architect, considered to be the only legitimate author-creator. In pre-configuring the relationship between local urban authorities and citizen participation, these 'cultural codes' (Gardesse, 2013) structure its practice and outcomes,[5] like a 'habitus' that plays a determining role in the definition of public territorial action. These cultural codes are particularly noticeable among the national deputies charged with redefining the *Politique de la Ville* plan for underprivileged urban zones. Noting that the concept of *concertation* had lost meaning over the years, the parliamentarians opted for the term 'co-construction', presented in the February 2014 law on Urban Cohesion and the City. However, this concept was weakened through its attachment to the newly created administrative tools – the 'citizen committee' and 'project house' – to be implemented for each new urban project. Open to associations and to local actors, these instruments for *concertation* appear as the pillars of the renewal of democratic practice in the *Politique de la Ville* priority districts. They are the result of a report by academic Marie-Hélène Bacqué and association leader Mohammed Mechmache, conducted in 2013 at the request of the Ministry for Urban Affairs. In their report (Bacqué and Mechmache, 2013), the authors recount the limited success of participative methods tried out in the underprivileged districts, all the while underlining the benefits of these actions for French society. The report's subtitle, 'It can no longer be done without us', clearly illustrates the population's expectations, yet the French Parliament remains reluctant to adopt the report's principal recommendations, such as financial support for residents' initiatives or the independent review of projects in order to guarantee their neutrality. One of the fears raised by the report's propositions again concerns the emergence of religious or ethnic-based opposition groups.

Presented as a 'flexible' tool whose organisation is to be adapted to local situations, the citizen committee is the latest addition to numerous existing administrative structures linked to citizen participation created within the *Politique de la Ville* urban and environmental regulatory codes. To be coherent and efficient, the citizen committee must respect certain criteria concerning skills and the role of experts, the parameters for action, as well as the capacity to mobilise citizens. This new entity has also encountered problems concerning the selection of participating residents and/or their representatives. For example, in their report, the two authors raise the issue of the right to vote for non-European residents as a prerequisite for the democratisation of public action in underprivileged districts, as promised by François Hollande during his 2012 presidential campaign. However, the government refuses to implement this on the basis that to pass such a measure would require a two thirds majority in both parliamentary houses, currently impossible to imagine. The implicit refusal to open a public debate on this question illustrates once again the lack of political conviction concerning the virtues of a genuinely deliberative procedure across local and national levels that associates elected political officers with ordinary citizens.

Political action renewed by citizen activism

In reconsidering urban actors and decision-making processes through the lens of cultural codes, it is important to not freeze institutional actors into a fixed role. If the arrival of residents in the urban project 'arena' is considered by some to threaten the legitimacy of administrative actors, leading them to fall back defensively on cultural codes, this arrival is also clearly shaking up these same codes and rules. In the simultaneous movement of 'opening out' to resident participation while 'closing down' in defence, local authorities and urban professionals find themselves in a state of permanent tension. This tension can only be resolved by a new generation of political and professional actors, a point of view confirmed by the most ambitious participative experiences conducted in France over the last few years. The speed of these changes and their acceleration in certain administrations depends on the strength and nature of local democratic cultures, found in relationships built over the years between elected officials and local civil society. Through public debate and other forms of collaboration, these relationships between political and associative leaders go beyond short-term electoral stakes. They create the right conditions for participation whereby residents are considered not as simple 'users' of urban territory, but as citizens with the right to express their needs, opinions and propositions concerning the environment in which they live. Such is the case for cities such as Strasbourg and Grenoble. Following the 2008 municipal elections in Strasbourg, the newly elected officials announced their shared commitment with local associations to a new approach to urban planning. The new left-wing municipal authority could rely upon strong local associative networks to democratise public action. In Grenoble during the 1960s, the associative movement was particularly strong in local politics, leading to the election in 1965 of one of their members, Hubert Dubedout, as city mayor. In 2014, the city's residents once again elected a 'civilian' mayor who, like his Strasbourg counterpart, built a political programme upon the two pillars of citizen participation and sustainable development. Today, in Grenoble and Strasbourg, a new generation of urban actors is composed of local politicians and professionals who work in tandem and are involved in innovative participative schemes on a national level.

The institutionalisation of citizen participation in France in the 1980s did not herald the disappearance of spontaneous resident actions, even if, at the beginning, one of its major objectives was to limit such initiatives. Instead of being contained, these resident initiatives multiplied and diversified, going beyond protest to take on new forms, for example, the co-housing processes in France that could lead to an important and necessary expansion of the country's housing stock. Going beyond the 1960s' and 1970s' utopian vision of communal living, the motivations guiding the people involved in these experiments are a pragmatic mix of the economic, social, environmental and political. These initiatives increasingly involve residents of all social origins, who organise themselves into collectives and associations at a national level in order to share their experiences. For the last 10 years, they have been putting pressure on public authorities on a local and ministerial level to gain support for their projects. In this way, today, both large and small city authorities, as well as housing developers, support participative projects in their urban operations, considering them to be a new entry point to the housing market (Devaux, 2014), as well as a lever for raising the attractiveness of old and new districts. They count on the dynamism of committed local resident groups to develop the conviviality, solidarity and sense of communal well-being in their urban designs.

Conclusion

Until the 2000s, the involvement of residents in urban planning in France, in terms of both conception and practice, was organised around two distinct rationales: the bottom-up 'urban struggles' of the 1960s and 1970s; and then a series of regulatory and administrative provisions that aimed to provide a framework for citizen participation but ended up by circumscribing it. Recently, European directives linking sustainable development and citizen participation have strengthened regulations on participation and urban management. The last decade has thus witnessed a converging discourse between different administrative actors to defend the principle of urban 'co-construction' with the population. The two rationales that have for so long been opposed to one another – one of participation organised by public authorities but, in fact, seen by observers as undermining it; the other a spontaneous mobilisation often considered to be underlined by conservative aims – are evolving in their respective objectives and implementation methods, and are increasingly overlapping.

On an institutional level, the regulatory framework developed over the last 30 years was initially designed to defuse conflicts with civil society and avoid the blocking of projects. Today, a growing number of political and urbanism professionals admit that while conflict may be a regular project phase, it can only be surpassed if it occurs within a well-organised framework of debate that allows for the full expression of diverse points of view. Furthermore, citizen participation is increasingly associated with innovative practices in the domains of habitat, transport and social welfare. The resident collectives and local or global associations who mobilise around urban projects are increasingly considered not only as experts on the subject, but also as potential drivers for propositions about the design of sustainable districts and the fight against exclusion in underprivileged 'sensitive urban zones'.

The virtues of 'community planning' tools have been (re)discovered by public authorities and urban professionals. Residents are getting organised at an early stage in urban development projects in order to have real impact on the improvement of their daily environment. Their actions are not necessarily oppositional; their protests are often accompanied by constructive proposals aimed at those public authorities ready to listen to and work with them (Gardesse and Grudet, 2015). Thanks to new communications possibilities, residents are able to build a shared culture around their participation practices that can also be developed and federated on a national level, often borrowing the language of urban ecology or underprivileged neighbourhood management to do so. Some groups aim for policy change on a local or national level, for example, in the housing sector, where residents contributed directly to the implementation of regulations encouraging different forms of participation.

Thus, it would seem that France is undergoing a renewal of methods and expectations regarding resident participation. For pragmatic reasons, public officials and professionals in charge of implementing public policy are increasingly inclined to work with residents to ensure the relevance and feasibility of their projects. Given the issues at stake over the management of declining resources and the transition to renewable energy, the development of the social economy, and the crisis in the traditional political model, there is a growing awareness that the spaces of our daily lives must be the product of cooperation between the different actors using and sharing them. Faced with the compartmentalisation of the public administration and its different technical divisions, residents' knowledge and input is crucial, especially given the recognised benefit of resident movements' actions for the *bien commun territorial* (common territorial good).[6] Although slightly unclear, this latter notion nonetheless allows urban planning professionals to develop a practice that closely links the concerns of living together, thinking together and acting together. This can encourage the development of citizen groups to define 'practice communities', without falling into communitarianism and the problem of minority rights.

While these reflections are today shared by diverse actors, the pervasiveness of certain cultural codes attached to both the framework of public action and the operational inertia of urban developers limits the possibility of fully integrating them into the daily practice of urban design and land-use planning. Despite a succession of grand speeches on the urgent necessity to reform and simplify the French administration, elected officials are hanging on to their often multiple political posts. The consequence is that the layers of territorial administration continue to overlap. This accumulation and entanglement only makes governance more opaque, with long decision-making processes that can discourage citizen participation and weaken its impact. In parallel, the reduction in public finances, along with the growing technical complexity of urban projects, has led to an increasing trend over the last years to transfer urban project management to private operators. This often has the effect of disempowering public authorities and giving free reign to private actors in the definition of planning and construction programmes. Experience has shown that participative processes are difficult to maintain in a committed and long-term way with private developers, who tend to be reluctant to involve residents, considering that such a process will hamper their work and objectives. Only strong local political willpower can create the conditions and support for ambitious, long-term citizen participation in France today. For this, local authorities also need the means to drive projects and work in partnership with developers and contractors in order to have an impact on outcomes. Many examples prove that local authorities, when renewed and jointly represented throughout all project phases by committed elected officials and ordinary citizens, are best placed to guarantee the 'common territorial good'. Put differently, to be effective, citizen participation still requires strong state leadership … perhaps another French exception?

Acknowledgements

The authors thank Sue Brownill and Quintin Bradley for their suggestions in the elaboration of this article, and Miranda Salt for her collaboration in the translation work.

Notes

[1]   Through the 'Code de l'Urbanisme' and the 'Code de l'Environnement'.
[2]   This term is used to designate all persons who feel concerned by the future of a place, whether they live or work there, or even maintain symbolic or emotional ties with the place.
[3]   During the first National Urban Renewal programme (2003–13), successive annual evaluation reports show that, in general, residents were not involved in either the design or development stages of urban planning, housing and infrastructure projects.
[4]   Notably through regulatory incentives for local authorities to commit to *ecoquartiers*, or ecodistricts, implemented following the Grenelle Environmental Forum in 2007.
[5]   By 'culture', we refer to a structure that organises actions in the function of contextualised political and social values, as well as, in the domain of urbanism, a series of norms that allows different actors to recognise and be recognised as belonging to this field.
[6]   *À la recherche du bien commun territorial*, *Urbanisme*, Hors Série no 52, March 2015.

References

Allmendinger, P. (2002) *Planning theory*, Basingstoke: Palgrave Macmilan

Bacqué, M.-H. and Gauthier, M. (2011) 'Participation, urbanisme et études urbaines', *Participations*, vol 1, no 1, pp 36–66.

Bacqué, M.-H. and Mechmache, M. (2013) 'Participation des habitants: le pouvoir d'agir des citoyens', report for the Ministry for Urban Affairs, July. Available at: http://www.territoires.gouv.fr/spip.php?article3494

Bacqué, M.-H., Sintomer, Y. and Rey, H. (eds) (2005) *Gestion urbaine de proximité et démocratie participative*, Paris: La Découverte.

Berke, P. (2002) 'Does sustainable development offer a new direction for planning? Challenges for the twenty-first century', *Journal of Planning Literature*, vol 17, no 1, pp 21–36.

Blondiaux, L. (2005) 'L'idée de démocratie participative. Enjeux, impensés et questions récurrentes', in M.-H. Bacqué and Y. Sintomer (eds) *La démocratie participative, histoire et généalogie*, Paris: La Découverte.

Bourdin, A., Lefeuvre, M.-P. and Mele, P. (eds) (2006) *Les règles du jeu urbain – Entre le droit et la confiance*, Paris: Descartes et compagnie.

Carrel, M. (2014) *Faire Participer les habitants? Citoyenneté et pouvoir d'agir dans les quartiers populaires*, Paris: ENS Edition.

Castells, M. (1973) *Luttes urbaines et pouvoir politique*, Paris: Maspero.

Conan, M. (1997) *L'invention des lieux*, St-Maximin: Théétète.

Devaux, C. (2014) *L'habitat participatif, de l'initiative habitante à l'action publique*, Rennes: Presses Universitaires de Rennes.

Dimeglio, P. and Zetlaoui-Léger, J. (2007) 'Les rapports ambigus entre politiques et citoyens: le cas du réaménagement du quartier des Halles à Paris', *French Politics, Culture & Society*, vol 25, no 2, pp 115–40.

Foucault, M. (1975) *Surveiller et punir. Naissance de la prison*, Paris: Gallimard.

Gardesse, C. (2011) 'La "concertation" citoyenne dans le projet de réaménagement du quartier des Halles de Paris (2002–2010): les formes de la démocratisation de l'action publique en urbanisme et ses obstacles', Thèse de 3e cycle en Urbanisme, Aménagement, Politiques Urbaines, Dir. J. Zetlaoui-Léger, Lab'Urba – Université Paris Est.

Gardesse, C. (2013) 'La double invisibilité des citoyens et de leurs expertises dans un dispositif participatif: le traitement de la dimension métropolitaine du site des Halles de Paris dans le projet de réaménagement du quartier, 2003–2010', in Ph. Hamman (ed) *Ville, frontière, participation : de la visibilité des processus démocratiques dans la Cité*, série 'Des textes et des lieux', Strasbourg: Editions Orizons, collection Universités.

Gardesse, C. and Grudet, I. (2015) 'Continuités et discontinuités de l'implication des habitants dans les écoquartiers: le cas de la Zac Pajol à Paris', *Développement durable et territoires*. Available at: https://developpementdurable.revues.org/10966

Lefebvre, H. (1968) *Le droit à la ville*, Paris: Anthropos.

Müller, P. (1992) 'Entre le local et l'Europe. La crise du modèle français des politiques publiques', *Revue Française de Science politique*, vol 42, no 2, pp 275–97.

Renaud, V. (2014) *Fabrication et usage des* écoquartiers. *Essai critique sur la généralisation de l'aménagement durable en France*, Lausanne: Presses polytechniques et universitaires romandes.

Rosanvallon, P. (2008) *La légitimité démocratique, les théories de l'intérêt général*, Paris: Seuil.

Schön, D. (1983) *The reflective practitioner*, San Francisco, CA: Jossey-Bass Publishers.

Wates, N. (2000) *The community planning handbook*, London: Earthscan.

Zetlaoui-Léger, J. (2015) 'Invention et réinvention de la "programmation generative" des projets: une opportunité de collaboration entre architecture et SHS pour des modes d'habiter "durables"', Revue CLARA, no 3, Université Libre de Bruxelles, pp 101–14.

Zetlaoui-Léger, J., Fenker, M. and Gardesse, C. (2015) 'La participation citoyenne dans les projets d'écoquartiers en France: quels "leviers d'expérimentation"?', in L. Mermet and D. Salles (eds) *Environnement et transition* écologique, Brussels: Éditions De Boeck.

THIRTEEN

Localism and neighbourhood planning in Australian public policy and governance

Paul Burton

Introduction

Localism is often used in confusing and contradictory ways in Australian political debate and policy discourse. While many state and territory governments extol the virtues of devolving responsibility for planning and service delivery down to local governments, they show no sign of relinquishing their constitutional authority over local government or of pressing for further devolution to more localised communities. State and territory governments continue to exercise their constitutional authority over local government in regulating their powers, responsibilities and finances, and, most symbolically, in enforcing the amalgamation of local councils in the name of efficiency and effectiveness, often in the face of staunch opposition from the councils concerned (Brown and Bellamy, 2006; Kembray, 2015; Sansom, 2015). While this may frame localism as the application of the subsidiarity principle in practice, it also reflects an increasingly complex system of multi-level governance based on a distinctive Australian system of federalism. This system does not yet give any constitutional recognition to local government, but it provokes considerable debate about overlapping responsibilities, bureaucratic duplication and cost-shifting. As most local governments in Australia cover relatively small populations, there is little or no political pressure for them to devolve powers and responsibilities to even more local levels, but this is not to say that they are not increasingly conscious of their statutory obligations and political commitments to develop more extensive and effective programmes of public participation and community engagement.

Paradoxically, while the colonial predecessors of the states and territories agreed to the formation of a federal Commonwealth of Australia in 1901 and those state and territory governments now determine the nature of local government in their jurisdictions, there are growing calls to resolve many of the problems of three-tier federalism by abolishing the states and territories in the name of localism (Twomey and Withers, 2007). However, it is unlikely that such a radical reform will gain much political traction in the foreseeable future.

Among the challenges for advocates of localism in Australia are the problems of political and bureaucratic capacity in an extremely diverse pattern of local governments, the nature of relations between levels of government and between adjoining councils, and problems of scale in a very large country with a relatively small but spatially concentrated population. This chapter explores these challenges, looking critically at the differences between the rhetoric and the reality of localism in practice. It uses examples drawn mainly from the state of Queensland, but places these in comparative context with other Australian and overseas experience.

Logics of localism

In their introduction to a special issue of *Policy Studies* on 'localism', Evans, Marsh and Stoker (2013a) propose a threefold classification of localism in Westminster-style democracies: representative, managerial and community-based. While these may be analytically distinct, they claim that, in practice, what counts is the particular mix of one or more of these types in any particular locality. They also suggest that of the three types, representative localism has tended to dominate media and public debate as it is preoccupied with electoral competition and the success or failure of candidates, parties or factions (Evans, Marsh and Stoker, 2013b). This is certainly the case in Australia, where extensive and often intense media scrutiny is concentrated on the federal and state levels of government and only occasionally on local levels, although the political machinations and performance of local government remain a staple of local newspaper coverage. One could, in fact, advance an argument of exceptionalism in which local governments only receive media attention outside of their locality when faced with extraordinary events such as natural disasters (in Australia, typically floods or bushfires) or instances of political corruption or malfeasance, although this is not, of course, an argument about local government confined to Australia. Finally, political leadership in Australian local government is subject to significant variation, with the leaders of local councils (typically called mayors) directly elected in some places and selected from among the set of local councillors in others. The legitimacy and efficacy of these different arrangements remains subject to debate, but some of the larger urban councils are moving closer to the Queensland model of requiring all to have directly elected mayors (Burton, forthcoming).

Managerial localism consists of the delegation of some powers and responsibilities from superordinate to subordinate bodies, within a specific regulatory framework. In Australia, this, in fact, characterises the entire system of local government in which powers and responsibilities given to local authorities could be taken away by state and territory governments if they choose. In Queensland, for example, a set of Priority Development Areas (PDAs) has been established by the state government, with a streamlined and focused approach to development assessment to stimulate localised economic growth. PDAs are not imposed on local governments against their will and, in most cases, are actively sought by them, but they can involve the loss of development assessment powers in the designated area. The operation of these PDAs is critically reviewed later in this chapter.

The third stand of localism is described by Evans et al as 'community localism' and entails the devolution of certain rights and responsibilities by government bodies directly to citizens as individuals and in groups. Although there may be instances of this in some European countries (Kersting and Vetter, 2013), it is not commonplace in Australia. State and territory governments can conduct referendums and non-binding plebiscites, which can be seen as particular instances of devolution in an otherwise representative system of government, but these are not common. Public participation or community engagement in certain aspects of local service planning and, of course, in land use and development planning is much more widespread. Again, this often takes the form of bilateral engagement between individual citizens and government representatives when responding to policy or development proposals or completing local opinion surveys, but it sometimes involves more collective forms. At the local level, public meetings are commonplace while more structured events such as focus groups or design charettes are less common but growing in popularity. Collective visioning events are sometimes organised at the state or territory level, and in 2013, the Queensland government of Premier Campbell Newman embarked on an extensive programme of community engagement. In preparing the Queensland plan, the government held a variety of events, including two major summits at which hundreds of people were invited to participate in preparing a shared vision for the state. The government claimed that 'it resulted in the largest community engagement activity of its kind ever undertaken in Queensland with individuals and groups from every corner of the state taking part' (State of Queensland, 2014) but, for some, it was an expensive exercise in manipulation that occupied one of the lowest rungs on Arnstein's (1969) ladder of participation (Remeikis, 2015). At the federal level, the government of Prime Minister Kevin Rudd held the Australia 2020 Summit in April 2008 to 'help shape a long term strategy for the nation's future'. This saw 1,000 of 'Australia's brightest minds' gather to discuss future prospects and priorities across 10 policy fields and, again, represented a collective form of public participation, but one that again was highly controlled in terms of its membership and agenda.

A brief history of local government in Australia

While local governments prefigured Australian state and territory governments and, indeed, the federal government of Australia, they now constitute the least powerful of all three levels of government and are dependent on their respective state or territory governments for their continued existence and the definition of their powers.

The first directly elected local council was formed in 1840 with the creation of the Adelaide Corporation to manage the affairs of that emerging city of free settlers. However, within three years, it had been suspended and the city was subsequently run by a small group of Aldermen commissioned by the colonial government. Morton (1996) calls this the beginning of a 'continuously abrasive relationship' between local, state and federal governments in South Australia. Across the country at large, and across the decades, this relationship between the three levels of government has never been entirely harmonious, and the latest attempt to secure 'financial' recognition for local government in the Constitution foundered (as described in the following) in the aftermath of the election of the Coalition federal government in 2013.

Local governments in Australia have typically been given, but have also embraced, what might be termed a minimalist position: collecting local rates to provide basic but important local services and facilities, such as the maintenance of roads and bridges, as well as the collection and disposal of waste. These can be described as mainly property-based rather than social services and reflect the fact that the liability to pay rates and the right to vote were tied initially to property ownership and therefore reflected the interests and needs of property-owners. However, throughout the 20th century, the role and scope of local government steadily expanded, first through the acquisition of powers to regulate development and then through providing more by way of social services to meet the needs of the full range of its local citizens. There remains, nevertheless, a tension between those wishing to limit the powers and hence the revenue-raising obligations of local government and those promoting greater local government intervention across a broader spectrum of local activities.

In comparison with local governments in the UK, Australian local governments are much more limited in their scope, with responsibility for education, social services, health, housing and policing all resting with state and territory governments. As these are all services that have a distinctly local dimension, local councils are not well placed to present themselves as the self-evident institutions of localism. This is not to say that many councils do not pursue these ambitions or that they are not seen in this light, but they are doing so without the opportunity or responsibility to intervene in a number of areas that are usually associated with localism in other settings.

Politically, Australian local government is characterised as much by parochialism as by localism and while there is little evidence of concerted and systematic attempts to give more power to the people in localities, in most cases, there is an enduring commitment among local politicians to their locality. In other words, many local councillors see themselves as the principal conduit of local opinion and remain suspicious of public participation and community engagement initiatives that appear (to them at least) to have the potential to undermine their role and responsibility as the foremost and formal representatives of the people of their area. Some of the larger councils have developed more systematic approaches to neighbourhood-level planning, but it is important to remember that many councils in Australia serve very small populations, often scattered over very large areas, and that notions of neighbourhood politics developed in metropolitan areas may not apply in remote and rural areas.

Nor is there evidence of any concerted campaign in Australia to transfer statutory responsibilities from the state and territory to more local levels, either the local government or even smaller spatial scales. The Australian Local Government Association (ALGA) is the peak national body for local government and is a member of one of the important national intergovernmental bodies – the Council of Australian Governments (COAG), which brings together the prime minister, all premiers and chief ministers of states and territories and the president of ALGA. ALGA has campaigned for a number of years for local government to be recognised in the Constitution. Following recent High Court rulings, the constitutional authority for the federal government to make payments to local government has been called into question. This is significant as local governments claim their ability to meet their statutory obligations, let alone pursue additional local goals, is now severely compromised by a structural funding problem. ALGA presents their case for this reform as follows:

> Of course, councils can't do the job of meeting the community's needs on their own. Local government must work in partnership with the other two levels of government – the Federal Government and the States and Territories – to deliver services and infrastructure at the local level. Providing the increasing range of services expected by the community is often beyond the limited resources of local communities, local ratepayers and therefore most councils. Grants from other levels of government are critical. And it is reasonable to expect that some of the taxes paid to the State and the Federal Government will be used to provide services and infrastructure at the local level. (ALGA, 2012, p 2)

Australian local governments have become increasingly reliant in recent years on federal grant programmes to cover local investment, especially in road maintenance and improvement. The constitutional standing of some of these funding regimes has been called into question (Hogg and Lawson, 2014), and this has provided the impetus for a campaign to change the Constitution to recognise the existence of local government and thereby allow it to receive grants directly from the federal government. In 2007, newly elected Prime Minister Kevin Rudd promised to progress the issue of constitutional recognition, and considerable effort by an ALGA Expert Panel and a Parliamentary Joint Select Committee on Constitutional Recognition saw the passage of the Constitution Alteration (Local Government Bill) 2013, with a referendum scheduled to occur in the latter half of that year. The reinstatement of Kevin Rudd as leader of the Australian Labor Party and hence as prime minister (replacing Julia Gillard) in June 2013 saw a snap election called for September that effectively rendered a referendum impossible in its intended time frame. The Coalition government led by Tony Abbott elected in September 2013 subsequently announced that it would not pursue a referendum of this type in the foreseeable future and the new (September 2015) Coalition government led by Prime Minister Malcolm Turnbull has given no indication to date that this will be a priority in its policy agenda.

Thus, an important element of any broader movement to strengthen the position of local government in Australia and to practically advance a localist agenda has been dropped and is unlikely to become a priority of any federal government in the foreseeable future. This is not to say that the federal government does not continue to provide financial support to local government across the country according to the principle of horizontal fiscal equalisation. In Queensland, for example, AU$450 million of (federal) Financial Assistance Grant was received by all 77 local government bodies in the state in 2015/16, with the city of Gold Coast receiving AU$18.4 million and Brisbane receiving AU$38.3 million, but these remain relatively small components of their total budgets. However, for smaller councils and especially those with small populations compared to their land areas, these Commonwealth funds can represent a more significant source of assistance in maintaining a dispersed network of minor roads and bridges vulnerable to the effects of flooding.

Localism in practice: Australian cases

One of the overriding features of Australian local government is its variety, as each state and territory has its own legislative base for local government, its own traditions and history, and a distinctive geography over which their local government system must operate. It is, therefore, unwise to see localism in Australia in general or national terms, and important to appreciate the significant variation across the states and territories. This section presents four short case studies of localism in practice drawn principally from one state, Queensland, with one from the Northern Territory. The Queensland cases illustrate different manifestations of localism: how parts of some local government jurisdictions are deemed worthy of special forms of intervention; the development of neighbourhood planning mechanisms in an uncharacteristically unified large metropolitan council; and the allocation of substantial budgets to divisional councillors in another large city. The Northern Territory case also touches on important issues of indigenous local politics, which are often neglected in Australian local government studies (Morton, 2012).

Priority Development Areas in Queensland

The Economic Development Act 2012 enables the Queensland government to work with local governments in the state to promote economic development for the benefit of local communities. One way it does this is through the designation of PDAs for particular localities, which results in the removal of the designated area from the provisions of the Sustainable Planning Act 2009 (SPA) and its successors. In short, the designated area becomes subject to a different, more streamlined planning regime that has fewer regulatory requirements than would apply under the SPA. Responsibility for preparing and implementing plans in a PDA can be delegated by the Queensland minister for economic development to any one of a number of bodies, including a local representative committee or the local council in whose area the PDA falls. The purpose of this initiative, which has some similarities with urban development corporations in other parts of Australia and overseas, is to encourage local economic development by speeding up the assessment process and relaxing regulations. As an explanatory brochure published by Economic Development Queensland (the state government body that oversees this process) says:

> The process for development assessment differs significantly between the Economic Development (ED) Act and SPA, due to the removal of the state agency referral process and appeals against development assessment decisions under the ED Act. The removal of state agency referrals is recognition of the collaboration with state agencies during the plan making process to resolve issues. The lack of an appeals process is to avoid potential delays to development within PDAs, which undermines the objectives of the ED Act to facilitate economic development. (EDQ, 2015, p 3)

The logic of this initiative is that the declaration of a PDA will accelerate development, provide greater certainty to the property market, unlock the development potential of government land in some cases and help particular major projects succeed. In the city of Gold Coast, for example, two PDAs have been declared: for the neighbourhood of Southport, which the city council recently designated as its official central business district; and for the old Parklands showgrounds next to Griffith University's Gold Coast campus, which will become the Athletes Village for the 2018 Commonwealth Games and subsequently part of the Gold Coast Health and Knowledge Precinct. Whereas the Parklands PDA is managed by Economic Development Queensland, planning in the Southport PDA remains the responsibility of a specialist team within the City of Gold Coast Council.

As noted earlier, what makes PDAs particularly noteworthy is the fact that responsibility for managing each one can and does vary according to local circumstances and that, in some cases, responsibility is retained by the local council. Indeed, PDAs are only declared with the support of local councils and are not imposed on them by the state government. In practice, if PDAs work in accordance with their principles, then residents will have lost some capacity to influence patterns of development in their locality as the PDA regime restricts third-party appeal rights and shortens the period in which development applications must be processed. To date, 26 PDAs have been declared and while many relate to large greenfield sites with few existing residents, there is little or no evidence of concerted opposition to them in general or in particular places and, in many cases, the general public is likely to be unaware of their existence. While the logic of their existence is based on a critique of the efficacy of normal local government planning regimes, local councils do not appear unduly concerned with PDAs either and tend to see them as useful vehicles for expediting development and growth in their area. In other words, a pragmatic acceptance of the benefits of local economic development typically outweighs any concern about the lack of local autonomy.

Neighbourhood planning in Brisbane

'Neighbourhood planning' is not a commonplace term or indeed one that is used with any degree of consistency across Australia. Sometimes, it refers to the preparation of local area plans within cities, which usually have some statutory weight and are used in the assessment of development applications; sometimes, it refers to the more general process of preparing urban design guidelines for particular neighbourhoods. It rarely refers to more comprehensive programmes of neighbourhood (or sub-municipality) planning for a range of local services, as it does in the UK and some other European countries. One exception to this is the process of neighbourhood planning in Brisbane.

In Brisbane, the city council decides which neighbourhoods within the city should have their own neighbourhood plan, and once approved, these become part of the panoply of plans regulating development across the city. So, the Brisbane City Plan 2014 provides the overall planning framework for the whole city over a 20-year period but this is supplemented by 72 neighbourhood plans. These neighbourhood plans are principally concerned with land-use planning, and development assessment addresses social, economic or environmental objectives mainly through land-use planning processes rather than through more direct intervention and spending programmes. Neighbourhood plans must be consistent with the City Plan, which always takes precedence in any disputes, just as city plans must be consistent with the principles of any state plan and remain constitutionally subservient to it.

Public participation and community engagement principles are certainly applied in this neighbourhood planning processes as there is a statutory obligation to do so. In Brisbane and elsewhere, some councils approach these public participation obligations enthusiastically and imaginatively, but not all do so. While there is little empirical and comparative research on the impact of public participation in practice, it is likely that variation in enthusiasm and imagination reflects a number of factors. Local councillors and mayors who are more politically mature and secure in their roles are more likely to see the benefits of public participation in local policy and decision-making, while others may see it as a threat to their standing and role as representatives. The great variation in size and, hence, capacity of local councils also influences their disposition towards public participation beyond the minimal statutory obligations and often relies on the enthusiasm of one or more key individuals. Of course, the existence of different levels or spatial scales of planning (neighbourhood and city-wide) also typically leads to different scales of participation and engagement and, hence, to the possibility of conflicting outcomes of these processes. In Brisbane, this has seen public debate and political conflict around competing planning principles that have emerged from neighbourhood and city-wide planning and participatory processes (McKechnie, 2015) and illustrates how greater participation does not necessarily lead to greater consensus in policy and decision-making processes.

Divisional budgets in the city of Gold Coast

Paradoxically, in most (but not all) local government areas, councillors are elected to represent local divisions and only mayors are elected at large with an unambiguous responsibility to take a strategic view of their whole jurisdiction. Divisional councillors are, of course, also expected to act in the best interests of the council area as a whole but, in practice, there are often incentives to behave parochially. In the city of Gold Coast, for example, each of the 14 divisional councillors is allocated an annual divisional budget (currently worth approximately AU$700,000) to spend on local projects that might otherwise fail to receive support from city-wide budgets. While this undoubtedly gives divisional councillors significant capacity to respond to local needs and issues, and, hence, to practice localism, it also fosters concerns about the hoarding of funds and pork-barrelling that are frequently aired in the local media. Councillors, unsurprisingly, see things rather differently and speak of the value of these funds in balancing the 'whole-of-city' perspective that characterises most of their work. Indeed, in its latest budget, the city council agreed to fund a city-wide kerbside collection programme that had previously only been offered in some areas, and which had been supported by some councillors from their divisional budgets.

Supershires in the Northern Territory

The Northern Territory only achieved a degree of self-government in 1978 when the Northern Territory Legislative Assembly was granted a set of delegated powers and responsibilities by the Commonwealth Parliament. One of its first actions was to pass a local government act to create a new system of local government comprising municipal councils in urban areas and a disparate set of 'community government councils' elsewhere in what is a very large but sparsely populated jurisdiction. The Northern Territory differs from the other states and territories in that almost 30% of its population of 231,000 consists of indigenous people, compared with 3% for the whole of Australia (ABS, 2013). The politics of local government in the Northern Territory is, therefore, inextricably a politics of indigeneity and perennial settler attitudes to place, size and efficiency in the delivery of services often run counter to indigenous perspectives and principles.

In the name of greater efficiency and in response to increasing concerns with the 'highly dispersed and differentiated system of local government', in which up to half the remote (indigenous) area councils were judged to be high-risk or dysfunctional, a simpler system was proposed comprising municipal councils for the main towns and cities and new 'regional shires' for the rest of the territory (Sanders, 2013, p 477). In late 2008, seven large remote area shires, or 'supershires', had been fully established but, as Sanders (2013) argues, for two main reasons, these came to represent a 'loss of localism'. First, in four of the new shires in the south of the territory, the headquarters of the councils were located outside their own boundary. Second, a substantial democratic deficit emerged as a repeating single-member election system saw councillors in some wards elected from a very small number of settlements while many more remote settlements were unrepresented. Moreover, the new system saw a clarification of the role of elected councillors vis-a-vis appointed officers in which the direct relationship that had previously existed was transformed into one based on a more traditional separation of powers between policymaking and implementation. Sanders (2013, p 485) suggests that this contributed to some representatives disengaging from the bodies to which they were elected because they were no longer able to work closely with officers in dealing with local issues and trying to solve the problems of local residents. It also reflects a possible point of difference between settler and indigenous perspectives on the nature of local government and the relations between elected and appointed officials.

Conclusions

In countries like the UK, an enduring challenge for territorial politics has been to mount a plausible case for the creation of a new tier of government between the central and the local, one that balances arguments about efficiency with more subjective notions of regional identity, sense of attachment and engagement with government (Young et al, 1996). To date, this has proved impossible and the 'regional agenda' appears to have all but disappeared. Instead, arguments for giving greater power to local governments and for devolving significant power and responsibility to even lower levels, such as neighbourhoods or parishes, have achieved greater prominence and political traction.

In Australia, this regional challenge was met, constitutionally at least, in the creation of the states and territories and in their agreement at the start of the 20th century to form a federal government to preside over the Commonwealth of Australia. This three-tier system provides, in theory at least, the opportunity to distribute responsibilities for government among the different tiers in such a way as to reflect efficiencies and economies of scale in the delivery of services and to maintain a sense of attachment and allegiance to long-standing territorial entities. However, in practice, there is widespread public dissatisfaction with contemporary Australian federalism and a belief that political responsibilities are blurred, costs are shifted and services duplicated or avoided because of this arrangement. There is no evidence that the public at large would like to see the introduction of a fourth tier of government through any process of giving more powers and responsibilities to neighbourhood-scale entities. The Australian Constitutional Values Survey suggests that, in general, Australians are happy with their local governments retaining a comparatively minimalist position, focusing on 'roads, rates and rubbish', and not taking on an expanded role that might significantly test their competence and capacity (Brown, 2014). Whether this is also the case for large metropolitan councils such as Brisbane and the Gold Coast (Burton, 2014) and whether the plethora of small councils that exist in most of the capital cities should be amalgamated is not so clear at this stage.

The case studies presented earlier highlight a number of other enduring issues associated with Australian localism, or, perhaps more accurately, with relations between different levels of government in which the precise degree of devolution of powers and responsibilities between levels is, to some extent, negotiable. These issues include the degree of trust that exists between levels of government, which, in turn, is related to perceptions of competence and capacity, as well as to the size and efficiency of governmental units and the extent to which these units promote a sense of attachment and democratic engagement (Markus, 2014; Edelman, 2014). There is a widespread sense that local councils should do all they can to contain local taxation in the form of rates, and building economies of scale through amalgamation is one way, albeit contested (Byrnes and Dollery, 2002), of achieving this. On the other hand, proposals to amalgamate local councils in the name of greater efficiency often bring to the surface strong local feelings about the importance of place and, in some cases, the de-amalgamation of councils is pursued even when local citizens are made aware of the significant costs of doing so (Drew and Dollery, 2014). Similarly, there is very little prospect of the state capital cities of Sydney, Melbourne, Perth or Adelaide choosing to take the path adopted by Queensland in 1925 when the City of Brisbane was formed through the merger of 20 previously separate local authorities. Although the city council's jurisdiction now includes only half the population resident within the greater metropolitan area (the Greater Capital City Statistical Area), it remains the only state capital city in Australia with a relatively consolidated council and stands in contrast to Sydney (with 35 councils) and Melbourne (with 28).

There are few calls for the creation of new forms of neighbourhood governance at the sub-municipal level; indeed, some have even argued that the widespread practice of electing local councillors for divisions (or wards) on a first-past-the-post basis should be replaced by elections at large using some form of proportional voting so as to avoid what is seen as an unduly parochial aspect of Australian local government (Tan and Grant, 2013). This is not to say that many local citizens would not welcome a more active role in local politics and decision-making through programmes of community engagement. However, as noted earlier, the benefits of greater public participation and community engagement in local governance remain, in Australia as elsewhere, mostly articles of faith rather than empirical certainties (Burton, 2009).

In summary, the enthusiastic application of localism and neighbourhood planning seen in the UK and some other European countries is not so evident in Australia. This may be because of the substantial variety in scale and capacity among Australian local governments and because each of the eight states and territories has its own local government legislative framework. The balance of powers and responsibilities is also different in the three-tier Australian system and local governments typically have a much more narrow range of responsibilities than their European counterparts. While public trust in federal and state governments is affected (often adversely) by volatility in leadership and control, and there is widespread dissatisfaction with duplication and cost-shifting between the different levels of government, there has not been a pronounced and concerted attempt to devolve power to the people either at the local government level or even closer to them at the neighbourhood level. Localism is, therefore, a principle yet to be applied with any degree of enthusiasm in Australia.

References

ABS (Australian Bureau of Statistics) (2013) 'Estimates of Aboriginal and Torres Strait Islander Australians, June 2011'. Available at: http://www.abs.gov.au/ausstats/abs@.nsf/mf/3238.0.55.001 (accessed 5 October 2015).

ALGA (Australian Local Government Association) (2012) 'The case for change: why local government needs to be in the Australian constitution'. Available at: http://councilreferendum.com.au/site/misc/alga_cr/downloads/COUNCIL_RESOURCES/ALGA_CaseForChange_WEB%20VERSION.pdf

Arnstein, R. (1969) 'A ladder of citizen participation', *Journal of the American Institute of Planning*, vol 35, no 4, pp 216–24.

Brown, A.J. (2014) 'Australian constitutional values survey 2014'. Available at: https://www.griffith.edu.au/__data/assets/pdf_file/0015/653100/Constitutional-Values-Survey-Oct-2014Results-2.pdf

Brown, A.J. and Bellamy, J. (eds) (2006) *Federalism and regionalism in Australia: New approaches, new institutions*, Canberra: ANU E Press.

Burton, P. (2009) 'Conceptual, theoretical and practical issues in measuring the benefits of public participation', *Evaluation*, vol 15, no 3, pp 263–84.

Burton, P. (2014) 'From white shoes to bold futures: the neoliberalisation of local government in an Australian city?', *Urban Studies*, vol 51, no 15, pp 3233–49.

Burton, P. (forthcoming) 'Popular leaders or rats in the ranks? Political leadership in Australian cities', in D. Sweeting (ed) *Directly elected mayors in urban governance: Impact and practice*, Bristol: The Policy Press.

Byrnes, J. and Dollery, B. (2002) *Do economies of scale exist in Australian local government? A review of the empirical evidence*, Working Paper Series in Economics 2002-2, Armidale: University of New England.

Drew, J. and Dollery, B. (2014) 'Separation anxiety: an empirical evaluation of the Australian Sunshine Coast Regional Council de-amalgamation', *Public Money & Management*, vol 34, no 3, pp 213–20.

Edelman (2014) 'Edelman trust barometer executive summary'. Available at: http://www.edelman.com/insights/intellectual-property/2014-edelman-trust-barometer/about-trust/executive-summary/

EDQ (Economic Development Queensland) (2015) *Introduction to priority development areas*, Brisbane: Department of Infrastructure, Local Government and Planning.

Evans, M., Marsh, D. and Stoker, G. (2013a) 'Understanding localism', *Policy Studies*, vol 34, no 4, pp 401–7.

Evans, M., Stoker, G. and Marsh, D. (2013b) 'In conclusion: localism in the present and the future', *Policy Studies*, vol 34, nos 5/6, pp 612–17.

Hogg, M. and Lawson, C. (2014) 'The watershed for Commonwealth appropriation and spending after Pape and Williams?', *Australian Journal of Administrative Law*, vol 21, pp 145–55.

Kembray, M. (2015) 'Council mergers: expert adviser Graham Sansom slams merger proposals', *Sydney Morning Herald (online edition)*, 20 December. Available at: http://www.smh.com.au/nsw/council-mergers-expert-adviser-graham-sansom-slams-merger-proposals-20151218-glrg0o.html (accessed 22 December 2015).

Kersting, N. and Vetter, A. (2013) *Reforming local government in Europe: Closing the gap between democracy and efficiency*, Wiesbaden: Springer.

Markus, A. (2014) *Trust in the Australian political system*, Papers on Parliament No. 62, Canberra: Parliament of Australia.

McKechnie, K. (2015) 'Brisbane City Council criticised over breaching own planning requirements', *ABC News website*, 4 May. Available at: http://www.abc.net.au/news/2015-05-04/brisbane-city-council-criticised-over-planning-requirements/6444070 (accessed 23 December 2015).

Morton, A. (2012) *Role and expectations of rural-remote and indigenous local government*, Sydney: Australian Centre of Excellence for Local Government, University of Technology.

Morton, P. (1996) *After light: A history of the city of Adelaide and its council, 1878–1928*, Adelaide: Wakefield Press.

Remeikis, A. (2015) 'Jackie Trad planning the plan to plan our future', *Brisbane Times (online edition)*, 28 July. Available at: http://www. brisbanetimes.com.au/queensland/jackie-trad-planning-the-plan-to-plan-our-future-20150728-gilxm3.html (accessed 22 December 2015).

Sanders, W. (2013) 'Losing localism, constraining councillors: why the Northern Territory supershires are struggling', *Policy Studies*, vol 34, no 4, pp 474–90.

Sansom, M. (2015) 'NSW council sackings threat real: local government expert', *Government News (online edition)*, 11 November. Available at: http://www.governmentnews.com.au/2015/11/nsw-council-sackings-threat-real-local-government-expert/ (accessed 22 December 2015).

State of Queensland (2014) *The Queensland Plan*, Brisbane: Queensland Government.

Tan, S.F. and Grant, B. (2013) *Local representation in Australia: A review of the legislation and the literature*, Sydney: Australian Centre of Excellence for Local Government, University of Technology.

Twomey, A. and Withers, G. (2007) *Australia's federal future: Delivering growth and prosperity*, Federalist Paper 1, Sydney: Council for the Australian Federation.

Young, K., Gosschalk, B. and Hatter, W. (1996) *In search of community identity*, York: Joseph Rowntree Foundation.

FOURTEEN

The many lives of neighbourhood planning in the US: much ado about something?

Larry Bennett

Introduction

Neighbourhood planning in the US can be traced to the settlement house movement at the turn of the 20th century. Over the course of subsequent decades, the aims of and mechanisms to further neighbourhood planning have shifted substantially. Indeed, in the last quarter-century, new forms of local political and civic action have seemed to supplant neighbourhood *planning* as a principal means of linking citizens and local government officials.

However, in one key respect, the evolution of neighbourhood planning in the US parallels the experience of the UK, as well as the other countries profiled in this volume. The fundamental purpose of neighbourhood planning and its variations can be construed, alternatively, in minimalist or more expansive terms. In the minimalist sense, neighbourhood planning serves cities and other localities by bringing professional planners and local residents together to craft physical plans or organise social action in a way that is responsive to local particularities. Planning that is responsive to local needs and wishes is presumably able to regulate land uses, site public facilities and deliver social services in a manner that best serves the well-being of local communities. The expansive vision of neighbourhood planning presumes that more is at stake than carefully sited public facilities or the equitable geographic distribution of hazardous land uses. In this view, neighbourhood planning is a tool for activating citizens, inducing them to study complicated issues and enabling them to engage in what political scientist Archon Fung (Fung, 2004; Fagotto and Fung, 2006) calls 'empowered participation'.

In the pages to follow, I first discuss the evolution of neighbourhood planning techniques in the US. This portion of the chapter emphasises the importance of the USA's federal system of government in generating a multitude of structural approaches to neighbourhood planning. In the early post-Second World War era, national initiatives such as Urban Renewal and the Community Action Program mandated neighbourhood consultation in the shaping and implementation of policy. Although the effectiveness of these consultative measures was the subject of much debate, they did seed many subsequent efforts to link planning and citizen participation. The latter part of this 20th-century policy tour touches on initiatives that have been mounted either by municipal governments or through the efforts of locally based activist movements. The remainder of the chapter profiles three contemporary variants of neighbourhood planning: what might be characterised as 'classic' neighbourhood planning by Portland, Oregon's neighbourhood council and New York City's community board systems; Chicago's community policing initiative; and the fashioning of community benefits agreements (CBAs) in several Californian cities. I conclude by reconsidering the most expansive inflection of the expansive view of neighbourhood planning: that neighbourhood planning can serve as a platform for achieving substantial social transformation.

US neighbourhood planning across the decades

Neighbourhood planning in the US, one could say, began in Britain. In 1888, a young Jane Addams, still on the trail of her life's calling, visited Samuel and Henrietta Barnett's pioneering Toynbee Hall in the East End of London. Within a few years, Addams had founded Hull House on Chicago's West Side, an exemplar of the US settlement house movement, which planted institutions in other industrial metropolises such as Boston, New York and Philadelphia. US settlement house 'residents', as they were called, sought to uplift immigrant neighbourhoods through programmes that encouraged neighbourly conviviality, celebrated and sought to retain immigrants' cultural heritage, but also served to 'Americanise' these urban newcomers. Beyond these direct efforts to serve local populations, settlements were also pioneers in data collection and local social analysis, typically using such information and insight to advocate expenditures on neighbourhood infrastructure and facilities by municipal governments (Knight, 2005, pp 275, 326).

Planning scholars William Rohe and Lauren Gates (1985, p 20) have described the settlements as 'established by the upper class to aid the lower class', but, in fact, key figures in the settlement movement such as Addams came from the 'middling' ranks of US society, often from communities at some distance from the burgeoning industrial centres (Davis, 1967, pp 33–9). Indeed, those settlement residents bear a distinct demographic resemblance to the cohort of younger Americans who have flocked to New Orleans following the Hurricane Katrina catastrophe (Goodman, 2014; Rivlin, 2015, pp 276–7).

However, Rohe and Gates's account of early neighbourhood planning surely is correct on another point: the work of settlement houses was a precursor to neighbourhood planning as that notion is understood today. *Professional* neighbourhood planning dates from the 1920s, particularly as advocated by Clarence Perry, whose notion of the 'neighbourhood unit' became an important component of the intellectual apparatus cobbled together by the nascent US city planning profession. As described by historian Robert Wojtowicz (1998, p 121):

> Perry's ideal neighbourhood unit was to be relatively self-contained, having its own residences, shops, churches, and recreational facilities. An elementary school was to be located strategically at its center with no house more than a half-mile distant from the school.

In effect, the residential portions of cities were to be assembled from such individual 'modules'. This assembling, by the way, would be the work of planners, other city officials and the real-estate interests actually building residential communities. As to the relationship between these elites and the residents of existing or planned neighbourhoods, Rohe and Gates (1985, p 29) describe it as 'paternalistic': the emergent planning profession was applying principles that would yield well-functioning cities. There was no expectation of dialogue between local knowledge and trained expertise.

In fact, the decade and a half spanning the 1930s into the mid-1940s was not a boom period for either city planning in general or neighbourhood planning in particular. The Great Depression brought to a halt residential construction in the US, and though the industrial mobilisation and war effort of the early 1940s called for much planning, *city* planning was not a priority. There is one notable exception to this generalisation. The three 'Greenbelt' towns developed by the Franklin Roosevelt administration during the 1930s were quite explicitly structured according to neighbourhood unit principles (Scott, 1971, pp 338–41). However, the Greenbelt towns constituted a 'one-off' effort. The US national government never became a large-scale, direct producer of housing, and the Greenbelt towns had little or no impact on local planning across the country.

The federal housing acts of 1949 and 1954, which jointly defined the Urban Renewal programme, did give a kick-start to both the US planning profession and neighbourhood planning. The 1954 legislation, in particular, through its commitment to residential neighbourhood revitalisation via 'conservation' – some clearance of properties, but also fiscal and other inducements to support private property improvement – brought neighbourhood planning to the centre of the nationwide effort to revitalise central cities:

> The rehabilitation game introduces neighbourhood people as the players with whom the redevelopment authority must negotiate. A successful rehabilitation project requires the involvement of enough residents to ensure that public investment in the renewal area will be matched by significant investment from the local community. Moreover, the federal requirement that a public hearing be held by the LPA [local public agency] to enable citizens to express their views on the merits of the proposed renewal plan dictates that there be people in the neighbourhood sufficiently sold on the plan to stand up and support it at that hearing. (Keyes, 1969, pp 6–7)

In *The rehabilitation planning game* (Keyes, 1969), Langley Carleton Keyes Jr's three case studies of Boston neighbourhood conservation efforts demonstrate how fraught the effort to 'sell' local plans could be. Also, across the country, the twin traumas produced by Urban Renewal and the routing of interstate superhighways through central cities produced widespread political conflict. Critics of these projects excoriated them for unnecessarily destroying long-standing working-class communities and pushing African-Americans away from desirable central city commercial and residential areas. The reputation of the planning profession was seriously damaged by these imbroglios, as was the technocratic approach to neighbourhood planning – widely viewed as little more than the manipulative promotion of preconceived real-estate deals – as post-war cities seemed to single-mindedly recast their downtowns and near-downtown neighbourhoods as workspaces and playgrounds for the prosperous (Gans, 1965; Wilson, 1966; Mollenkopf, 1983; Fogelson, 2001, pp 317–80).

Nonetheless, the next major push for a variety of neighbourhood planning was once more a component of federal government policy, in this instance, the Johnson administration's War on Poverty of the mid-1960s. Determined to make his own mark on US public policy, Lyndon

Johnson was drawn to the 'community action' model of neighbourhood development. On the one hand, Johnson hoped to mount a domestic policy campaign that would not fire the wrath of fiscal conservatives. Budget-busting job creation through public infrastructure investment, for instance, was to be avoided. On the other hand, in several east coast cities, a series of small-scale neighbourhood development initiatives that had emphasised local resident participation and empowerment had won the admiration of, among others, Attorney General Robert F. Kennedy, the late President Kennedy's brother (Marris and Rein, 1967; Lemann, 1992, pp 123–9). As Johnson's policy team formulated what came to be known as the Community Action Program, an initiative directing federal funds to neighbourhood-based organisations in support of social services and, to some unspecified degree, local resident political mobilisation, a more emphatic vision emerged:

> The heart of the War on Poverty was an institutional critique rather than a program. Community action was the method for 'shaking the system' and forcing change on reluctant school administrators, welfare and employment service officials, and even settlement houses and Community Chest [a variety of citywide philanthropic funding] leaders ... 'the board ladies' and 'the bureaucrats'. (Katz, 1989, p 100)

The passage of the Economic Opportunity Act of 1964 was followed by the rapid formation of 'community action agencies' (CAAs) across the country. These local organisations typically recruited neighbourhood residents to their governing boards, and, in many cases, also hired locals to serve on their staffs. In the main, the CAAs developed neighbourhood improvement plans focusing on social services – job training, neighbourhood health clinics and legal aid offices – and they also sponsored other federally funded initiatives such as the pre-school Head Start programme. On occasion, they hired community organisers to, for instance, seek to empower local renters as a constituency advocating for improved landlord practices. Among municipal elites, the CAAs were profoundly unpopular: a few of them stirred up trouble, they *all* were viewed as diverting federal funds that could be better used by municipal officials and, worst of all, their formation coincided with the riot-disrupted mid-1960s (Cloward and Piven, 1974, pp 271–83; Self, 2003, pp 177–255). Across the US, mayors and city councillors accused the CAAs of fomenting civil unrest. During the last two years of the Johnson administration (ie within just a couple of years following its enactment), congressional support for the War on Poverty withered, and by the early 1970s, the Nixon administration had terminated the Community Action Program.

On the streets, US cities' turbulent 1960s could not be so easily halted. In many low-income neighbourhoods, CAAs or their organisational descendants managed to stay afloat even without federal funding. It is also a truism of the War on Poverty experience that though many CAAs struggled to have a measurable programmatic impact, they did birth cohorts of activists who, in subsequent years, would go on to influence neighbourhood and broader city politics. Possibly most consequentially, emerging trends such as deindustrialisation provoked neighbourhood activism in working-class areas that had not been the focus of War on Poverty efforts (Boyte, 1980).

During the 1970s, many US municipal governments – even as major federal initiatives such as Urban Renewal were scaled back – created neighbourhood advisory systems to, among other things, review large-scale physical development proposals, advise municipal officials regarding the dispersal of lingering federal aid programmes such as Community Development Block Grants or, more broadly, serve as vehicles for citizen–public official intercommunication.

At present, it is a safe generalisation that *many but not all* US cities have developed structures that allow local resident comment on proposed land-use matters and, to some degree, mandate local resident advice on future private and public physical development within the boundaries of their neighbourhoods (Scavo, 1993). There is much variation in the particulars of how neighbourhoods and the organisations representing them are determined and structurally organised (neighbourhood planning has become a municipally driven process, with municipal governance structures reflecting the variations to be found in the 50 states' constitutional and statutory enactments). It is a very safe generalisation to note that in the case of major land-use decision-making, the recommendations of local boards or councils are invariably *advisory*, as such, subject to reversal by city planning departments, citywide planning commissions or special-purpose districts such as airport and public transit authorities.

However, in addition, 'a funny thing happened' on the way to broadening citizen participation in planning and land-use decision-making, which is that since the 1960s, there has also been a noteworthy *functional* expansion of what neighbourhood residents in US cities can seek to influence or plan. Probably the most consequential of these participatory innovations has been the adoption by many cities of some form of public school decentralisation, through the creation either of multiple-school 'sub-districts' within a citywide system or, more radically, local councils that manage the affairs of each school within a citywide system (Ornstein, 1989).

Community policing is an innovation dating to the 1980s, which, in one form or another, has been widely adopted by US municipalities. One of its proponents has characterised its aims in the following way: 'The philosophy rested on giving individual officers ownership of a specific neighbourhood where they could work with people, as individuals and in groups, to address the community's priorities' (Bucqueroux, 2014). Community policing is often described as a problem-solving effort based on mutually respectful and ongoing communication between police officers and neighbourhood residents. While the ultimate aim is to enhance the security of urban neighbourhoods, 'along the way', so to speak, local issues such building abandonment or inadequate youth recreational facilities may well be addressed. The latter, obviously, overlaps with the kinds of issues typically falling under the rubric of community or neighbourhood planning.

In some respects, even farther afield than community policing from conventional neighbourhood planning is another emergent practice that, nevertheless, seeks to 'socialise' the positive impacts of private investment in neighbourhoods. This is what is known as the 'community benefits agreement' (CBA), a document negotiated between interests representing particular neighbourhoods and private investors (Parks and Warren, 2009). Among the typical 'benefits' that are specified by such agreements are job 'set-asides' (and/or training programmes) for local residents and affordable housing set-asides. The 'stick' employed by local coalitions of community and neighbourhood organisations, labour unions, and immigrants' rights groups to bring real-estate interests to the negotiating table has been the threat to oppose the development incentives (zoning exceptions, tax increment financing, etc) that many local governments use to 'sweeten' new real-estate investment. Actual neighbourhood, labour and immigrant mobilisation has been the political foundation for inducing otherwise unwilling negotiating partners to make community-directed job and housing commitments.

Neighbourhood planning in Portland and New York City

Collaborative neighbourhood planning in Portland – through which municipal officials work with neighbourhood residents on more or less equal terms – dates from 1974 when the city of Portland created the Office of Neighbourhood Associations (ONA). In the preceding decade, Portland had experienced a series of neighbourhood–

municipality confrontations over the latter's Urban Renewal and expressway plans. By 1974, a new city administration, led by Mayor Neil Goldschmidt, took to heart the complaints that had been articulated by neighbourhood activists and formalised a system of ongoing neighbourhood–municipal communication and collaboration (Abbott, 1983, pp 183–206). A striking feature of the formation of ONA (subsequently renamed the Office of Neighbourhood Involvement [ONI]) was the designation of existing neighbourhood organisations as the representatives for particular local areas within the city. Of the original network of approximately 30 local neighbourhood associations, historian Carl Abbott (1983, p 205) observes:

> Neighbourhood associations in the 1970s largely ignored the carefully defined neighbourhood units of the Comprehensive Development Plan when they set their own boundaries. The neighbourhoods on the 1966 map are compact and tidy units that float between arterial streets like the bubbles in a carpenter's level. The map of neighbourhood association boundaries maintained by ONA is an untidy hodgepodge. Several associations claim overlapping territories and still other sections of the city have no active associations.

The structural 'looseness' of Portland neighbourhood planning persists to this day. The municipal government recognises 95 neighbourhood associations, of which 93 are grouped into seven neighbourhood coalitions. Five of the seven neighbourhood coalitions are, effectively, independent units controlled by their constituent neighbourhood associations. In the wake of neighbourhood-level conflicts in the 1990s, two of the neighbourhood coalition offices were attached to the city government and municipal employees comprise their staffs (Leistner, 2008, p 5). At present, there are also 41 business district associations recognised by the municipal government (City of Portland ONI, 2015). ONI specifies its agenda by way of four initiatives: the Community Neighbourhood Involvement Center (CNIC); crime prevention; information and referral; and neighbourhood liveability services. CNIC accounts for approximately half of ONI's annual budget appropriation of US$8 million (City of Portland ONI, 2014), and, in particular, supports the seven neighbourhood coalitions and 95 recognised neighbourhood associations. A number of years ago, Portland neighbourhood activist and Fellow at the Portland State

University Center for Public Participation Paul Leistner (2008, p 7) typified ONI's neighbourhood planning work in the following way:

> Neighbourhood associations do a tremendous amount of good work in their communities. They organize neighbourhood cleanups, block parties, and community celebrations; they produce and distribute neighbourhood newsletters, host websites, hold forums on controversial issues, pursue community improvement projects, build relationships with other community groups, tap the wisdom and experience in the community, leverage community resources, and engage with city government to help shape city projects, policies, and programs.

As for the seven district coalitions, they 'provide a wide range of technical support for neighbourhood associations and a vehicle for neighbourhood activists to share experiences and work together on issues that transcend a single neighbourhood' (Leistner, 2008, p 7).

Neighbourhood planning in Portland has not been an unmitigated success. Leistner (2008, p 8) reports that there was a period from the mid-1990s to the early 2000s during which the city government seemed to lose its enthusiasm for working with the neighbourhood associations and district coalitions, and, further, that the neighbourhood associations perform quite unevenly (some are virtually professional in their operations; others do not approach that standard), as well as that, across the city, more prosperous homeowners are over-represented in neighbourhood planning efforts. Nonetheless, among US cities, Portland had achieved a very strong 'quality of life' reputation (*Monocle Magazine*, 2015). Portland has also avoided the extreme resident income polarisation characteristic of some US metropolises (Berube, 2014). Neither of these positive traits is a straightforward consequence of effective neighbourhood planning, but one does feel confident in asserting that Portland's strong neighbourhood planning record substantively contributes to the city's broader reputation for progressive local policies, reasonably harmonious governance and liveability.

The less auspicious record of New York City's community board system should be viewed not as a counter-example of failed neighbourhood planning, but, rather, as an alternative model working within a radically different metropolitan context. New York City's community boards – currently numbering 59 – date from 1963. Each community board serves a rationally calibrated ('bubbles in a carpenter's level') local area; the 50 members of each board are appointed by the borough president within which their communities are located. Substantively, community boards engage with two varieties of planning: (1) reactively speaking, as local advisory bodies within the city's multi-stage Urban Land Use Review Procedure (ULURP); and (2) proactively, as initiators of neighbourhood plans via what is known as the 197-a process.

Close observers of local planning in New York City tend to be sceptical of community board performance in either planning mode. Regarding community boards as reviewers of developers' proposals within the framework of ULURP planning, political scientist Bruce Berg (2007, p 277) has observed: '[C]ommunity board participation in ULURP is advisory, and there have been instances ... when the community board voted unanimously to oppose the project, yet it was approved at higher levels of the process'. Berg goes on to add that some community boards – those representing prosperous neighbourhoods of high reputation – have had success in blocking undesirable land-use changes. These outcomes, however, are largely attributable to the social capital and political influence that such locales can marshal. In reference to 197-a planning, in 2008 – that is, nearly two decades following the enactment of the 197-a mandate – planning scholar and long-time local activist Tom Angotti (2008, p 171) noted that very few community boards had actually initiated and carried through 197-a plans:

> Each community board has a full-time district manager and assistant whose days are filled with answering complaints and going to meetings. Most are not trained in planning. Successive [mayoral] administrations have avoided providing effective professional planning assistance to community boards, despite the mandate in the city charter to do so.

Elsewhere, Angotti (1999) asserts that '[t]he real success stories of community based planning are more likely to be found in the many unofficial movements, particularly in neighborhoods whose official institutions have less access to decision-making power – low-income neighborhoods and communities of color'.

Ultimately, the mixed history of neighbourhood planning in New York City does seem to be a matter of context. In a global metropolis subject to intensive development pressures – and in which municipal government has tended to view ever-more intensive development favourably – neighbourhood voices animated by local concerns have often been stifled by more powerful political and economic interests (Fainstein, 2010, pp 87–112).

Community policing in Chicago

In 1993, the Chicago Alternative Policing Strategy (CAPS) began as a trial initiative in five police districts. Within two years, the programme was expanded to the entire city. At the heart of the programme are monthly police 'beat' meetings that bring together police officers and neighbourhood residents (CCPEF, 2004; Dumke, 2011). There are currently 285 designated police beats. As described on the Chicago Police Department (2016) website, 'the CAPS partnership is tackling serious crime problems, as well as those neighbourhood conditions that breed crime – conditions such as abandoned buildings and vehicles, vacant lots, drug houses, and graffiti'. So characterised, the CAPS agenda is typical of community policing efforts across the US, being premised on more and better communication between neighbourhood residents and law enforcement representatives, and aiming to do more than simply lower the incidence of crime.

The evolution of CAPS is also illustrative of multiple hazards that can beset long-term participatory structures. During the late 1990s, resident participation in CAPS beat meetings increased, and, concurrently, there was a downward trend in serious crime rates (CCPEF, 2004, pp ii–v). However, in the early 2000s, resident participation in CAPS beat meetings levelled off, and from the middle of that decade, city of Chicago budgetary shortfalls yielded fiscal cutbacks in CAPS. In 2008, overtime pay for the police officers attending beat meetings was rescinded; two years later, 200 officers were reassigned from the CAPS office (Dumke, 2011). In some sections of Chicago, CAPS has also been politicised. Sociologist Jan Doering (no date, p 8) writes of the North Side Uptown neighbourhood:

> The assessment that CAPS in Uptown served as a political platform for pro-development interests may or may not have been correct.... However, the efforts by Alderwoman Shiller [City Council representative for the 46th ward] and her supporters to delegitimize CAPS certainly helped to make it one. CAPS activists frequently voiced their dissatisfaction with Shiller and her apparent disinterest in crime and public safety, as neither she nor her staff attended the CAPS meetings.

In regard to CAPS's most expansive aim – to improve the quality of neighbourhood problem-solving – more than a decade ago, community policing expert Wesley Skogan and his team of researchers commented:

An analysis of hundreds of beat-level plans ... found that efforts to solve local priority problems have not been very effective. District-level priorities get more sustained attention, but the same problems, in about the same locations, persist year after year. Over time the effectiveness of beat meetings in setting problem-solving agendas for the public has declined. Officers have had no refresher training in problem-solving, and most of a decade has passed since resident activists were offered any training opportunities. (CCPEF, 2004, p 155)

As a mechanism for improving urban policing, community policing is subject to particular challenges growing out of the often-contentious relationship between quasi-militarised police forces and neighbourhood residents, especially the residents of largely African-American or Latino neighbourhoods. However, the CAPS experience in Chicago also speaks to fundamental perils threatening any structure dedicated to neighbourhood planning or engagement: how to maintain municipal commitment over time, but also how to maintain inclusive and energetic resident participation over time.

Community benefits agreements

A CBA is a pact signed by development interests and representatives of a neighbourhood that will be the site of a major physical project such as a shopping complex or professional sports arena. In return for local groups pledging to support the development proposal, the developers agree to offer jobs to neighbourhood residents, build affordable housing or in other ways guarantee that the local area will tangibly benefit from the new facility. Typically, the development group will use the local residents' pledge of support to leverage aid from local government. Local government assistance can run the gamut from expedited planning approval to some variety of fiscal support, such as land acquisition assistance or tax abatement. The normative assumption driving CBAs is that 'everyone' – neighbourhood residents, the municipality at large and developers – should gain from real-estate development.

In the US, the first CBAs were drafted around the beginning of the new millennium. To a considerable extent, the formulation of the CBA concept was the brainchild of a particular group, the Los Angeles Alliance for a New Economy (LAANE), an organisation that has sought to ally neighbourhood activists and labour unions in the effort to promote more equitable economic development (Parks and Warren, 2009). An organisational offshoot of LAANE, the Partnership for Working Families, offers support to local groups across the US that seek to draw developers into CBA negotiations. At present, the Partnership website identifies 17 operational CBAs across the nation; of these, 13 have been signed by developers and community representatives in Californian localities (Partnership for Working Families, 2015).

CBAs seek to accomplish something – the delivery of material benefits to neighbourhood residents – that past highway, Urban Renewal and private 'megaproject' developments have so often failed to do. CBAs also reflect the 'neoliberal turn' in contemporary urban policy (Raffol, 2012). Rather than the national or municipal governments initiating local development action, private sector development drives growth and progressive interests seek to extract a 'piece of the pie'. The execution of CBAs has been uneven. On occasion, developers have pledged to set aside jobs or other benefits for local residents and simply failed to honour their commitments. It is also the case that providing real job opportunities to highly marginalised neighbourhood constituencies can be a complicated process of recruitment and training even before actual jobs can be offered (Saito and Truong, 2015, pp 277–80).

Like community policing, CBAs represent a participatory process – in terms of both the initial mobilisation of support *and* subsequent negotiations with developers – that bears a resemblance to conventional neighbourhood planning but is not, strictly speaking, planning with the aim of improving the social and physical character of particular locales. Note the following commentary by two observers of the 'L.A. Live' entertainment district project in Los Angeles:

> [R]esidents ... revealed that they did not wish to live in the area because the construction of the Staples Center [an adjoining sports arena] and L.A. Live erased much of the physical and social structure of their community, and events created problems such as vandalism, traffic, noise, and bright lights at night.... With these concerns in mind, funding went to four CDCs [community development corporations] building projects outside the immediate LA. Live area in neighbourhoods with large numbers of low-income and working-class Latino residents. (Saito and Truong, 2015, p 273)

To put the matter bluntly, the L.A. Live CBA has, in effect, endorsed the obliteration of an older neighbourhood in favour of what is currently viewed as a cutting-edge commercial project. Incumbent residents have been compensated via a sophisticated job creation programme and an affordable housing commitment *in other locales*.

Neighbourhood planning ... to what end?

The scholars, journalists and activists who have assessed the varieties of and variations on neighbourhood planning that I have discussed can be likened to aesthetes for whom 'beauty is in the eye of the beholder'. For planners Susan Fainstein and Clifford Hirst (1996), the great virtue of the Minneapolis Neighbourhood Revitalization Program of the early 1990s was its record of improved municipal–local resident consultation in the ongoing process of locating public facilities and anticipating the consequences of private development. For political scientists such as Archon Fung (Fagotto and Fung, 2006) and the team of Berry, Portnoy and Thomson (1993), the central question is whether neighbourhood planning improves local civic culture. The title of the latter's study of neighbourhood planning in Birmingham, Alabama, Dayton, Ohio, Portland, Oregon, St. Paul, Minnesota and San Antonio, Texas – *The rebirth of urban democracy* – a volume that devotes virtually no space to the analysis of particular planning efforts, speaks directly to their main interest. For geographer Virginia Parks and political scientist Dorian Warren (2009), who I will characterise as qualified admirers of the CBA process, the ultimate attraction of CBA mobilisation efforts is their prospective seeding of broader community–labour political collaborations.

Irrespective of the varied expectations brought to the analysis of neighbourhood planning, there are empirical points accepted by every close observer of these measures. Homeowners and the more affluent often dominate neighbourhood planning processes and institutions. Neighbourhood planning is an inherently 'uneven' process: some neighbourhoods simply have a greater capacity – via long-established local organisations, due to the educational and professional backgrounds of local residents – to envision achievable goals, to negotiate with public officials and private development interests, and to *sustain* action over time. There is, of course, that other side to neighbourhood planning's unevenness: the leadership of some local areas will use neighbourhood planning to deflect unwanted public facilities or affordable housing development.

Cities such as Portland that have maintained a firm commitment to official–resident dialogue via neighbourhood planning have managed to reduce the negative effects of the aforementioned tendencies.

Nevertheless, the ubiquity of these issues – elite domination of processes, neighbourhoods unable to 'scale up' to effective planning and 'NIMBYism' – also speaks to how the careful analyst should calibrate his/her expectations of neighbourhood planning. Municipally led processes, such as neighbourhood planning boards, local school councils and even community policing, can clearly improve the quality of local life, and, more broadly, can enhance both the reputation and governance of cities. To expect neighbourhood planning – however it is construed functionally or organisationally – to drive more fundamental social change vastly overestimates the prospective impact of what represents, objectively speaking, a sensible but inherently limited restructuring of municipal governance.

References

Abbott, C. (1983) *Planning, politics, and growth in a twentieth-century city*, Lincoln, NE: University of Nebraska Press.

Angotti, T. (1999) 'Race, place and waste: community planning in New York City', *New Village Journal*, September. Available at: http://www. newvillage.net/Journal/Issue1/1angotti.html (accessed 22 July 2015).

Angotti, T. (2008) *New York for sale: Community planning confronts global real estate*, Cambridge, MA: MIT Press.

Berg, B.F. (2007) *New York City politics: Governing Gotham*, New Brunswick, NJ: Rutgers University Press.

Berry, J.M., Portney, K.E. and Thomson, K. (1993) *The rebirth of urban democracy*, Washington, DC: The Brookings Institution.

Berube, A. (2014) *All cities are not created unequal*, 20 February, Washington, DC: The Brookings Institution. Available at: http:// www.brookings.edu/research/papers/2014/02/cities-unequal-berube (accessed 29 August 2015).

Boyte, H.C. (1980) *The backyard revolution: Understanding the new citizen movement*, Philadelphia, PA: Temple University Press.

Bucqueroux, B. (2014) '11 reasons community policing died', *Lansing Online News*, 7 December. Available at: http://lansingonlinenews. com/news/11-reasons-community-policing-died/ (accessed 5 August 2015).

CCPEF (Chicago Community Policing Evaluation Forum) (2004) *Community policing in Chicago, year ten*, April, Chicago, IL: Illinois Criminal Justice Authority.

Chicago Police Department (2016) 'What is CAPS?'. Available at: http://home.chicagopolice.org/get-involved-with-caps/how-caps-works/what-is-caps/ (accessed 22 September 2016).

City of Portland ONI (Office of Neighbourhood Involvement) (2014) 'FY 2014–15 adopted budget'. Available at: https://www.portlandoregon.gov/oni/article/509278 (accessed 28 August 2015).

City of Portland ONI (2015) 'Neighbourhood involvement directory', July. Available at: https://www.portlandoregon.gov/oni/article/391493 (accessed 28 August 2015).

Cloward, R.A. and Piven, F.F. (1974) *The politics of turmoil: Essays on poverty, race, and the urban crisis*, New York, NY: Pantheon.

Davis, A.F. (1967) *Spearheads of reform: The social settlements and the progressive movement 1890–1914*, New York, NY: Oxford University Press.

Doering, J. (no date) 'Race as a tool: the politics of crime and race in multiracial neighbourhoods', unpublished paper.

Dumke, M. (2011) 'Community policing is caught in a crossfire', *New York Times*, 8 January.

Fagotto, E. and Fung, A. (2006) 'Empowered participation in urban governance: the Minneapolis Neighbourhood Revitalization Program', *International Journal of Urban and Regional Research*, vol 30, no 3, pp 638–55.

Fainstein, S.S. (2010) *The just city*, Ithaca, NY: Cornell University Press.

Fainstein, S.S. and Hirst, C. (1996) 'Neighbourhood organizations and community planning: the Minneapolis Neighbourhood Revitalization Program', in D.W. Keating, N. Krumholz and P. Star (eds) *Revitalizing urban neighbourhoods*, Lawrence, KS: University Press of Kansas, pp 96–111.

Fogelson, R.M. (2001) *Downtown: Its rise and fall, 1880–1950*, New Haven, CT: Yale University Press.

Fung, A. (2004) *Empowered participation: Reinventing urban democracy*, Princeton, NJ: Princeton University Press.

Gans, H.J. (1965) 'The failure of urban renewal: a critique and some proposals', *Commentary*, April, pp 29–37.

Goodman, L. (2014) 'The city through newcomers' eyes and ears', *New York Times*, 9 March.

Katz, M.B. (1989) *The undeserving poor: From the war on poverty to the war on welfare*, New York, NY: Pantheon.

Keyes, L.C., Jr (1969) *The rehabilitation planning game: A study in the diversity of neighbourhoods*, Cambridge, MA: MIT Press.

Knight, L.W. (2005) *Citizen: Jane Addams and the struggle for democracy*, Chicago, IL: University of Chicago Press.

Leistner, P. (2008) 'Hopes and challenges of democratic governance: Lessons from Portland, Oregon', paper presented at the National League of Cities conference, Orlando, Florida, November.

Lemann, N. (1992) *The promised land: The great black migration and how it changed America*, New York, NY: Vintage.

Marris, P. and Rein, M. (1967) *Dilemmas of social reform: Poverty and community action in the United States*, New York, NY: Atherton.

Mollenkopf, J.H. (1983) *The contested city*, Princeton, NJ: Princeton University Press.

Monocle Magazine (2015) 'The Monocle quality of life survey'. Available at: http://monocle.com/film/affairs/the-monocle-quality-of-life-survey-2015/ (accessed 29 August 2015).

Ornstein, A.C. (1989) 'Centralization and decentralization of large public school districts', *Urban Education*, vol 24, no 2, pp 233–5.

Parks, V. and Warren, D. (2009) 'The politics and practice of economic justice: community benefits agreements as tactic of the new accountable development movement', *Journal of Community Practice*, vol 17, nos 1/2, pp 88–106.

Partnership for Working Families (2015) 'Policy & tools: community benefits agreements and policies in effect'. Available at: http://www.forworkingfamilies.org/page/policy-tools-community-benefits-agreements-and-policies-effect (accessed 14 September 2015).

Raffol, M. (2012) 'Community benefits agreements in the political economy of urban development', Advocates Forum, University of Chicago School of Social Service Administration. Available at: https://ssa.uchicago.edu/community-benefits-agreements-political-economy-urban-development (accessed 4 August 2015).

Rivlin, G. (2015) *Katrina: After the flood*, New York, NY: Simon & Schuster.

Rohe, W.M. and Gates, L.B. (1985) *Planning with neighbourhoods*, Chapel Hill, NC: University of North Carolina Press.

Saito, L. and Truong, J. (2015) 'The L.A. Live community benefits agreement: evaluating the agreement results and shifting political power in the city', *Urban Affairs Review*, vol 51, no 2, pp 263–89.

Scavo, C. (1993) 'The use of participative mechanisms by large US cities', *Journal of Urban Affairs*, vol 15, no 1, pp 93–109.

Scott, M. (1971) *American city planning*, Berkeley, CA: University of California Press.

Self, R.O. (2003) *American Babylon: Race and the struggle for postwar Oakland*, Princeton, NJ: Princeton University Press.

Wilson, J.Q. (ed) (1966) *Urban renewal: The record and the controversy*, Cambridge, MA: MIT Press.

Wojtowicz, R. (1998) *Lewis Mumford and American modernism: Eutopian theories for architecture and urban planning*, New York, NY: Cambridge University Press.

Part Four:
Reflections and conclusions

In this concluding section, Chapter Fifteen draws together the themes that run through the book to question whether a more progressive form of localism can emerge from the practices of neighbourhood planning. Drawing on the debates and evidence presented in the preceding chapters, Quintin Bradley and Sue Brownill discuss the possibilities for new forms of democratic engagement and a planning practice that is informed by place attachment and focused on delivering social purpose. They explore the extent to which this progressive potential can be realised within the current constraints of localism apparent in England and elsewhere. The aim of this section is to clarify the emerging counter-narratives of localism and neighbourhood planning, to reassert their significance in an international context, and to identify the progressive outcomes and potential. While neighbourhood planning may or may not represent 'power to the people', it is obvious that it has changed the landscape and the dynamics of planning, and will do so in ways that will continue to impact on planning thought and planning practice for many years to come.

FIFTEEN

Reflections on neighbourhood planning: towards a progressive localism

Quintin Bradley and Sue Brownill

Introduction

At the time of writing in the summer of 2016, 1,900 neighbourhood plans were under way across England, and more than 200 had passed referendum and were being used to help make development decisions (Planning Aid England, 2016). A movement of citizen-planners had responded with pragmatic enthusiasm to the conditional and much-circumscribed opportunity to influence the look and feel of their communities. In no other case study of devolution, across a broad international canvas, do we see so vividly the liberatory and regulatory conflicts that arise from the assemblages of localism, or the tangled relations of power and identity that result. In this concluding chapter, we review the contribution of this edited book to the study of neighbourhood planning and discuss what it reveals about the contradictory processes inherent to state strategies of localism, and the deepening of democratic practice in participatory planning. In particular, we ask whether the propositions of spatial liberalism have called up counter-narratives from the practice of neighbourhood planning and whether a different kind of localism, a more progressive localism, might be emerging. We begin by debating what we mean by a progressive practice of localism. We then review the discussion in previous chapters to examine our understanding of neighbourhood planning as democratic practice, as development planning and as contributing to a definition of sustainable development. We conclude with an assessment of the significance of neighbourhood planning in charting the topology of progressive localism.

Photo 15.1: Democratic planning: announcing the referendum on a neighbourhood plan

Source: Alamy stock photo available from www.alamy.com

Towards a progressive localism

In 2012, David Featherstone et al (2012, p 179) argued for an outward-looking and expansive localism that addressed itself to 'emergent agendas for social justice, participation and tolerance'. The authors outlined a model of progressive localism that contrasted with government austerity strategies and pointed to the potential for local projects of mutualism and self-organisation to evolve into universal services and a new collective settlement. Other theorists have been inspired by the ambiguities of localism to imagine how radical traditions of local democracy integral to ideas of neighbourhood planning might bring about fundamental changes in the hierarchies of power (Levitas, 2012; Newman, 2014; Williams et al, 2014). These scholars call for a more sympathetic reading of the opportunities for political experimentation in the 'cracks and fissures' of localism and they argue that those who focus on devolution only as a regulatory project ignore, and may even help to suppress, the possibilities for more progressive outcomes (Williams et al, 2014, p 2798).

The search for a progressive localism necessarily implies that what we experience now is a regressive opposite, and as Brownill warns in Chapter Two, these dichotomies may not make a particularly helpful diagnostic. Localism is messy and 'multi-vocal' (Larner, 2000); it invokes both regulatory freedom and liberatory rule, and it can be difficult to tell the difference between them. The subtitle of this book, 'Power to the people?', ends in a question mark intended to indicate the essential uncertainty in this project. If we understand power as a relational effect, then power connects those exercising it and those on the receiving end and it acts upon relationships and actions. It has direction and takes a specific form and it is always power of a particular kind, so it dominates, or seduces, coerces or incites (Allen, 2006). Localism cannot be said to empower, nor does it involve a seizure of power. Instead, it acts upon the connections of power to bring actors into different conjunctions, to change the direction of power relations and to transform the particularities of power. Localism brings about changes to the social interaction between citizens and institutions, ideologies and discourses (Newman, 2014). This might mean that power exercised as authority instead becomes a power that cajoles and entices. A relationship of domination might be mediated by new opportunities for negotiation and bargaining. Localism constructs the neighbourhood but it also changes the power relations of the neighbourhood, expanding its reach and bringing it into new proximities that may change the scalar hierarchies that we are familiar with. The impact of localism is to loosen the fixity of place as socio-spatial positioning and to make specific action easier or, indeed, more difficult (Foucault, 1982). We might call these new possibilities 'bottom-up localisms' but they are essential components in the assemblage of spatial liberalism (Clarke, 2009, p 13). The statecraft of localism could not be effective unless it responded to, and found recognition in, a stock of desires and capabilities already present at the local level and amassed over many years. Clarke (2009) argues that localism should be understood as a populist social construction that addresses a wide range of liberal concerns. While the state implementation of localism might have liberal market goals, other preoccupations of liberalism are also explored through the local, and the neighbourhood has been, and continues to be, a site for experiments and ethical inquiries into liberty, autonomy and belonging (Robinson, 2015).

It is this idea of civic inquiry that motivated Ruth Levitas (2012, p 335) to read localism through what she calls, with a nod to the French philosopher Paul Ricoeur, the 'hermeneutics of faith'. She also looks towards its progressive possibilities. Acknowledging that a return to community self-organisation is not enough to spark a renewal of cooperation and collective solidarity, Levitas articulated seven principles through which localism might shake off its liberal identification and point the way towards a more progressive society. These principles pose questions about what is valuable in development, how sustainability can be made central to human practice, how we can prioritise well-being and how we can promote equality, particularly across a gendered divide, and revalue the unpaid labour of care. Levitas regards the neighbourhood as a suitable site for the re-evaluation of human relations and human flourishing, and, in this, she reflects many feminist scholars who have aligned the geography of localism with an ethics of care (Staeheli, 2002; Newman, 2012). She encourages us to regard the practical application of localism in the neighbourhood as a process of civic inquiry that is enabled and shaped by liberal statecraft but is not defined by it. This inquiry might be progressive in seeking to develop renewed forms of democracy, solidarity and care, and in articulating different values to questions of economic growth, human well-being and sustainability. It would, at best, be an emergent inquiry (Healey, 2012), and progressive only in its expansion of the liberal project into further conflicting pathways (Newman, 2014). When there are limited opportunities to implement change, any inquiry that questions the 'rules of the game' may be considered an opening to new possibilities of political assemblage (Barnes et al, 2007; Williams et al, 2014). The policy agenda of neighbourhood planning in England has been articulated around four propositions of localism: to create spaces of empowerment; to create spaces of economic growth; to remake planning's publics; and to remake planning as a collaborative activity. These conflicting propositions invite further inquiry into the possibilities of localism's democratic imaginary and its quandaries of sustainability, citizenship, power and knowledge. In the next section, we begin our review of the significance of neighbourhood planning by reflecting on its democratic practices and questioning its contribution to a more progressive model of participation.

Democratic practice and neighbourhood planning

One of the stated objectives of neighbourhood planning was to foster democratic participation, not only to engage citizens in decisions over land-use planning, but to inspire a renewed engagement in the democratic process (DCLG, 2011). Neighbourhood planning policy appears to draw on participatory democratic theory and to embed participative forms of decision-making within the institutions of representative democracy (Brownill, 2009; Brownill and Downing, 2013). Long-held criticisms of participatory democracy have been mobilised against the logics of localism and their devolutionary promises (Ercan and Hendriks, 2013), and in this section, we critique the potential for neighbourhood planning to develop innovation in democratic practice.

Neighbourhood planning was intended to reduce the space for democratic political debate over land and property market decisions (Stanier, 2014). It was a technology of agency that offered citizens the right to plan in order to secure their consent for policies that they might otherwise oppose. It went further than any previous participatory initiative, however, in awarding statutory recognition to neighbourhood groups and delegating to them decision-making power within regulatory parameters. The key question concerns the constraint of those parameters and the degree to which they restrict the scope of devolved decision-making. Fung's (2002) distinction between administrative and the participatory devolution is useful here. Administrative devolution means authorising lower agencies to make decisions that are predetermined from above. This may result in more responsive decision-making but does 'not alter political forms or create new avenues for engagement' (Fung, 2002, p 68). Participative engagement, on the other hand, requires 'profound changes in the architecture of governance' (Ercan and Hendriks, 2013, p 426) in that it potentially leads to the formation of 'effective democratic publics' or self-organised citizens who 'come together to reflect upon collective affairs and state actions to jointly discover and create new, more effective approaches and possibilities' (Fung, 2002, p 68). Although, in practice, Fung refers to mechanisms of co-production and deliberative democracy, his theoretical engagement is closer to Fraser's (1997) idea of 'counter-publics', which was rooted in the contentious politics of 1960s' and 1970s' participatory democracy. In participatory democratic theory, citizens are directly involved not only in deliberating on decisions, but in making them (Hilmer, 2010). Bradley has argued in Chapter Three of this book that neighbourhood planning is distinctive in championing collective participation by endorsing the formation of counter-publics in neighbourhood forums and in the steering groups of town and parish councils. This is a fundamental change in the architecture of planning, one that signals a return to notions of citizen control popularised in the US, and still evident in the neighbourhood councils that Bennett describes in Chapter Fourteen. The juridical framework for neighbourhood planning may have confined the decision-making power available to collectives to the 'design and precise location' of development (DCLG, 2011, p 10), but its participative devolution has enabled the formation of collective political identities that cannot be so firmly delineated. Collective practice may create and open up new possibilities for political action (Levitas, 2012, p 336), but much depends on the practical outcome of the neighbourhood plan and its impact on development. Parker, in Chapter Five, points to the curtailment of democratic debate in neighbourhood planning by local authorities and consultants when it strays outside defined land-use issues. McGuinness and Ludwig illustrate in Chapter Six how the constraints surrounding the content of neighbourhood plans immediately close down the choices open to participants and reduce the scope of democratic inquiry. Participatory democratic theory suggests that citizens need to see that their deliberations and decisions have significant effect before they can feel a heightened sense of political efficacy and become more effective and more demanding in exerting control over decisions that directly affect them (Hilmer, 2010). Nevertheless, there is much in this book to suggest that the process of plan-making itself, and therefore the experience of constrained but tangible democratic participation, initiates feelings of efficacy, even when it is confined to limited influence in the management of development.

A common critique of participative democracy and an objection to neighbourhood planning is that it acts to reinforce existing power inequalities and installs self-selected elites in the place of egalitarian and representative government (Allmendinger and Haughton, 2012; Davoudi and Cowie, 2013). To establish that neighbourhood localism has progressive possibilities, it is necessary to demonstrate that it extends democratic inclusion to those previously excluded or marginalised (Pieterse, 2001). Advocates of participative democracy argue that the opportunities for engagement in decision-making are open to all, and therefore enfranchise previously excluded social groups. In neighbourhood planning, the forums in urban areas hold open elections and publically advertised events, while parish and town councils usually establish open steering groups. The argument that there are no structural barriers to participation ignores, however, the capacities required to take part in neighbourhood planning and the resulting obstacles to engagement in communities with the least resources. In Chapter Six of this book, McGuinness and Ludwig demonstrate that substantial specialist support is required for there to be realistic opportunities to participate in plan-making, while considerable civic capacity is needed to maintain commitment throughout the project (Wills, 2016). The process of writing planning policies is necessarily something that only small groups can undertake and this task becomes more exclusive when consultants are involved. There is a danger that participation becomes confined to particular phases of plan production (Parker et al, 2015). In Chapter Eight, Colomb points to the risk that neighbourhood planning might be colonised by specific publics for their own particular interests. Neighbourhood forums, in particular, appear open to capture by elites, in that they are self-selecting and at least initially unelected (Davoudi and Cowie, 2013). In parish and town councils, elections are frequently uncontested, with councillors co-opted rather than voted in (Bishop, 2011). Bradley (2014, 2015; see also Chapter Three) argues that neighbourhood planning groups are made accountable by neighbourly interaction and that their democratic representation is ensured by 'living in nearness'. Nearness may recede as the size and complexity of the neighbourhood grows, and, as Colomb argues, some urban neighbourhoods are characterised more by distance and 'tolerable coexistence' than any sense of collective belonging (Albrow, 1997, p 52). Gardesse and Zetlaoui-Léger's study of participation in France, in Chapter Twelve, reminds us of the remit of the state in addressing issues of spatial justice, and local planning authorities in England, especially those in more diverse municipalities, have taken steps to redress the uneven geographies of neighbourhood planning by supporting planning aspirations in more deprived communities, as Parker notes in Chapter Five (see also Chapter Seven). Ercan and Hendriks (2013) maintain that institutional policy design has an essential role to play in ensuring that participatory practices are equal and open. Neighbourhood planning was designed to sit within systems of representative democracy, and local authorities retain the power to rule on questions of representation and inclusion, and act to moderate the uneven practices of participatory engagement. Concerns over the equality and fairness of planning decisions are, in any case, not confined to neighbourhood planning, and the system of local and national plan-making established through representative democracy has long been shown to favour elites (Sturzacker and Shaw, 2015). The claims of a professional class to more equitably arbitrate on matters of the public good have been challenged by citizen-planners, who are undoubtedly no less fallible. Inequality and low participation are inextricably entwined and 'a more equitable and humane society requires a more participative political system' (Macpherson, 1977, p 94). Therefore, the opportunities for engagement in participative decision-making in neighbourhood planning add to, rather than detract from, the institutional architecture of a democratic planning system.

A progressive localism is defined, according to Featherstone et al (2012), not only by its commitment to spatial justice, but by its outward-looking and expansive character – its engagement with the global in the local (Massey, 1994; Harvey, 1996). The international chapters in this book illustrate the ubiquitous convenience of the neighbourhood as a unit of governance to marshal populations by market differentiation and the effectiveness of public services. Neighbourhood planning in England is significant in that it imagines the self-contained and self-sufficient locality as a manifestation of a collective public aligned to market forces (Hall and Massey, 2010; see also Brownill, Chapter Two). In the absence of state redistributive programmes, neighbourhoods are considered market actors, charged with shouldering the responsibilities of a residual public sector, dependent on their ability to maximise their resources and mobilise volunteer labour (Newman, 2014). It is difficult to maintain, in these circumstances, that neighbourhood planning isolates the local from the global since it directs citizen-planners to an awareness of the development market and to direct engagement with multinational actors. Neighbourhoods have little choice but to concern themselves with the structural inequalities that influence the politics of place; their planning powers are oriented to the trends of global property markets and their calculations of public good are dependent on the outcomes of uneven development. Community activists whose political horizon was formerly fixed on the power brokers of local government have acquired an understanding of how their neighbourhood is impacted by market forces, although they may be woefully ill-equipped to respond (Bradley, 2015). The basic conditions of neighbourhood planning, and the continuing centralisation of planning powers, enforce awareness of international and national regulation, although they continue to promote a local response to global issues. While considerable work has gone into networking individual groups, there is, as yet, no national organisation of neighbourhood planning groups, and it could be argued that there is a disconnect between neighbourhood planning and wider civil society and social movements. In Chapter Four, Bradley et al identify some slender links made between neighbourhood plans and civil society groups advocating environmental innovation, but they point to the restrictions on the practical application of these ideas in the defined remit of planning policy. Self-help projects in social welfare or environmental sustainability developed by neighbourhood planning groups present a patchwork politics that may remain defensively parochial; only the active engagement of civil society associations and social movements with political objectives can piece together a new collective settlement (Bradley and Haigh, 2015).

At the time of writing, the average voter turnout at referendum for neighbourhood plans was a respectable 34%, with the highest turnout at 71% (DCLG, 2015; Planning Aid England, 2016). These figures compare favourably with municipal elections, and bestow an equivalent legitimacy, but inner-city areas have attracted much less support; for example, Heathfield Park, a former urban regeneration area in Wolverhampton, registered only an 8% voter turnout in its neighbourhood referendum. The strength of the ballot in small rural communities suggests that the referendum provides an endorsement of place attachment and neighbourhood identity rather than a vindication of a development plan, as Bradley explores in Chapter Ten. The low results in some urban areas militate against the assumption in neighbourhood planning that shared residence confers shared knowledge and that this can be simply mobilised around a shared vision. The stubborn fact remains that many citizens do not identify with the significance of shared residence and disagree on what knowledge is important and what vision should be pursued (Young, 2016). Colomb's case study of the Stamford Hill Forum in Chapter Eight illustrates this clearly, but she also acknowledges the potential for community groups to construct frames of collective identity that resonate around the issues of shared residence (Tilly and Tarrow, 2007). The process of political engagement in neighbourhood planning that emerges from the case studies in this book appears more intimate and complex than suggested by the aggregative democracy of a referendum's majority decision (Clarke and Cochrane, 2013). Rather than the assumption of a homogeneous space of local knowledge, it implies an attempt to assemble a polity of common interest or the political construction of what participatory democratic theory calls 'unitary democracy' (Mansbridge, 1983, p ix). Consultation and engagement become political processes when the referendum result may be liable to influence from oppositional voices in neighbourhoods complexly networked by kinship, friendship or obligation. A process of political bargaining is necessary, with compromise on contested planning policies to achieve a majority vote of support. Neighbourhood planning can be an emotional journey for participants, with contentious views expressed, and disputes ending in lasting disagreements as difficult decisions are made. It is planning with passion, and the process of engagement and decision-making is perhaps more compelling than the completed plan. The function of participatory democracy is an educative one, as its theorist Carole Pateman (1970, p 42) said: 'Participation develops and fosters the very qualities necessary for it; the more individuals participate the better able they become to do so'. Neighbourhood planning is constrained by the statecraft of localism, but it can rehearse the spatial practices through which an empowered participatory democracy might be realised. In the next section, we review the planning practice and spatial outcomes of neighbourhood planning and consider the possibilities for a more progressive, more sustainable development.

Towards a progressive planning

Neighbourhoods in England may enjoy more democratic rights to engage in planning but their influence is confined only to development requiring planning permission. They cannot produce community plans that shape the future delivery of public infrastructure, or conceive strategies of resource redistribution. In other parts of the devolved UK, as Pemberton explains in Chapter Eleven, a more holistic form of community planning continues to be practised. A neighbourhood plan that was genuinely designed around the specific outcomes required by its community would identify needs and distribute resources fairly for employment, environment, education and well-being. Crucially, it would also include the option to say 'no' to growth (Laurence and Bua, 2016). This section is concerned with the ability of neighbourhood planning participants to push the boundaries of their regulation and to work pragmatically with the tools at hand to widen the scope of development planning towards progressive ends.

Neighbourhood planning has been lauded by government for its success in convincing communities to accept development, especially housing growth, but it is by no means clear that neighbourhoods are planning to meet government priorities. They have proved capable of accommodating differing goals. Chapters Four and Nine have outlined a dramatic ethical divide emerging over house-building. Far from saying a simple 'yes' to development, neighbourhoods appear to be promoting a different model of housing delivery, supporting small and medium builders and affordable and custom-build housing. Given the task of reconciling economic development with social and environmental concerns, neighbourhood plans have prioritised the need to define and foster place identity, to protect green space, and to uphold local distinctiveness. In contrast to, and in acknowledgement of, the requirement to deliver the exchange values of sustainable development, they have positioned the neighbourhood as the defender of fundamental use values (Cox and McCarthy, 1982). Neighbourhood plans might be seen to be taking up the daunting challenge of negotiating the place of the local in a global market, and of promoting an outward-looking sense of belonging (Clarke, 2013). This strategy – if something so uncoordinated can be called a strategy – has deepened the political complexity of planning decisions, triggering the increased legal action by developers discussed in Chapters Four and Nine, and requiring government intervention to maintain a balance between devolution and support for deregulated property markets. This unequal contest over property and place seems likely to deepen the political conflicts of planning and, as Roy (2006) suggests, ultimately lead to questions of redistribution, the missing ingredient of neighbourhood planning. Government localism seeks to territorialise the neighbourhood as a homogeneous space of capital so that competition between regions and urban centres can be devolved further downwards in expectation of a more entrepreneurial response to the state's retreat from collective consumption. However, competition is taking place within the locality as neighbourhoods try to defend themselves against capital disinvestment and state neglect by mobilising unpaid labour to maintain and develop community facilities, and prop up residual welfare services. A new public is coalescing around the rights and responsibilities of neighbourhood planning. It may adopt some of the subject positions offered in the statecraft of localism, and form up into little platoons to fill the hollowed space of collective responsibility, but there are other identities clustered around the theme of active citizenship (Newman, 2014). Participants in neighbourhood planning do not appear to be dutifully making straight the path for growth. It would perhaps be more true to say that they are activist citizens who are adding land-use planning skills to their repertoires of contention (Tilly and Tarrow, 2007; Inch, 2015). They appear to be asserting a more social purpose of planning, utilising rights to community land ownership and pursuing a grass-roots model of sustainability and housing need. The pragmatic enthusiasm with which communities have greeted neighbourhood planning suggests that the statutory recognition conferred by the process is most prized. Plan-making bestows a legal identity on the neighbourhood that provides additional leverage to negotiate relationships and positions in the politics of collective consumption.

Neighbourhood planning purports to establish the citizen as volunteer planner and to democratise land-use decisions, as if to demonstrate the triumph of local knowledge. Case studies in this book suggest, on the contrary, that neighbourhood planning has reinforced planning's arcane privilege. The coded language of planning policy can be adapted to draft what approximates to a manifesto of community need. However, it is common for a neighbourhood plan to take several years to complete. The process takes its toll; participants drop out, leaving an ever-smaller group of people to share the task of encrypting experiential knowledge into the cipher of planning policy. Neighbourhood participants begin by questioning 'what counts as knowledge, and the narrowness of the sources of knowledge considered relevant' (Wainwright, 2003, p 23).

They try to find a way to communicate the passion for place they feel, and to record for the plan some of the strength of feeling that is conveyed to them in consultation events (Jupp, 2013; see also Chapter Ten). However, the path they have chosen eventually forces them to reassert the value of planning's restricted knowledge as they squeeze community concerns into the ill-fitting clauses of planning policy. Government funding for neighbourhood planning has galvanised a market in small planning consultancies tailoring their services to provide communities with standardised policy templates, reinforcing the democratic deficit in planning practice. While opposition to neighbourhood planning from the development industry might suggest that a more ethical politics of liberalism is developing around the value of place and belonging, Brownill reminds us in Chapter Two that place attachment and identity were passions enlisted by government to achieve the desired behavioural shift in support of economic growth (Locality, 2014). The government's community rights programme promoted asset transfer, community land trusts and community-run services but these local initiatives struggle to make inroads in a speculative land market commanded by global finance and corporate traders (Hetherington, 2015). Neighbourhood plans exist in creative tension with government objectives, and the regulatory parameters of what can be achieved are redrawn in response to market interests, and planning policy is centralised as quickly as it is devolved. Against this contradictory policy background, it would be surprising if, as chapters in this book suggest, the majority of neighbourhood planning policies were not quietly conservative. Many neighbourhood planning groups feel dismayed by their inability to express community views in planning policy that is reserved only to matters of land use (Parker et al, 2015, see also Chapter Six).

The democratisation of planning through neighbourhood localism is reliant on a matching response from the state and local planning authorities to the emergence of an activist citizenry enmeshed in deregulatory practices. The reaction of local government to the initiative appears divided, with some authorities resolving not to promote neighbourhood planning, and being correspondingly slow and grudging in dealing with applications for designation and support. Other planning authorities, notably, metropolitan localities adapting with resilience to the harsh agenda of austerity (Lowndes and McCaughie, 2013), have taken the lead in coordinating and directing neighbourhood plans and steering them towards strategic priorities. There are indications of a shift in organisational culture, where individual planning officers have reappraised their relationship with communities, adapting their practice to envisage the neighbourhood as the client of the planning authority, or adopting a non-directive pedagogy and a planning practice that 'gets its hands dirty' (see Chapter Seven). Local authority strategies illustrate a 'will to empower' (Cruickshank, 1999) that advances corporate priorities and is seldom willing to tolerate contentious difference at the neighbourhood level. In Chapter Nine, Brownill cites the incorporation of neighbourhood planning into the process of local plan production by the authority in Herefordshire, while in Chapter Eight, Colomb notes the use of a council-led area action plan to replace controversial attempts to author a neighbourhood plan in Stamford Hill. In these ways, planning authorities commandeer the neighbourhood process to harvest local knowledge while adroitly recuperating any disruptive effects of empowerment. There are clear signals that central government intends to recruit the neighbourhood in its ongoing struggle with the local state, suggesting that the topology of community governance is likely to become even more fraught. The agonistic relationship between the neighbourhood and the planning authority is perhaps the key dynamic in developing the possibilities for a more progressive planning practice, as Bradley argues in Chapter Three, but there will be many losses for citizen-planners in the ensuing conflicts over the governance of space.

Progressive possibilities of neighbourhood planning

To conclude this chapter, and pull together the themes of the book, it is necessary to judge the progressive possibilities of neighbourhood planning according to the processes in land-use governance that they complement or supplant (Crisp, 2015). Neighbourhood planning has instated formal community-led participatory democratic practice in the statutory framework of development planning and has, as a consequence, significantly reconfigured the power relations between citizens, the state and the development industry. The uneven geography of its take-up and its barriers to participation can in no way detract from this advancement given the continuing remit of the local state in development planning and the inequities currently evident in the regulation of property markets. From this new infrastructure of participatory democracy, a chorus of discordant voices has begun to challenge the paradigms of planning to assert its social purpose and promote the primacy of place and well-being against the imperatives of growth. Neighbourhood planning is constituted by and constitutive of the statecraft of localism, and this experimentation in democratic planning has already exceeded its boundaries and contributed to new complexities in land-use regulation and territorial governance. Its participants are active agents in a process of political change and the neighbourhood has been mobilised as a polity from which new formulations of liberalism may emerge (Larner, 2000; Wills, 2016). The limitations on what can be achieved are formidable and there is nothing intrinsic to the changed connections of power enacted by neighbourhood planning to guarantee progressive ends. There is a keen awareness of the constraints, challenges and setbacks among participants in neighbourhood planning. There is also an enthusiasm, an unleashing of feelings of efficacy, that is unlikely to be easily pacified, and that may generate multiplying sites of conflict over questions of sustainability, well-being and fairness. Neighbourhood planning has changed the institutional architecture of planning and it is likely to unleash a new and disturbing dynamic in the liberal inquiries of localism.

References

Albrow, M. (1997) 'Travelling beyond local cultures. Socioscapes in a global city', in J. Eade (ed) *Living the global city: Globalisation as a local process*, London: Routledge.

Allen, J. (2006) *Lost geographies of power*, Oxford: Blackwell.

Allmendinger, P. and Haughton, G. (2012) 'Post-political spatial planning in England: a crisis of consensus?', *Transactions of the Institute of British Geographers*, vol 37, pp 89–103.

Barnes, M., Newman, J. and Sullivan, H. (2007) *Power, participation and political renewal: Case studies in public participation*, Bristol: Policy Press.

Bishop, J. (2011) 'What chance for neighbourhood plans?', *Town & Country Planning*, vol 80, no 2, pp 72–6.

Bradley, Q. (2014) 'Bringing democracy back home: community localism and the domestication of political space', *Environment & Planning D: Society & Space*, vol 32, no 4, pp 642–57.

Bradley, Q. (2015) 'The political identities of neighbourhood planning in England', *Space and Polity*, vol 19, no 2, pp 97–109.

Bradley, Q. and Haigh, D. (2015) 'Sustainable communities and the new patchwork politics of place', in M. Dastbaz, I. Strange and S. Selkowitz (eds) *Building sustainable futures: Design and the built environment*, London: Springer.

Brownill, S. (2009) 'The dynamics of participation: modes of governance and increasing participation in planning', *Urban Policy and Research*, vol 27, no 4, pp 357–75.

Brownill, S. and Downing, L. (2013) 'Neighbourhood plans – is an infrastructure of localism emerging', *Town & Country Planning*, vol 82, no 9, pp 372–6.

Clarke, N. (2009) 'In what sense "spaces of neoliberalism"? The new localism, the new politics of scale and town twinning', *Political Geogaphy*, vol 28, no 8, pp 496–507.

Clarke, N. (2013) 'Locality and localism: a view from British human geography', *Policy Studies*, vol 34, nos 5/6, pp 492–507.

Clarke, N. and Cochrane, A. (2013) 'Geographies and politics of localism: the localism of the UK's coalition government', *Political Geography*, vol 34, pp 10–23.

Cox, K.R. and McCarthy, J.J. (1982) 'Neighbourhood activism as a politics of turf: a critical analysis', in: K.R. Cox and R.J. Johnston (eds) *Conflict, Politics, and the Urban Scene*, Harlow: Longman, pp 196–219.

Crisp, R. (2015) 'Work clubs and the Big Society: reflections on the potential for progressive localism in the cracks and fissures of neoliberalism', *People, Place and Policy*, vol 9, no 1, pp 1–16.

Cruikshank, B. (1999) *The will to empower: Democratic citizens and other subjects*, London: Cornell University Press.

Davoudi, S. and Cowie, P. (2013) 'Are English neighbourhood forums democratically legitimate?', *Planning Theory and Practice*, vol 14, no 4, pp 562–6.

DCLG (Department of Communities and Local Government) (2011) *Impact assessment to the Localism Bill: Localism Bill: neighbourhood plans and community right to build*, London: DCLG.

DCLG (2015) *Notes on neighbourhood planning 16*, London: DCLG.

Ercan, S. and Hendriks, C. (2013) 'The democratic challenges and potential of localism: insights from deliberative democracy', *Policy Studies*, vol 34, no 4, pp 422–40.

Featherstone, D., Ince, A., Mackinnon, D., Strauss, K. and Cumbers, A. (2012) 'Progressive localism and the construction of political alternatives', *Transactions of the Institute of British Geographers*, vol 37, pp 177–82.

Foucault, M. (1982) 'The subject and power', in H. Dreyfuss and P. Rabinow (eds) *Michel Foucault: Beyond structuralism and hermeneutics*, Brighton: The Harvester Press.

Fraser, N. (1997) *Justice Interruptus: Critical reflections on the 'post socialist' condition*, London: Routledge.

Fung, A. (2002) 'Creating deliberative publics: governance after devolution and democratic centralism', *The Good Society*, vol 11, no 1, pp 66–71.

Hall, S. and Massey, D. (2010) 'Interpreting the crisis', *Soundings*, no 44(Spring), pp 57–71.

Harvey, D. (1996) *Justice, nature and the geography of difference*, Oxford: Blackwell Publishing.

Healey, P. (2012) 'Re-enchanting democracy as a mode of governance', *Critical Policy Studies*, vol 6, no 1, pp 19–39.

Hetherington, P. (2015) *Whose land is our land?*, Bristol: The Policy Press.

Hilmer, J. (2010) 'The state of participatory democratic theory', *New Political Science*, vol 32, no 1, pp 43–63.

Inch, A. (2015) 'Ordinary citizens and the political cultures of planning: in search of the subject of a new democratic ethos', *Planning Theory*, vol 14, no 4, pp 404–24.

Jupp, E. (2013) '"I feel more at home here than in my own community": approaching the emotional geographies of neighbourhood policy', *Critical Social Policy*, vol 33, pp 532–53.

Larner, W. (2000) 'Neoliberalism: policy, ideology, governmentality', *Studies in Political Economy*, vol 63, pp 5–25.

Laurence, R. and Bua, A. (2016) 'Powerhouse or power failure: what devolution means for Britain', *Red Pepper*, Issue 206, February/March.

Levitas, R. (2012) 'The just's umbrella: austerity and the Big Society in Coalition policy and beyond', *Critical Social Policy*, vol 32, no 3, pp 320–42.

Locality (2014) *The power of neighbourhood planning*, London: Locality.

Lowndes, V. and McCaughie, K. (2013) 'Weathering the perfect storm? Austerity and institutional resilience in local government', *Policy & Politics*, vol 41, no 4, pp 533–49.

Macpherson, C.B. (1977) *The life and times of liberal democracy*, Oxford: Oxford University Press.

Mansbridge, J. (1983) *Beyond adversary democracy*, Chicago, IL: University of Chicago Press.

Massey, D. (1994) *Space, place & gender*, Oxford: Polity Press.

Newman, J. (2012) 'Making, contesting & governing the local: women's labour and the local state', *Local Economy*, vol 27, no 8, pp 846–58.

Newman, J. (2014) 'Landscapes of antagonism. Local governance, neoliberalism and austerity', *Urban Studies*, vol 51, no 15, pp 3290–305.

Parker, G., Lynn, T. and Wargent, M. (2015) 'Sticking to the script? The co-production of neighbourhood planning in England', *Town Planning Review*, vol 86, no 5, pp 519–37.

Pateman, C. (1970) *Participation and democratic theory*, Cambridge: Cambridge University Press.

Pieterse, J. (2001) 'Participatory democratisation reconceived', *Futures*, vol 33, pp 407–22.

Planning Aid England (2016) 'Forum for neighbourhood planning news'. Available at: www.ourneighbourhoodplanning.org.uk (accessed 26 July 2016).

Robinson, E. (2015) 'Defining progressive politics: municipal socialism and anti-socialism in contestation, 1889–1939', *Journal of the History of Ideas*, vol 76, no 4, pp 609–31.

Roy, A. (2006) 'Praxis in the time of empire', *Planning Theory*, vol 5, no 1, pp 7–29.

Staeheli, L. (2002) 'Women and the work of community', *Environment & Planning A*, vol 35, part 5, pp 815–31.

Stainier, R. (2014) 'Local heroes: neighbourhood planning in practice', *Journal of Planning and Environmental Law Occasional Papers*, Issue 42: OP105-115.

Sturzacker, J. and Shaw, D. (2015) 'Localism in practice: lessons from a pioneer neighbourhood plan in England', *Town Planning Review*, vol 86, no 5, pp 587–609.

Tilly, C. and Tarrow, S. (2007) *Contentious politics*, London: Paradigm Publishers.

Wainwright, H. (2003) *Reclaim the state: Experiments in popular democracy*, London: Verso.

Williams, A., Goodwin, M. and Cloke, P. (2014) 'Neoliberalism, Big Society and progressive localism', *Environment and Planning A*, vol 46, pp 2798–815.

Wills, J. (2016) 'Emerging geographies of English localism: the case of neighbourhood planning', *Political Geography*, vol 53, pp 43–53.

Young, I.M. (2016) 'Inclusion and democracy', in S. Fainstein and J. Defilppis (eds) *Readings in planning theory* (4th edn), Oxford: Wiley Blackwell.

Index

Note: Page numbers in *italics* indicate tables, figures, boxes and photographs.

A

Adelaide Corporation 218
administrative devolution 255
affordable housing 154
agonistic politics 47–48
Allendale, North Pennines 172–173
Alnwick Friends of the Earth (FoE) 68
appeals 117
area action plans (AAPs) 136–137
assemblage 148–149
  and the nature of planning 152–154
  Neighbourhood Development Plans
    (NDPs) as a form of 149–152
  temporal shifts 154–158
austerity governance 6
Australia
  history of local government 218–221
  localism 215–218, 226–228
    case studies 221–226
Australia 2020 Summit 218
Australian Constitutional Values Survey
  226
Australian Local Government Association
  (ALGA) 219–220
autonomous neighbourhood 45
autonomy 40–41
Aylesbury Vale 151

B

balcony analogy 194
Barratt Homes 59
Being and time (Heidegger, 1962) 165
bien commun (common good) 200
bien commun territorial (common territorial
  good) 211
Big Society 23, 104, 148
Boston Spa, Leeds 69
boundaries 45–47, 48–49, 194
Brisbane 221, 223–224, 227
Broughton Astley 60
brownfield sites 61, 62
building regulations 65–66

C

Camden 130
Camden Council 150
Cameron, David 23
capacitation citoyenne (empowerment) 201
capacity building 99, 107–108, 110
Carbon Budget 65
central government 76, 87, 88, 110–111,
  194
  North Shield Fish Quay
    Neighbourhood Plan (FQNP) 97
  Upper Eden Neighbourhood Plan
    (UENDP) 105
  see also power relations
Central Stamford Hill Neighbourhood
  Area 136
centralism 6, 30, 32, 41–42
Chatsworth Road Neighbourhood Forum
  138–139, 170–171
Chatsworth Road Traders and Residents
  Association 138
Chicago Alternative Policing Strategy
  (CAPS) 241–242
Christie Commission 191
citizen committees 208
citizen participation *see* participation
citizen-planners 32–33
citizens' control 40
citizenship 40, 201
Clifford Neighbourhood Planning Group
  29
Climate Change Act 2008 65
Coalition government 193
Cockermouth, Cumbria 28
co-construction 207, 210
Code for Sustainable Homes (CSH) 65
collaborative planning 146
collective action 40, 42–45, 167–169
collective identity 48, 168, 169
collective interest 199–200
common good 200
common territorial good 211
communitarianism 204
community action 40–41
community action agencies (CAAs)
  235–236
Community Action Program 235–236

community benefits agreements (CBAs) 237, 242–244
community boards 239–240
Community Empowerment (Scotland) Act 2015 191
community groups 168–169
community identity 168
Community Infrastructure Levy (CIL) 31, 64, 116
community involvement policy 115
community localism 217–218
Community Neighbourhood Involvement Centre (CNIC) 238
community planning partnership (CPP) 188
community policing 237, 241–242
community projects 64
community protests 40, 42–45
community right of appeal 117
community rights 26, 28–29, 262
community strategy partnerships (CSPs) 187
community-based planning 183–186
  implications for planning and governance 193–195
  strategic-relational approach (SRA) 190–193
  temporal, structural and spatial variations 186–190, 189
  see also neighbourhood planning
community land trust 28-29, 31, 61–62, 262
concertation 202–204, 206–207
conflict 34, 48
consultants 122–124, 152
Council of Australian Governments (COAG) 219
counter-publics 40, 255
Cringleford 157
cultural codes 207, 208–209, 211–212
culture 212n
custom-build 61, 260

D

"Dasein" 165
Daws Hill Neighbourhood Forum 49
democratic participation 47–50, 254–260
  see also participation
deprivation 63–64, 78, 88
  Index of Multiple Deprivation (IMD) 84–85
Deregulation Act 2015 65
developers 124–126, 152
development see growth; housing development
Devises 155

devolution 24, 255
  and community-based planning 183–186
  implications for planning and governance 193–195
  strategic-relational approach (SRA) 190–193
  temporal, structural and spatial variations 186–190, 189
diversity 140n
  London 129–132
  London Borough of Hackney 132–139
divisional budgets 224–225

E

East Shoreditch Neighbourhood Forum 133
ecodistrict projects 206
Economic Development Act 2012, Australia 221
Economic Development Queensland 222
economic growth see growth
Economic Opportunity Act 1964, US 235
Eden District Council (EDC) 102, 103, 104, 105–106
Egan Review 2004 187–188
emplacement 164–167
empowerment 2–5, 20–21, 30, 40, 201
  see also power
England 184, 187, 188, 189, 192–193, 194, 258
environmental discourse 205–206
environmental movements 43, 44–45
environmental organisations 67–68
environmental policies see low carbon policies
ethnicity see diversity
European Union (EU) legislation 65, 66
Exeter St James 64

F

facilitators 100–101, 107, 108–109, 110
  see also consultants
federal housing acts 1949 and 1954, US 234
federalism 215–216, 226
Feed-in-Tariff (FiT) 69
"filling in" 184–185
financial support 28, 33, 34, 35n, 78, 104, 119, 220, 221
Fish Quay Heritage Partnership 96
Fishwick and St. Matthews 62–63
Folk Interested in Shields Harbour (FISH) 96
Fortune Green & West Hampstead Neighbourhood Development Forum 64

France
  citizen participation 210–212
    cultural adaptation to 206–208
    environmental discourse 205–206
    limitations 203–204, 211–212
    and political action 208–210
    regulatory framework 201–203, 210
  political culture 199–201
Friends of the Earth (FoE) 67, 68
frontier effects 49
Frontrunners 77–78
funding *see* financial support
Fung, A. 255

G

general interest 199–200
gentrification 138–139
global perspective 6
globalisation 20
Gold Coast 221, 222, 224–225
"government through community" 19–20
grants *see* financial support
Great Depression 233
Green Party 67–68
Greenbelt towns 233
greenhouse gas emissions (GHG) 65
Grenoble 209
growth 30–31, 32, 46, 261
growth-dependent paradigm 5

H

Hackney, London Borough of 132–139, 170–171
Hackney Planning Watch 134–135
Harborough District Council 60
Haredi Jewish community 134–135, 140n
Hargreaves, T. 69
Heathfield Park 63–64, 259
Heidegger, Martin 165
heterogeneity 128, 131
hierarchy of the English statutory planning system 26
Highgate Neighbourhood Forum 138
Holbeck neighbourhood forum 3, 88, 173–174
"hollowing out of the state" 20, 184
homogeneity 34, 47, 127, 131
Houghton, G. 4
Housing and Planning Act 2016 49–50
housing development 58–62, 103, 116
  Cringleford 157
  Linton 113–114, 115
  Thame 155–156
  Upper Eden 103
  see also developers
Hyde Park neighbourhood forum, Leeds 43, 118, 158, 165
hydro energy 68–69
hyper-diversity 129–132

I

identity 48, 165, 168
  see also place identity
identity talk 169
immigrant neighbourhoods 232
Index of Multiple Deprivation (IMD) 84–85
Inner East Preston 62–63
insurgent citizenship 44
insurgent planning 44–45
international perspective 6
international trends 19–20

J

John Thompson and Partners 204
Johnson, Lyndon 234–235

K

Keyes, Langley Carleton Jr 234

L

L.A. Live 243–244
landowners 114–115, 152
land-use planning 40, 42–45, 86–87
Larkfleet Homes 60
Laurence Weston, Bristol 154
Leeds City Council (LCC) 115
Lefevbre, H. 166, 168
liberalism 41
  see also neoliberalism
l'intérêt collectif (collective interest) 199–200
l'intérêt général (general interest) 199–200
Linton 113–116
local area agreements (LAAs) 188
local authorities 49
  see also local planning authorities (LPAs); planning authority voices
local citizen-planners 32–33
local enterprise partnerships (LEPs) 193
Local Government Act 2000 187
Local Government (Scotland) Act 2003 187
local planning authorities (LPAs) 24, 28, 30, 34, 150, 151, 156
local service agreements (LSAs) 188
local service boards (LSBs) 188
local strategic partnerships (LSPs) 187
localism
  aims 29–34
  characteristics 2–4
  classification 216–217
  global perspective 6
  neoliberal 76–77
  pro-development 193
  progressive 6–7, 252–254, 257
  rise of 19–20
  understandings of 21–22
  see also neighbourhood planning

Localism Act 2011 23–24, 30, 45, 104,
150, 184, 192
localism agenda 1
Localism Bill 2010 23
"Localism in London" (London Assembly,
2014) 129
localist trap 154
Locality 28, 78
London 129–132
London Assembly 128–129
London Borough of Hackney 132–139,
170–171
Los Angeles Alliance for a New Economy
(LAANE) 242–243
low carbon policies 65–70, 66–67
luttes urbaines (urban struggles) 202

M

managerial localism 217
Mechmache, Mohammed 208
Melbourne 227
Mobius strip 147
Mouffe, Chantal 47–48
multi-agency approach 78

N

National Planning Policy Framework
(NPPF) 24, 59, 81
neighbourhood area designation 132–139
neighbourhood associations 238
Neighbourhood Development Orders
(NDOs) 26, 28
Neighbourhood Development Plans
(NDPs) 24–29
costs 78–79
and empowerment 30
as a form of assemblage 149–152
and growth 30–31
interactive map 79
non-professionalism 33–34
social goals 62–65
temporality 154–158
neighbourhood forums 43, 49
legal requirements 133–134
legitimacy 130–131
London Borough of Hackney 132–139
neighbourhood planning
democratic participation 47–50,
254–260. see also participation
global perspective 6
government definition 1
international trends 19–20
non-professionalism 33–34
partners 79–80, 88–89
policy content 86–87
political identities 45–47
progressive planning 260–263
progressive possibilities for 263–264

purposes of planning 5–6
support for 77–79, 88–89, 99–101, 105
take-up 77–80
diversity of 84–86
estimated and actual 81
geographical 82–84, 82, 83
speed and timing of 80–82
User experience study (Parker et al, 2014)
86, 87–88
see also community-based planning;
localism
neighbourhood planning groups 48
neighbourhood planning steering group
122
neighbourhood units 233
neighbourhood voices 113–118
neighbourhood-as-planning-polity 46
neighbourhoods 34, 45–47, 205–206
neoliberal localism 76–77
neoliberalism 21–22, 31, 40, 243
see also liberalism
networks 102
New Labour 29, 32, 148
New York City 239–240
Newman, J. 22
"NIMBY" 42–43
Nixon, Richard 236
North Hackney Neighbourhood Forum
134–136
North Shield Fish Quay Neighbourhood
Plan (FQNP) 95–102
planning stages 96–98
positive aspects of local government
structures 102
process 98–101
product: quality of plan 101
reflection on 109–111
North Tyneside Council (NTC) 95–96,
97–98, 99
Northern Ireland 187, 188, 189, 190–191
Northern Territory, Australia 225–226

O

Office of Neighbourhood Associations
(ONA) 237, 238
Open source planning (Conservative Party,
2010) 24

P

Paris City Hall 206–207
participation 32–33, 39–42, 43–44, 49
France 210–212
cultural adaptation to 206–208
environmental discourse 205–206
limitations 203–204, 211–212
political action renewed by 208–210
regulatory framework 201–203, 210
motives and aims of participants 87

North Shield Fish Quay
   Neighbourhood Plan (FQNP) 98–99
Upper Eden Neighbourhood Plan
   (UENDP) 106–107
participatory democracy *see* democratic
   participation
participatory democratic theory 254–256
Partnership for Working Families 243
path dependency 193–194
permitted development rights (PDRs) 155
Photovoltaics (PV) 68–69
Pickles, Eric 23, 32, 155
place affect 169
place and emplacement 164–167
place attachment 164, 167–169, 173
place definition 168, 169
place dependence 169
place framing 168
place identity 165, 168–169, 170–174
place social bonding 169
planning *see* land-use planning;
   neighbourhood planning
Planning (Wales) Act 2015 192
Planning Aid England 78
Planning and Compulsory Purchase Act
   2004 103
planning authority voices 118–122
planning officers
   North Tyneside Council (NTC) 97–98,
      99, 101
   Preston Council 63
planning system *26*
policing *see* community policing
policy content 86–87, 119
Policy Studies 216
political action 208–210
political engagement 40, 259
political identities 45–47
Politique de la Ville 205, 207–208
Portland 237–239
positivism 200
power 253
   topologies of 146–149, 158–159. *see also*
      assemblage
   see also empowerment
power relations 40, 41–42, 46, 48, 49, 145
   see also assemblage
Preston 62–63
Priority Development Areas (PDAs) 217,
   221–223
private sector 79, 124–126, 243
pro-development localism 193
production of space, The (Lefebvre,
   1991[1974]) 166
progressive localism 6–7, 252–254, 257
progressive planning 260–263
project officers 104, 105, 106–107
   see also consultants; facilitators

protest 40, 42–45
public service boards (PSBs) 188, 192

Q

Queensland 217–218, 221–223

R

regional assemblies (RAs) 193
regional development agencies (RDAs)
   193
rehabilitation planning game, The (Keyes,
   1969) 234
"relational" filling in 184–185
religion 140n
renewable energy 65, 68–69
representative localism 216–217
Review of Public Administration (RPA)
   187, 188, 190
Review of public services in Wales (Williams
   Commission, 2014) 192
right of appeal 117
Roosevelt, Franklin 233
Royal Town Planning Institute (RTPI) 78
rural protests 44

S

scale 145
Scotland 187, *189*, 191–192
Scottish National Party 191
self-organisation 40–41
settlement house movement 232–233
skills 99, 102, 107–108, 110
Skogan, Wesley 241–242
social goals of neighbourhood plans 62–65
social identity 165
socio-economic diversity 130, 131,
   138–139
socio-economic profiles 84
Somers Town, London 31, 149, 150,
   153–154, *153*, 156
South Oxfordshire District Council
   (SODC) 149, 155
space 34, 166
spatial hierarchies 146–149
spatial imaginaries 34–35
spatial liberalism 34
spatial practices 61–62, 64, 70–72, 86–87
spatial variations in community-based
   planning 187–190, *189*
Stamford Hill Area Action Plan *137*
Stamford Hill Neighbourhood Forum
   134–136
statutory planning system *26*
Strasbourg 209
strategic-relational approach (SRA)
   185–186, 190–193
"structural" filling in 184

structural variations in community-based planning 187–190, *189*
subjectivity 166
super-diversity 129–132
supershires 225–226
Supplementary Planning Document (SPD) 95–96, 101
sustainability 205–206
  see also low carbon policies
Sustainable Planning Act 2009 (SPA), Australia 222
Sydney 227

T

Tattenhall, Cheshire 59–60
technical support 78
"technologies of agency" 33
"technologies of citizenship" 33
temporal shifts 154–158
temporal variations in community-based planning 186–187
Thame, South Oxfordshire 149–150, 152, 155–158, 171–172
"There Being" 165
topologies of power 146–149, 158–159
  see also assemblage
transition initiatives (TIs) 67–68
trust 99, 102, 108, 119, 227, 228
Tyneside *see* North Shield Fish Quay Neighbourhood Plan (FQNP)

U

Upper Eden Community Plan (UECP) 103
Upper Eden Neighbourhood Plan (UENDP) 102–109
  governance arrangements 103–104
  planning stages 104–106
  process 106–109
  product: quality of plan 109
  reflection on 109–111
Uppingham, Rutland 60
urban neighbourhoods 62–64, 88, 128
urban regeneration 194
Urban Renewal programme, US 234
urban struggles 202
US 231–232
  neighbourhood planning 244–245
    across the decades 232–237
    New York City 239–240
    Portland 237–239
User experience study (Parker et al, 2014) 86, 87–88

V

Voluntary Action Camden 150

W

Wainhomes 59
Wales 187, 188, *189*, 192, 194, 195
War on Poverty 234–236
Well-being of Future Generations (Wales) Act 2015 188
West Ferring, Sussex 31
Westminster 130
Williams Commission 192
wind energy 68–69
Winsford, Cheshire 173
Wivenhoe 68
Wolverhampton 63–64
Wycombe District Council 49